Culture and Identity in Early Modern Europe
(1500–1800)

Natalie Zemon Davis. (Photo: Denise Applewhite, 1993.)

Culture and Identity in Early Modern Europe (1500–1800)

Essays in Honor of Natalie Zemon Davis

Edited by
Barbara B. Diefendorf
and Carla Hesse

Ann Arbor

THE UNIVERSITY OF MICHIGAN PRESS

Copyright © by the University of Michigan 1993
All rights reserved
Published in the United States of America by
The University of Michigan Press
Manufactured in the United States of America

1997   1996   1995   4   3   2

A CIP catalogue record for this book is available from the British Library.

Material from Chapter 8 is reprinted from *Beneath the Cross: Catholics and Huguenots in Sixteenth-Century Paris,* by Barbara B. Diefendorf. Copyright © 1991 by Oxford University Press, Inc. Reprinted by permission.

Library of Congress Cataloging-in-Publication Data

Culture and identity in early modern Europe (1500–1800) : essays in
  honor of Natalie Zemon Davis / edited by Barbara B. Diefendorf and
  Carla Hesse.
       p.   cm.
    "Bibliography of Natalie Zemon Davis' work" : p.
    Includes bibliographical references and index.
    Contents: Pt. 1. Spiritual identities. Hearing lay people's prayer
  / Virginia Reinburg — The Huguenot psalter and the faith of French
  Protestants in the sixteenth century / Barbara B. Diefendorf —
  Rituals of conversion : Catholics and Protestants in seventeenth-
  century Poitou / Keith P. Luria — Confessors, penitents, and the
  construction of identities in early modern Avila / Jodi Bilinkoff —
  Pt. 2. Social identities. Writing and the power of speech : notaries
  and artisans in baroque Rome / Laurie Nussdorfer — People of the
  Ribers : popular politics and neighborhood identity in early modern
  Barcelona / James S. Amelang — The social transformation of the
  French parish clergy, 1500–1800 / Andrew Barnes — Deep play in the
  forest : the "War of the Demoiselles" in the Ariège, 1829–1831 /
  Peter Sahlins — Pt. 3. Cultural identities. Between oral and
  written culture : the social meaning of an illustrated love letter /
  Elizabeth S. Cohen — Print's role in the politics of women's health
  in early modern France / Alison Klairmont Lingo — Deadly parents :
  family and aristocratic culture in early modern France / Jonathan
  Dewald — Revolutionary histories : the literary politics of Louise
  de Kéralio, 1758–1822 / Carla Hesse.
    ISBN 0-472-10470-5
    1. France—Civilization. 2. Europe—Civilization. 3. Social
  change. 4. Church history—Modern period, 1500– 5. Written
  communication—Europe—Influence. 6. Oral communication—Europe.
  7. Politics and culture—Europe—History. 8. Davis, Natalie Zemon,
  1928- —Bibliography.   I. Diefendorf, Barbara B., 1946- .
  II. Hesse, Carla Alison.   III. Davis, Natalie Zemon, 1928- .
  DC33.3.C82   1994
  944—dc20   93-27169
                                                              CIP

Preface: Dialogues with the Past

In November 1990, a symposium in cultural history entitled "Dialogues with the Past" was held at Boston University in order to honor the historian Natalie Zemon Davis as teacher and as scholar. The articles in this book are products of that symposium. Written by former students of Natalie Davis from her years at the Universities of Toronto, California at Berkeley, and Princeton, they are dedicated to her as a token of our appreciation for the contributions that she has made both to our personal growth as historians and to the profession at large.

The symposium was organized around a concept central to Natalie Davis's scholarship and to her identity as historian and as teacher. This is the concept of history as a dialogue with the past. In an interview conducted in 1981 by members of the Radical Historians' Organization, Davis described the practice of history as "a dialogue and sometimes a debate with the past." It is a dialogue in which "our own scholarly theories and cultural values" necessarily play a part, but one in which the principal challenge is this: "How can I re-create these people without molding them in my image?"[1] Davis suggested that her technique for meeting this challenge was to try to give her subjects their own voice, even when she did not agree with them. This deceptively simple suggestion contained an important response to the historian's dilemma of how to understand the past: Listen to your subjects, she told us, and actively interrogate them. Why do they act and think as they do? What shapes their beliefs and the actions that derive from them? And how do they define themselves in relation to the larger structures of family, community, and polity? She drew our attention to both the language and the logic of our subjects' thought, encouraged us to examine their systems of values without assuming that they shared our own.

But if history is a dialogue with its subjects, it is also a dialogue with other historians. This is the image that Davis evoked in her presidential address to the American Historical Association in 1987. Wishing to leave her audience with an image of history "that would suggest the complexity, commitment, and multiple vision that [she believes] must be at its heart," she concluded her address by saying: "My image of history would have at least two bodies in it, at least two persons talking, arguing, always listening to the other as they gestured at their books."[2]

The articles in this book are intended to exemplify both aspects of Natalie Davis's concept of dialogue. They are dialogues with the past—explorations in cultural history by scholars attentive to the need to give their subjects their own voice. They are dialogues with other historians as well, first and foremost with the teacher and scholar in whose honor they were conceived. All of the articles are rooted in one way or another in Davis's own work, either in the subjects they address or the approaches they take or, often, in both. Many aspects of Davis's work are represented here, from her early interest in the problem of religious choice during the French Reformation, to studies of the dynamics of social groups—families, neighborhoods, and corporate bodies—to the influence of gender on cultural values and social strategies. Several articles take their point of departure from questions she has raised about the meaning of the written word in a largely illiterate society; others build upon her explorations of the cultural and political messages embedded in the nonverbal communication of ritual and symbol.

If these articles are somehow rooted in Natalie Davis's own scholarship, that does not mean they are blandly derivative and uncritically accepting of the questions and approaches that provided their seed. Indeed, the concept of dialogue forbids these essays to be simply encomia, as it forbids Natalie Davis's works to be taken as icons or her ideas as given truths. In her 1987 presidential address, Davis mused on "the anxiety of influence—both the influence of one's teachers and the influence over one's students and successors," and she related an incident that suggests her own preferred solution to the problem of influence. Recounting how the medievalist Eileen Power, while advising the younger scholar Sylvia Thrupp, told Thrupp, "You want to follow my example." Davis went on to quote Thrupp's spirited reply: "We're moving in the same direction." "What better tribute to a historian," Davis asked, "than that she could elicit such an independent response?"[3]

As a teacher and mentor, Natalie Davis always tried to elicit an independent response. As her students, we carried out dialogues with the past that were dialogues with Davis as well, "talking, arguing, always listening to the other." With an energy, intensity, and intellectual curiosity that few in the profession can match, Davis opened our minds and imaginations with a constant string of questions: "Have you read this?" "Have you looked at that?" "Have you thought about the broader meaning, or what an anthropologist might say?" She listened to our answers, pointed out connections we had overlooked, and then she sent us back to our libraries and archives. She urged us to dig deep in primary sources but also to search wide—to examine the complex interrelationships among socioeconomic, intellectual, and cultural phenomena. She taught us that historical contexts are multidimensional and urged us to learn from, but not be dominated by, the methods and discoveries of other disciplines, to ask big questions but never to forget the telling detail.

One thing she never did was to ask us to follow her. Rather, she encouraged us each to develop what was best in our own historical vision. For this we are grateful. If these essays nevertheless show that "we're moving in the same direction," it is because the path that Davis indicated to us is a broad one, because the dialogues begun with her as many as twenty years ago are ongoing ones. For this too, we are grateful.

As the organizer of the symposium "Dialogues with the Past," and as coeditor of this volume, I have other debts of gratitude that need to be acknowledged as well. I would like to thank the Florence Gould Foundation and the Boston University Humanities Foundation for providing financial support for the symposium. They made it possible to bring together twenty-one participants from two continents for three days of formal presentations and informal discussion. The staff of the history department at Boston University, in particular our department administrator, James Dutton, provided invaluable assistance with the organizational and administrative details of the conference. Caroline Walker Bynum, Stephen Greenblatt, Nancy Lyman Roelker, Lawrence Stone, and Louise Tilly chaired sessions of the symposium and contributed wit and wisdom to the event, as did

Sherrill Cohen, Barbara B. Davis, and Lynn Hunt, three participants whose papers will be published elsewhere. I am grateful for the contribution these individuals made to the symposium and to the book of essays that is its product.

In addition, Carla Hesse and I would like to offer special thanks to Caroline Bynum, Jeffry Diefendorf, Laura Engelstein, Lynn Hunt, Virginia Reinburg, and Randolph Starn. We are grateful to Katharine Norris for her work in preparing the bibliography, to Andé Lambelet for his assistance with the page proofs and index, and to Joyce Harrison, our editor at the University of Michigan Press.

—Barbara B. Diefendorf

NOTES

1. Interview conducted during the summer of 1981 by Rob Harding and Judy Coffin and republished in *Visions of History* by MARHO, The Radical Historians' Organization, ed. Henry Abelove, Betsy Blackmar, Peter Dimock, and Jonathan Schneer (New York, 1983), 114.

2. Natalie Zemon Davis, "History's Two Bodies (Presidential Address)," *American Historical Review* 93 (1988): 29–30.

3. Ibid., 29 and 27.

Contents

Introduction: Culture and Identity

Barbara B. Diefendorf and Carla Hesse

Culture and identity have been subjects of central importance in Natalie Davis's work, from her earliest studies in the social and religious history of sixteenth-century Lyons to her current research on the cross-cultural experiences and exchanges of Europeans who went abroad in increasing numbers during the sixteenth and seventeenth centuries. Though historians in the United States often identify Davis as an American descendant of the French *Annales* school of sociocultural history, her work has in fact always been as much a challenge to as a continuation of the methods and inquiries of those practitioners of the history of *mentalités*. Rather than regarding cultural experience as something that exists above, but ultimately depends upon, first economic and then social realities, from her earliest writings Davis found common cause with a new generation of English Marxist historians, most notably E. P. Thompson, in her insistence that cultural practices and processes are not simply reflections or articulations of socioeconomic experience but rather constitutive of it. Like Thompson, Davis departed from earlier generations of social historians (Marxist, modernizationist, and *Annaliste* alike) in her view of cultural life as the infrastructure of a given social order rather than as its superstructure. Cultural activity in her view thus becomes the central mechanism by which the very categories of social life—the notions of collective and individual identity—are constituted and transformed.

For Davis, the central question facing the social historian has never been, How is this society ordered, but rather, How does this society order itself? What systems of meaning or categories are employed? And by whom? What are the terms of the relationships established among different groups within a given social order? And how are points of contact and exchange established across social, religious, or political boundaries? Over the years, these questions have led Davis into an active dialogue with anthropologists and literary theorists. Yet, while Davis makes use of the insights to be gained from employing the methods of other disciplines, she has never lost sight of her specifically historical concerns. As she explains in the introduction to *Fiction in the Archives:*

> I have been much helped by what literary specialists have shown us about how narratives are put together, but my historian's eye will not focus on morphologies of the tale, on production from a universal grammar, or on arrangements of functions, "indices," and propositions that might be found in any time or place. Rather I am after evidence of how sixteenth-century people told sto- ries...how through narrative they made sense of the unexpected and built coherence into immediate experience.[1]

It is not the universal but rather the specific—the historical—that she is seeking in her texts. How did cultural practices specific to the sixteenth century influence the way people listened to or told their stories?

For Davis, moreover, the lines between social and cultural pro- cesses inevitably are blurred. As a member of a panel addressing the question of the relation between art and society, Davis defined herself as a "historian working on sixteenth-century processes of social and cultural exchange." She went on to explain the blurring of lines this reciprocity entails:

> You will notice that I say "social and cultural," for it is hard for me to distinguish absolutely between parlements, plows, mortality rates, and the sexual division of labor on the one hand, and under- standings and ideas on the other, whether they be found in royal decrees, woodcuts, or poems. The sixteenth century writes after all of the art of agriculture, the art of metallurgy, the art of war, and the art of the prince.[2]

To some, Davis's work may appear too eclectic—insufficiently theo- retical—precisely because of this refusal to "distinguish absolutely" between artifacts and ideas, between societies and cultures. Davis's history is not made up of distinct strata but of intersections. She does not ask us to watch her peel off one layer of truth in order to reveal another but rather holds up an image, an incident, or an artifact and asks us to look at it from first one perspective and then another and another. Although she engages in the close reading of texts, she never allows her texts to become ends in themselves. Rather they remain cultural artifacts that disclose the logic of the societies and cultures that produced them.

Les Cultures du peuple, the title of the French translation for Natalie Davis's now classic collection of articles, *Society and Culture in Early Modern France,*[3] in fact better reflects Davis's appreciation of the multiformity of the past than does the English title. It better captures her realization that wherever we turn our focus on the past—on the Protestant printer, the Catholic nun, the repentant prisoner, the peasant wife—the individuals who capture our attention must not be viewed as members of a single, monolithic cultural system but rather as participants in intersecting cultures, with different and even conflicting founding assumptions, value systems, and expectations. As Davis has pointed out, people in early modern times defined themselves largely in collective and corporate terms. "The exploration of self in sixteenth-century France," she writes, "was made in conscious relation to the groups to which people belonged."[4] Identity was necessarily multiple, deriving as it did from membership in a family and a corporation or estate, from residence in a particular neighborhood and parish, and from participation in devotional societies or sodalities. It was thus inevitable that competing or even conflicting sets of values could develop. At the heart of Davis's work is a persistent search for new ways to understand the intersecting value systems, the seldom-articulated premises that underlay behavior and belief in early modern France.

In her early essays Davis was centrally concerned with understanding how social experience affected individual or group consciousness. Seeking to discover the factors that aided or discouraged the penetration of Calvinism in the French cities, she focused on such questions as corporate affiliation, gender roles, geographical mobility, and literacy and asked how these factors might have shaped patterns of behavior and belief. The examination of the symbolic meanings acted out in popular festivities and crowd violence in the seminal essays

"Women on Top" and "The Rites of Violence" marked a turn toward what would prove to be a continuing preoccupation with the symbolic languages of ritual and gesture as means of recapturing the unwritten, and often unspoken, meanings disclosed through accounts and artifacts of lost cultural practices.[5]

Earlier concerns were not abandoned but rather were enriched as the analysis of ritual and gesture provided new ways of looking at old questions. "The Sacred and the Body Social," for example, offered a fresh way of looking at how the Protestant and Catholic faiths "worked" in an urban setting by asking where each faith located the sacred in the city.[6] Analyzing the use of public space in Catholic and Protestant rituals, the calendars of work and rest adopted by each church, and the metaphors each group used to express its conception of the "body social," Davis delineated two contrasting styles of urban behavior, each with its own sense of place, rhythm, and community. Asking how each religion "functioned as a source of safety and solidarity within the city," she offered a new way of understanding the successes and failures of Calvinist ideas in the French cities.[7]

Along with ritual and gesture, another central preoccupation was the dynamics of reading, writing, and printing. This led to reflections on the ways books might be used and the varied meanings they might acquire in the hands of different audiences. The essay on "Printing and the People" in *Society and Culture* responded to a growing literature on "popular culture" with an analysis of the patterns of interaction between literate and oral culture in the French countryside and among the *menu peuple* (common people) of French towns. Davis's continuing interest in the penetration of Calvinism was given a new twist in this essay, which used reading practices in the French countryside—in particular the custom of the *veillée* (an evening social gathering)—to explain why Calvinist books had little appeal for the French peasantry. Assumptions about how to read a book, Davis found, could be as important as the theological content between its covers: "For most peasants, the religion of the Book, the Psalm, and the Consistory gave too little leeway to the traditional oral and ritual culture of the countryside, to its existing forms of social life and social control."[8] Davis cautioned, however, against assuming that either peasants or the urban *menu peuple* were "passive recipients" of the written word. "Rather they were active users and interpreters of the printed books they heard and read, and even helped give these books form."[9]

The same essay reveals Davis's deepening concern for the role of the historian as interpreter of the past. Spelling out her interpretive practices in the introduction to *Society and Culture,* Davis wrote:

> First, I have tried to be especially attentive to the context of a change, an occurrence, or a decision.... But second, I have not assumed that either context or any single attribute of these peasants and city people—whether their sex, or their relation to property and production—in itself determined their behavior. Rather I have imagined these features of their lives as shaping their condition and their goals, as limiting or expanding their options; but I have seen them as actors, making use of what physical, social, and cultural resources they had in order to survive, to cope, or sometimes to change things.[10]

This hermeneutical insistence on respecting the historical individual as an actor who improvises from a variety of roles available for persons of a given age, gender, and social standing, also characterizes her later work. Broadened into collective terms, it provides us with a distinctive perspective on the "location" of historical change. In the article "Ghosts, Kin, and Progeny," for example, Davis calls our attention to the processes set in motion by the growing tendency of families in the sixteenth and seventeenth centuries to plan consciously for the future. "What we see here," she points out,

> is historical change flowing from the decisions of myriad small groups, some rich and powerful, but many of only middling affluence in provincial towns and smaller rural centers. Their push toward planning, toward manipulation of property and persons for private goals, and their blending of beliefs in virtue with beliefs in stock were assisted by the growth of the state and of commercial capitalism and the professions, but were also in defiance of some of the forces of their time, both demographic and social.[11]

Insisting on the interactive character of historical change, Davis further emphasizes that the processes of change are neither uniform nor unidirectional. In "Ghosts, Kin, and Progeny," for example, she identifies within Catholicism a "disjuncture between privatistic family values and the more corporate values, often accepted by these same families, which were embodied in [certain Catholic customs and belief]," and she proposes that this disjuncture may be a creative one. Initially startling, the suggestion that we consider "why religion or any cultural system can sometimes carry along contradictory values and keep little-used options open for centuries" is nevertheless consistent with Davis's insistence on the multiplicity of the past.[12]

The problem of the historical construction of identity is most explicitly explored in *The Return of Martin Guerre*.[13] The book reconstructs two parallel histories of self-invention and their complicity with one another. The first is a story of imposture, recounting the success that Arnaud du Tilh enjoyed in passing himself off as the returned Martin Guerre—how Arnaud insinuated himself into the bosom of Martin's family and the bed of his wife—and the events that finally led to the unraveling of this imposture. The second, intimately related story is that of Martin's wife, Bertrande de Rols, and of Bertrande's role in these events. Rejecting the contemporary sixteenth-century interpretations of Bertrande as a simple woman thoroughly deceived by the wily imposter, Davis sets out not only to demonstrate Bertrande's complicity in the deception but also to show how this supposedly simple peasant woman in fact displayed "a shrewd realism about how she could maneuver within the constraints placed upon one of her sex."[14] Within horizons limited by custom and tradition, Bertrande created her own identity: she made choices that ultimately determined both who she was and how she lived. As a woman, Bertrande's options were particularly limited, but the options open to men in the peasant society of the Artigat were narrow as well. As Davis presents it, Martin's choice to run away and seek service in the army of the king of Spain represents a desperate flight from the suffocating constraints that tied him too young to the burdens of family and land. Meanwhile, Arnaud, having already experienced the soldier's life, voluntarily assumes the life that Martin has abandoned, an ironic reversal of roles that serves to emphasize the limited nature of the available options.

The story of Martin Guerre fascinated contemporaries, as it continues to fascinate today. Yet what makes Natalie Davis's retelling so masterful—what makes it significant as history and not just a "prodigious story"—is the painstaking care with which the historian strips bare the unarticulated assumptions and beliefs, the traditional practices and customs, that operated to condition without altogether determining the responses of Bertrande de Rols, Arnaud du Tilh, and Martin Guerre to the circumstances that they encountered. The complex interplay of culture and identity is a constant theme throughout the book. If Davis begins her story by describing the Guerre family's roots in the French Basque country and their move to Artigat when Martin was only two years old, it is less to describe the physical setting in which the story takes place than to set out the particular customs—the patterns of landholding and exploitation, inheritance laws, and traditions of patriarchal authority—that shaped the understanding each individual would have had about his or her place within the family, his or her relation to the land. In the same way, the possibility that Bertrande de Rols and Martin Guerre were secretly attracted to the new Protestant teachings that were beginning to spread in the region at just the time this story takes place is introduced not to prove that they did or did not convert but rather to demonstrate how the new attitudes toward marriage introduced by the Protestants might have allowed Bertrande and Martin to view their own relationship in altered terms. As Davis points out, Protestantism allowed them at least "the possibility of *conceiving* of marriage as something that was in their hands to make, indeed, as in their hands alone."[15] In the hands of Davis, the historian, this tale becomes a history of how peasant men and women—living in conditions of severe material, legal, social, and familial constraint—nonetheless shared in that eminently Renaissance impulse to shape their own lives. And indeed, for an albeit elusive moment, they succeeded.

The concept of "self-fashioning," the conscious and unconscious shaping of identity through cultural choices, is also an explicit theme in Davis's book *Fiction in the Archives,* which examines how common folk who also happened to be convicted felons constructed narratives of their actions that they hoped would buy back their lives by convincing the king to grant them pardon for their crimes. Davis shows how these "pardon tales" artfully deployed rhetorical and narrative strategies drawn from traditions of both popular storytelling and courtly literature in an attempt to recast their crimes into culturally acceptable—and therefore excusable—forms. For men, this usually meant to show how they had been moved by uncontrollable rage to commit a crime of passion. Women, however, had to be wary of offering this excuse; uncontrollable rage was more forgivable in a man than in a woman. Cultural stereotypes thus forced women to devise more subtle strategies to explain away their crimes.

If *Fiction in the Archives* is about self-fashioning, it also reveals Davis's continuing fascination with the intersections and interactions between literate and oral, and learned and lay, cultures. Information and values, she writes, moved "across the lines of class and culture" as the stories told by the pardon-seekers circulated among the notaries, clerks, attorneys, and judges of the court. "We have here," Davis concludes, "not an impermeable 'official culture' imposing its criteria on 'popular culture,' but cultural exchange, conducted under the king's rules. The stakes were different for supplicants, listeners, and pardoners, but they were all implicated in a common discourse about violence and its pacification."[16] These notions of cultural permeability and cultural exchange—so central to Davis's thought—point again to her insistence on the imperative for social historians to examine how cultural practices paradoxically work to articulate social, political, or spiritual boundaries and conflicts, while at the same time opening up possible channels of communication and reconciliation across those very same boundaries. The articulation of differences, Davis reveals time and again, not only differentiates social actors, it also establishes relations among them.

No single volume could ever hope to offer an exhaustive account of either the range or the depth of Natalie Davis's impact on the field of European history. The twelve essays gathered in this volume nevertheless reflect the enduring centrality of the questions her work raises concerning the formation of identity at the intersection of various social and cultural processes. Though spanning the period from the eve of the Reformation to the aftermath of the French Revolution, and encompassing Italy and Spain as well as France, these essays come together in their common concern with how early modern Europeans were able to create both individual and collective identities for themselves, within, alongside, and sometimes against, the prescriptive norms imposed by traditional political, religious, or cultural authorities. The essays are grouped into three distinct and yet inevitably intersecting sections, which examine in turn the construction of spiritual, social, and cultural identities.

Spiritual Identities

The first group of essays examines ways in which the spiritual identities of both lay people and clerics were reshaped in response to the major social, political, and religious upheavals of the sixteenth and seventeenth centuries. Each of the four essays focuses on a different devotional practice—prayer, the reading of scripture, conversion, and confession—and asks how these practices were used to change, affirm, or subvert spiritual identities. All four essays have their origins in questions about how religious consciousness was formed, what faith meant in the daily lives of ordinary believers, and how the metaphors in which belief was encapsulated and the rituals through which it was expressed acquired new meanings and opened up new paths for spiritual self-realization in different social and political settings.

Virginia Reinburg asks us to listen to the daily prayers of ordinary people on the eve of the Reformation and to consider how Protestant assaults on saintly intercessors and the rapid expansion of monarchical authority in the sixteenth century affected the social metaphors lay people used to construct their spiritual identities. Reformation theologians, she suggests, created a new devotional literature that suppressed saintly intercessors of both sexes as spiritual interlocutors. Instead, they encouraged lay people to express their relationship to God in the more narrowly patriarchal terms of father and child.

Barbara Diefendorf examines the impact of the Huguenot psalter—the vernacular translation of the Book of Psalms by Clement Marot and Theodore Beza—on the faith of French Protestants in the later sixteenth century. She argues that the psalter not only provided the language with which French Protestants expressed their fundamental beliefs but also that, through the Huguenots' identification with the psalmist David, it had a formative influence on their faith. It armed them not only with militancy but also with a particular understanding of persecution as a trial by God—a concept that helped them weather the storms of religious war and proved critical in their reaction to the massacre of Saint Bartholomew's Day.

The third essay, by Keith Luria, looks at the Catholic counteroffensive mounted for the reconversion of the Huguenots in seventeenth-century Poitou. Taking up the question of the "location of the sacred" in Catholic and Protestant cultures, Luria first establishes how, despite their many differences and their very recent history of bloody war, the substantial Protestant minority and the Catholic majority in the Poitou established a relatively comfortable coexistence in the years following the Edict of Nantes in 1598. He then proceeds to show how, beginning in 1617, Catholic missionaries in the Poitou mounted public rituals of conversion that ultimately redrew not only the sacred but also the social boundaries of the community along doctrinal lines.

Examining the relationships established between male confessors and their female penitents in Counter-Reformation Spain, Jodi Bilinkoff takes up yet another aspect of the problem of spiritual identity. She shows how the spiritual lives and religious careers of five prominent Spanish churchmen were transformed through their encounters with the exceptional women whose confessors, spiritual directors, and biographers they became. Not only was the relationship between confessor and penitent more reciprocal than one might imagine, but also the priests came to look favorably upon forms of religious expression that were more direct and ecstatic than those usually sanctioned by the Catholic church. By preaching, teaching, and writing in favorable terms about these forms of spirituality (forms that, significantly, were usually gendered as "feminine" by disapproving churchmen), they not only altered their own religious identities but also helped articulate the major shift in values associated with "baroque" spirituality.

Social Identities

The second section of this volume offers four inquiries into the processes at work in the formation of social identities, especially collective ones. It opens with an essay by Laurie Nussdorfer that examines the collective petitions composed orally by Roman artisanal groups and transcribed by paid public notaries. Nussdorfer shows how the employment of public notaries by artisans and guilds not only equalized access to the power of the legal contract between literate and nonliterate artisans but also made it possible for the artisanal corporation to constitute itself as a collective body and a legal force in local politics. Paradoxically, the written word gave illiterate Roman artisans a voice; but it was a collective voice. As Nussdorfer points out, the only particular voice to which the notary drew attention in his text was his own. And so, in the end, "the artisans' dependence upon the notary attests to the ultimate triumph of the written word over the power of speech. The oral played through the texts of their meetings, giving them authority, but the invisible pen was what inscribed and gave potency to their voices."[17]

Popular politics and collective identity are again examined in an urban setting in James Amelang's essay, which looks at the formation of neighborhood identity in early modern Barcelona. Amelang shows how a particular area in Barcelona, that known as the Ribera, took advantage of its social complexity and of the weakness of royal, municipal, and ecclesiastical authorities, in order to create its own forms of cultural and political representation. Through actions that ranged from street violence to poetry and theater, the people of the Ribera forged an identity as a neighborhood and acquired through it an effective means of political empowerment.

An essay by Andrew Barnes examines the social processes at work in the formation of a new identity for post-Tridentine Catholic clergymen. The key relationship for Barnes is that between the country priest and his parish. Barnes suggests that a post-Tridentine insistence on seminary education for all priests transformed the social composition of the rural clergy by making access to this vocation at once more difficult for the peasantry and more appealing to the urban middle classes. This policy, he concludes, resulted in a widening of the social gap between the priest and his parishioners. Moreover, the unprecedented stress this seminary education placed on moral rectitude as an ideal of priestly conduct ultimately led to the psychological isolation of the clergy from the laity. The post-Tridentine rural priest thus emerged as an outsider whose social affinity and function within the community had been severely diminished. These policies, Barnes suggests, help to explain both the increase in popular anticlericalism and the radicalization of the lower clergy in the eighteenth century.

This section closes with an essay by Peter Sahlins that seeks to further explain the growing tension between traditional, peasant culture and reforming elites. Sahlins takes us to the forests of the Ariège in order to explore why male peasants dressed up as women in order to chase out forest guards and charcoal makers. They took these actions to demonstrate opposition to the passage of a national forest code that excluded their exercise of traditional rights of usufruct in the private and state forests of the Pyrenees, and the riots thus represent an act of political resistance. Sahlins's analysis focuses on the ritual forms this resistance took, its relation to the rites of carnival and *charivari*. He explores the multivalent symbolism of women in the riots—the rioters identified themselves with the forest "raped" by the guards, but they also identified themselves as young men "married" to the forest, and they evoked the image of "disorderly women"—and the linkages between these symbols and the place of the forest in peasant culture. He argues that the ritual reversal of gender roles was also a dramatic enactment of community in relation to the state, and that it must be seen as a cultural ordering of political relations.

Cultural Identities

Examining four different genres of the written word—the love letter, the vernacular medical treatise, classical drama, and the history of women—the essays that comprise the closing section of the volume look at the cultural process of identity formation in the narrower and more traditional sense of culture as the product of intellectual and aesthetic training. Yet, while focusing specifically on questions of literary and learned culture, the authors of these essays share a common conception of the history of literate culture as the study of a complex process of sociocultural exchange that must inevitably include consideration not only of the formal content of the texts in hand, but also of the circumstances of their writing, printing, publishing, and reading as well.

The section opens with an essay by Elizabeth S. Cohen that assesses the personal power an individual gained through literacy. Her essay is one of several in this collection that reexamine the meaning and consequences of having access to the written word—as reader, as writer, and as published author. Cohen's approach to the problem is that of the case study. She examines a love letter written by a Roman youth to his illiterate girlfriend. The letter, which combines epistolary formality with adolescent whining and romantic pleading, bears graphic sexual decoration both inside and out. Preserved because of a libel suit the girl's parents brought against its young author in 1602, the letter poses interesting questions for the study of literacy. Why write a letter to a girl who cannot read? More particularly, why write a compromising letter, when someone else will have to see and decipher it? What accounts for the letter's strikingly erratic style? In the course of answering these questions, Cohen challenges traditional assumptions of neat divisions between images and texts, between oral and written cultures, elite and popular forms of intimate exchange, and public and private modes of communication.

Alison Klairmont Lingo's essay, which explores the impact of printing on the transmission of knowledge about women's health care in the sixteenth and seventeenth centuries, provides a further examination of the relations of power implicit in access to the written word. In the essay "Printing and the People," Natalie Davis called attention to what she called "the central paradox in the impact of printing on the people":

> On the one hand, it can destroy traditional monopolies on knowledge and authorship and can sell and disseminate widely both information and works of imagination.... But printing can also make possible the establishment of new kinds of control on popular thought.[18]

Lingo affirms and illustrates this paradox by showing just how the rapid proliferation of vernacular texts on childbirth and female medical complaints unsettled the monopoly of the learned male medical elite on representations and knowledge of the female body. By permitting the participation of lay practitioners in both the public transmission of different midwifery techniques and the sensitive religious and ethical debates then occurring about medical intervention in the reproductive process, printing offered women unprecedented access to knowledge about their bodies. It also allowed them some participation in the debates about medical practice and ethics. At the same time, as Lingo documents, a rising group of male medical practitioners, the surgeons, used the controlling capacities of print in their struggle to appropriate lifesaving obstetrical practices as male prerogatives and thereby displace the traditional, empirical medicine of female midwives.

Jonathan Dewald's essay takes its point of departure from the insight that the reworking of literary tropes—in this case the figure of the "deadly parent" in the classical drama of seventeenth-century France—can tell us something important about social and cultural values. He shows us how Racine's reworking of the Theban story "inverts our expectations about Oedipal relations" and asks us to consider why themes of family violence became so pervasive in the dramas most popular with Parisian high society in the age of Louis XIV.[19] Why the preoccupation with family murder, conflicted inheritance, and incest? Above all, why does the father become the primary symbol of danger and destruction? The answer, he suggests, lies in the mythical form these dramas gave to the conflicts generated by the underlying tension between personal ambition and familial obligation in a social world organized according to principles of patriarchal authority and political absolutism.

Like Racine, Louise de Kéralio, the subject of Carla Hesse's essay, used stories of family conflict to reveal the cruelties of absolutism and the tensions it generated. But in Kéralio's works the gender roles are reversed: mothers and daughters compete for lovers in novels whose plots revolve around complex tales of female rivalry, maternal tyranny, and domination. Kéralio was a historian as well as a novelist, and Hesse shows how, in her authorial persona as well as her writings, she invented a unique identity for herself as a historian of women by "bending the rules of both gender and genre as far as they could bend without breaking them."[20] The fact that Kéralio's career spanned the tumultuous changes brought about by the French Revolution meant that she was forced to adapt to several distinct transformations in the unspoken codes that governed women's public and private roles.

True to the spirit of the historical writings of Natalie Zemon Davis, the essays gathered in this volume do not add up to a single grand narrative recounting the cultural transition from the medieval to the modern world. Indeed, the historians writing here have, for the most part, followed Natalie Davis in rejecting the traditional conceptualization of the early modern period that finds its unity in the teleological notion of an "age of transition." In place of the overdetermined unity offered a generation ago by those espousing various modernizationist paradigms, the essays in this volume seek to interpret each of the major transformations in early modern European history—the Reformation, Counter-Reformation, urbanization, the advent of print, absolutism, Enlightenment, and revolution—as the result of a series of uneven and discontinuous changes welling up from within a patchwork of social, spiritual, and cultural realities. These studies in the history of cultural practices, it is hoped, will thus further our appreciation of the fact that the greatest historical events may in fact be the result of discrete yet intersecting social, spiritual, and cultural movements, whether of individual or collective invention.

NOTES

1. Natalie Zemon Davis, *Fiction in the Archives: Pardon Tales and Their Tellers in Sixteenth-Century France* (Stanford, 1987), 4.

2. Natalie Zemon Davis, "Art and Society in the Gifts of Montaigne," *Representations* 12 (Fall 1985): 24.

3. Natalie Zemon Davis, *Society and Culture in Early Modern France* (Stanford, 1975); in French, *Les Cultures du peuple. Rituels, savoirs et résistances au 16e siècle* (Paris, 1979).

4. Natalie Zemon Davis, "Boundaries and the Sense of Self in Sixteenth-Century France," in *Reconstructing Individualism: Autonomy, Individuality, and the Self in Western Thought,* ed. Thomas C. Heller, Morton Sosna, and David E. Wellbery (Stanford, 1986), 53.

5. "Women on Top," in *Society and Culture,* 124–51. "The Rites of Violence," in ibid., 152–87, was originally published in *Past & Present* 59 (1973).

6. Natalie Zemon Davis, "The Sacred and the Body Social in Sixteenth-Century Lyons," *Past & Present* 90 (1981): 40–70.

7. Ibid., 68.

8. "Printing and the People," in *Society and Culture,* 203.

9. Ibid., 225.

10. Ibid., xvii.

11. Natalie Zemon Davis, "Ghosts, Kin, and Progeny: Some Features of Family Life in Early Modern France," *Daedalus* 106 (1977): 108.

12. Ibid.

13. (Cambridge MA, 1983).

14. Ibid., 29.

15. Ibid., 47 (Davis's italics).

16. Davis, *Fiction in the Archives,* 112.

17. See Laurie Nussdorfer, "Writing and the Power of Speech," in this volume.

18. Davis, *Society and Culture,* 224–25.

19. See Jonathan Dewald, "Deadly Parents: Family and Aristocratic Culture," in this volume.

20. See Carla Hesse, "Revolutionary Histories," in this volume.

Part 1
Spiritual Identities

Hearing Lay People's Prayer

Virginia Reinburg

This is what Martin Luther had to say about lay people's prayer in his *Betbüchlein* (1522):

> Among the many harmful books and doctrines which are mislead-
> ing and deceiving Christians and give rise to countless false beliefs,
> I regard personal prayer books as by no means the least objection-
> able. They drub into the minds of simple people such un-Christian
> tomfoolery about prayers to God and his saints! Moreover, these
> books are puffed up with promises of indulgences and come out
> with decorations in red ink and pretty titles. . . . These books need
> a basic and thorough reformation if not total extermination.[1]

Two years later Guillaume Farel cautioned readers of his devotional
treatise *Le Pater Noster et le Credo en françoys* against "rattling their lips"
without understanding the words of their prayer.[2] Similarly, Calvin's
friend and Lausanne reformer Pierre Viret criticized "the little books
called 'Hours'" and their readers, those who through a foolish fantasy
believed—as magicians did—that there was more value in written or
spoken words than in God's word.[3] Luther, Farel, and Viret wished
to replace the evils of the book of hours with the virtues of their own
devotional books. In the process they thought they would transform
the way "simple people" prayed.

Protestant reformers' accusations of superstition and emptiness in
the prayer practices of their day have continued to inform our understanding of those practices. Commenting on the external emphasis
of popular devotion in a tone less ridiculing than the sixteenth-century reformers but nonetheless condescending, Pierre Chaunu calls

medieval Christianity "a religion of doing, not of knowing." "The exact content of the rite is lost."[4] Jacques Toussaert writes that "the vulgar manner adopted" with regard to the saints "was often only a deformation" of true worship.[5] Johan Huizinga comments: "The signs of the everlasting divine grace multiplied endlessly; a host of special benedictions sprang up side by side with the sacraments; in addition to relics we find amulets; the bizarre gallery of saints becomes even more numerous and variegated." And furthermore, "religious customs tended to multiply in an almost mechanical way." There was, as Huizinga described it, "an irresistible urge to reduce the infinite to the finite, to disintegrate all mystery. The highest mysteries of the creed become covered with a crust of superficial piety. Even the profound faith in the Eucharist expands into childish beliefs." Huizinga's portrait of late medieval piety in *The Waning of the Middle Ages* (1924)—its oppressive, obsessive, morbid character—is persuasive because it shows us a religious culture groaning under the weight of its own oversaturated emotion, on the verge of collapse, a collapse we all know will take place hours after his book closes.[6]

Modern historians have inherited a central assumption of the sixteenth-century reformers: the belief that proper or "true" Christianity implies clear boundaries between sacred and profane, between spiritual and material, between heaven and earth. This view has important consequences for our understanding of lay religious life of the late Middle Ages. Today when we open a fifteenth-century prayer book we have been conditioned to find there meaningless rote prayers, prayers in a language few could read, absurdly inflated indulgences, superstitious magical charms. But what if we were to listen more closely to the voices in the prayer books themselves, voices we will have to strain to hear over the condemnatory din made by sixteenth-century reformers and modern historians? If we explore the relationships, feelings, and hopes people expressed in their prayers to God, the Virgin Mary, and saints, and then return to the reformers' critique, we will see more clearly what lies at the root of their charges of superstition.

The prayers I discuss are found primarily in manuscript and early printed books of hours from northern France and Flanders.[7] The book of hours—the best-selling book of the late Middle Ages—was a collection of offices, litanies, and prayers originally adapted from the clerical breviary but designed explicitly for use by lay men and women. The earliest books of hours were probably compiled by the spiritual advisers and chaplains of nobles, in collaboration with scribes and illuminators. Like the breviary, the book of hours included offices—patterns of daily and hourly prayer based on different combinations of psalms, antiphons, and readings. But unlike the breviary, the book of hours also contained numerous prayers addressed to God, the Virgin Mary, and saints; prayers for special intentions and occasions; and illustrations that might also be used for private meditation. No two manuscript books of hours were exactly alike. The enormous variety in design, contents, and devotional style we find among surviving books of hours testifies to the malleability of the genre. An individualized anthology of prayers and religious images, the book of hours was thus open to multiple devotional uses. Undoubtedly many owners wished to have a book of hours among their possessions for reasons of artistic taste and social prestige. But scattered and fragmentary evidence also suggests that owners did use books of hours in their practice of prayer.[8]

Marks of individual ownership in surviving manuscript and printed books of hours allow us to identify most owners as members of noble, bourgeois, and professional families. Between the twelfth and the fourteenth centuries, manuscript books of hours were produced for and owned by wealthy, literate nobles. We have evidence that after that time ownership of books of hours moved down the social hierarchy. Members of bourgeois and robe families owned them in increasing numbers. Even prosperous, literate artisans owned books of hours by the midfifteenth century. By that time manuscripts were being mass produced by scribal workshops and, after about 1485, printed as well.

Sold in scribal and print shops, sometimes copied by owners themselves, inherited from family and friends, the book of hours was remarkably free of any form of clerical supervision. Owners added illustrations, vernacular texts, family diaries, amulets, and other personal material to books they purchased or inherited. As a genre, the book of hours was capable of accommodating diverse personal tastes and religious concerns. While the sources do not provide straightforward answers about which devotees said which prayers in what specific way, books of hours are nevertheless a rich mine of visual and textual information about the practice of prayer among literate lay people.

At first glance, it seems that far more prayers in books of hours address the Virgin Mary and saints than God. In the sixteenth century, humanists and church reformers accused ordinary Christians of idolatry, for praying to God's creatures instead of to God. Calvin believed it "the height of stupidity, not to say madness, to be so intent on gaining access to the saints as to be led away from God, apart from whom no entry lies open."[9] While of course omitting condemnation on doctrinal grounds, historians have pointed out the same propensity of common people to appeal to lesser heavenly patrons than God—or at least strongly implying that prayer to saints was less worthwhile than prayer to God. As Francis Oakley has commented, devotees charged "a swarm of minor saints with the most refined and gross of specialties."[10] Such a sharp distinction between prayer to God and prayer to other heavenly persons was probably not clear to ordinary lay people, for God's presence permeates prayers to the saints. Devotees often invoked God's power and wishes when they prayed to saints. Likewise, saints often appear in prayers addressed to God. They assist and honor him in the heavenly court. For example, a French prayer penned onto a blank page of a book of hours from Amiens shows how close God and the Virgin were in the devotee's mind: "God, Father, be with me at the end to guard from tribulation my soul, my heart, and my body that I present to you; mother of God be present at my end."[11]

For readers of books of hours, prayer is a highly mediated activity, in fact a system of patronage in which a devotee asks one person to speak to a more influential one. Even prayers addressed to the Trinity emphasize the interdependence of three distinct persons at the center of a patronage network. Father, Son, and Holy Spirit rule jointly; they sit on the divine throne together, as illustrations in books of hours explain. If human-supernatural relationships constituted a network of spiritual patronage, to pray was to participate in a system of exchange within that network. A human devotee offered petitions, praise, and donations, and expected an answer or assistance from the person or persons to whom she prayed or dedicated herself. Thus hierarchy and reciprocity governed relations between devotee and supernatural patron, as was true in most social relations of the sixteenth century.

In their prayers devotees addressed saints by a wide variety of titles drawn from the social world. Saint Barbara is "my honorable mistress" to the devotee in a prayer from fifteenth-century Lorraine.[12] The owner of a Flemish book of hours could pray, "Holy angel of God, to whose care I, Ançola, an unworthy sinner and your unworthy servant, commend myself."[13] The Apostle John was called "beloved friend of Christ."[14] A prayer from Rouen has the devotee call Saint Mary Magdalene "honorable lady of the manor," and herself the saint's "human goddaughter."[15] In a more complex fusion of roles, the devotee in one prayer calls Jesus "sovereign bishop, father, shepherd of our souls."[16]

Not only were the forms of address familiar from secular life, the very modes of relating to heavenly persons suggested the support, responsibility, and protection expected from relatives and patrons. People appealed to Saint Sebastian, a courageous Roman soldier martyred in the second century, to protect them from the "diabolical ambushes" of the plague and asked for his "defense in these anxious times."[17] In one prayer a devotee declares unequivocal faith in the influence of the Virgin and Saint John: "I indeed believe firmly and accept without any doubt that he who wants to be yours will belong to God, and he who does not want to be yours will not belong to God, for you can obtain whatever you ask from God without delay."[18] This prayer has the air of an oath, a formal and oral declaration of fidelity to a lord.

Sometimes the oath was depicted visually, as in the Hours of Isabelle de Coucy (Walters MS. W. 89). An owner's portrait in this late fourteenth-century Parisian manuscript portrays Isabelle praying before the Virgin and child Jesus. (See fig. 1.) This painting makes a precise statement about the relationship among Isabelle, Mary, and Jesus. Mary inclines her head toward Isabelle, signaling attentiveness, while Jesus grasps Isabelle's folded hands in his hand. Each gesture performed here—Isabelle kneeling and folding her hands, Jesus holding Isabelle's hands between his own—constitutes an element in the ritual of homage by which a lord and a vassal made a mutual vow of service and protection. The iconography of homage to the Virgin and Jesus was borrowed from rituals of homage practiced by lords and vassals, as illustrated, for example, in a fourteenth-century legal manuscript (Harvard Law School MS. 12).[19] (See fig. 2.) Isabelle de Coucy's vow was individual, but a community might also take a vow, as for example in a text entitled "Vow made by the city of Cervières in October 1628, to Saint Roch, confessor, taken as patron." Here the village as a body appeals to Saint Roch to preserve it from the plague and pledges to honor him as patron in return for his protection. The village asks the saint "to be a very good friend to us, before Jesus, the heavenly king." In response Saint Roch replies that he has presented their petition to God, who, for his part, promised to curb the plague's spread.[20] This hierarchy of appeal—from devotee to saint to God— conforms to late medieval notions of salvation, a business laboriously conducted through avenues of spiritual patronage, entailing intricate exchanges of favors and gifts. Isabelle de Coucy expects Jesus' protection in return for her service and fidelity. The village of Cervières hopes that Saint Roch's friendship with God will enable him to gain God's ear, while the villagers' gifts of prayers and a chapel should encourage the saint to listen to them.

As a person might do when requesting favors from a patron, devotees sometimes invoked particularities of a saint's relationship to God. Prayers to Saint Mary Magdalene emphasized the mutual love between the saint and Jesus. In one fourteenth-century text, Mary Magdalene is called Jesus' intimate friend (*amie, amanz*), his "loyal handmaiden and good disciple." The devotee asks the saint to request from God on the devotee's behalf the same love and mercy she herself received. The devotee then turns her own voice to Jesus, pleading with him not to despise the prayer of his "miserable," "unworthy" servant, who is trying to serve him loyally.[21] The prayer's language evokes not only patronage but also contemporary practices of charity and almsgiving, in which beggars customarily acknowledged absolute dependence on the generosity of the more fortunate and powerful.[22] Another prayer to Mary Magdalene even calls her *doulce aulmonière*, a word that can mean almsgiver or almspurse.[23] Devotional language was rich and varied in its use of metaphor.

The best examples of this richness of language and social metaphor may be found in prayers to the Virgin Mary. Among all the saints in God's heavenly court, the Virgin held a place of special honor. She was "queen and duchess of the heavenly saints," to quote a text from Langres.[24] She was often called "lady" or "mistress" (*dame, maitresse*), titles that through familiarity have now lost their late-medieval associations with courtly and noble modes of relationship. Mary was sometimes addressed in obviously feudal language, as in this prayer to Notre-Dame du Puy, the black virgin of the Auvergne:

Fig. 1. Isabelle de Coucy kneeling before Virgin Mary and child Jesus. Hours, use of Paris, ca. 1380 (Hours of Isabelle de Coucy). Walters Art Gallery (Baltimore), MS. W. 89, fol. 3v. Reproduced with permission.

Fig. 2. Exchange of homage and fealty. Statutes of England, 1326. Marginal illustration from Harvard Law School (Cambridge, Mass.), MS. 12, fol. 33v. Reproduced with permission.

I pray you humbly, in your oratory, before your very holy image, to protect me faithfully as your own, while I do you total homage with body and soul. Defend me from dishonor and harm, for in you, lady, is my entire hope. Protect me in this uncertain world, so that I will live forever before the high judge. Amen.[25]

Another prayer to Notre-Dame du Puy has the devotee declare, "I offer myself to you in soul and in body, and all that I have...."[26] Kristen Neuschel has shown how sixteenth-century French nobles spoke a language of humility and deference in their political and social relations; use of this language could only have nourished the devotional meaning of fidelity and reciprocity in prayers to the Virgin.[27] Similarly, calling Mary "advocate" would have carried connotations of legal representation before a court or judge.[28] Calling Mary "the merciful one," or even "Mother of mercy," emphasized her power and willingness to ask God to grant pardon to sinners, in much the same way that a king's relative might plead for mercy for a criminal. Here the double meanings of *mercy, pardon,* and *intercede* are far from accidental. Sixteenth-century clerics believed this kind of symbolism rendered the Virgin overly familiar and the devotees' appeals excessively concrete. But we might also say that concepts familiar from secular life enriched devotees' prayer by layering associations from different worlds of experience.

Prayers to the Virgin Mary are best known for their maternal imagery. Mary is the mother of Jesus, and spiritually the mother of all men and women. The "Obsecro te," a prayer almost invariably found in books of hours, opens by addressing Mary as "mother of God ... most glorious mother ... mother of orphans." As the prayer continues, the devotee cites significant episodes in Mary's life as Jesus' mother—the Annunciation, Jesus' birth and crucifixion—pausing to contemplate briefly her physical and emotional experiences of each. The text graphically describes Jesus' agony at Calvary, and sensitively evokes Mary's suffering. Through this suffering, Mary is asked to listen to the devotee's prayer.[29] Thus the prayer combines petition and meditation. The devotee appeals to the Virgin for assistance, acknowledging her as *mediatrix.* But the Virgin also interceded in another way, by providing the eyes through which to see Jesus' suffering and death. Jesus' mother was a model for the onlooker's emotional participation in the passion.

The imaginative effort this prayer requires was not unique. Mary also acted as the devotee's eyes in the popular Stabat Mater, an anonymous thirteenth-century sequence from the Mass of the Seven Sorrows of the Virgin Mary that often appeared in books of hours. The sequence recreates a moment of Jesus' passion: the time when the sorrowful mother weeps beside her son's cross. Mary's grief has two stages: first she sees Jesus' pain, then she suffers her own pain. The devotee learns to participate in the passion by watching the Virgin watch Jesus and identifying with her pain. One line of the prayer asks plaintively, "who would not weep to see the mother of Christ in such torment?" As a devotional experience, the Stabat Mater progresses from vision to feeling, and from Mary to devotee, ultimately creating within the devotee an empathetic fusion with Jesus' grieving mother.[30]

Prayers to the Virgin Mary refer to a parent's grief at a child's suffering. But Mary is also the mother of all humanity. The same prayers just cited for their sensitive portrayal of a mother's pain are also appeals from human devotees to their own heavenly mother. The Obsecro Te recalls Jesus' promise at his ascension not to leave his followers orphans. He gives them the consolation and aid of his mother, whom the prayer calls "mother of orphans." The Obsecro Te binds bereaved mother to bereaved follower of Christ by placing the devotee, a descendant of those Jesus left behind, in Mary's care. The prayer promises motherly protection for orphaned children. Mary also consoles the sick and dying. The closing lines of the prayer express hope that the Virgin will be present at the devotee's deathbed:

And at the end of my life show me your face, and reveal to me the day and hour of my death. Please hear me and receive this humble prayer and grant me eternal life. Listen and hear me, Mary, sweetest virgin, mother of God and of mercy. Amen.

In some books of hours, rubrics attached to the text promise that the Virgin will appear to announce the hour of death to those who say the prayer faithfully.[31] And one fifteenth-century Parisian prayer book expresses the pledge visually: a miniature depicts the Virgin and child Jesus peeking inside a window of a dying woman's bedchamber (Bibliothèque Nationale MS. lat. 1164).[32] (See fig. 3.) Rooted in widespread fear of sudden, unprepared death, the desire to see Mother Mary's face expresses the devotee's wish for proof of the Virgin's intercession at this crucial moment before individual judgment. But we can also hear a longing for kind, motherly comfort during pain and insecurity.

When the sixteenth-century reformers faced this rich variety of social metaphor in devotional language they heard idolatry, superstition, and excessive familiarity with the sacred. Protestants argued strenuously for a solid scriptural basis for prayer, and for intellectual comprehension. Luther, Farel, Viret, and their colleagues published commentaries on the Lord's Prayer that they hoped would replace the "deceptions" of the book of hours and teach lay people how to pray in a simpler, more direct, more heartfelt way. But listen more carefully to what Protestant authors are saying in the works they write to instruct lay people about prayer. They encourage devotees to pray the Lord's Prayer, Jesus' most direct instruction about prayer—but also a scriptural passage that emphasizes paternal imagery in devotion. Here it is important to note that of the several scriptural models available for conceptualizing the relationship between human being and God, the reformers chose first that of father and child, and secondarily that of master and servant. In the writings of Calvin and Viret, the divine father figure is extraordinarily demanding, almost domineering. The child—ordinarily a son—declares complete dependence on the father and complete obedience to his wishes. *Le miroir du pénitent,* an anonymous Protestant work published in Lyons in 1549, consistently employs father-son imagery to describe the God-devotee relationship, occasionally also referring to God as king, Jesus as the king's son, and the faithful devotee as a subject. God is sometimes a judge.[33] Pierre Viret likewise emphasizes a particular model of father-son relationship, one in which the father is stern, severe, and strict. If the father decides to be merciful and understanding of the son's faults, it is not out of any obligation on his part to do so.[34] A reformed prayer book of the early 1530s describes God as a father who is "powerful, wise, and good." The anonymous author notes that God's request that human beings call him "father" is a sign of his love, yet this loving father is not described as also gentle and nurturing.[35] Reformed Catholics hardly differed from Protestants in favoring this kind of father-son relationship as a model for devotion. To be sure, Catholics did not generally begin their discourses on prayer with

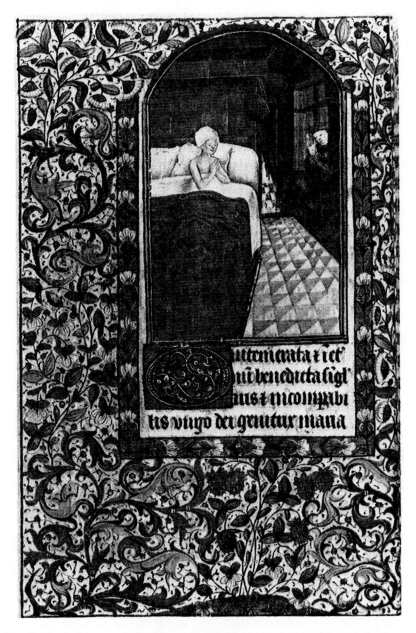

Fig. 3. Virgin Mary and child Jesus appearing to woman in sick bed. Book of Hours, use of Paris, mid or late fifteenth century. Bibliothèque Nationale (Paris), MS. lat. 1164, fol. 24v. Reproduced with permission.

scriptural justification. Yet Catholic writers also encouraged their readers to think of God as "the good and just father" who governed humanity as a father governed a family.

In most devotional books and commentaries written by Protestant and Catholic reformers, God and the saints take on different personalities and roles from those they display in books of hours. Most obviously, female saints retreat. Protestant reformers removed all saints, whatever their sex, as well as the Virgin Mary, from the devotional universe. In a subtler way, Catholic reformers also transformed female metaphors and figures in prayer texts. The Jesuit Emond Auger encouraged his readers to pray to the Virgin but instructed them carefully to think of her primarily as a model of sanctity and obedience. His *Formulaire de prières catholiques* (1584) contains only one prayer to Mary, out of twenty-six texts.[36] Parisian parish priest René Benoist composed a prayer to Saint Mary Magdalene, but the text actually serves as an excuse for a venomous diatribe against women who abuse and emasculate their husbands and sons.[37] Female saints play a very small role even in Pierre Coton's devotional book addressed explicitly to women.[38] The removal of female figures is accompanied by a full reordering of gender imagery. Gentle, nurturing qualities ordinarily associated in books of hours with Jesus' mother and familiar patron saints are assumed by a fatherly God, or also, in Catholic writings, by Saints Michael and Peter. Rather than being patrons with particular relationships to communities or individuals, however, these divine or saintly male figures protect devotees by means of great strength and virtue. The local and multiple devotional voices we can hear in prayers in books of hours, addressing a well-populated spiritual universe of God and saints, have been replaced with a singular kind of appeal to a universal source of heavenly assistance. God, and for the Catholics, a few powerful male saints, have assumed all the personal characteristics and specialties attached to a wide variety of heavenly persons in lay books of hours. The devotional universe of Protestant and Catholic clerics was governed by a clear, simple, male hierarchy that ruled with sovereign authority.

Both Protestant and Catholic reformers encouraged use of particular modes of political relationship in devotion. Slightly more pronounced in reformed Catholic writers than in Protestants is the metaphor of God as "sovereign lord." Auger refers consistently to the kingship and lordship of God in terms that are resolutely paternal and monarchical. The notion of God as lord seems so familiar to us from Anglican and Roman versions of Christian hymns that perhaps we do not think easily of its connotations for fifteenth- and sixteenth-century lay people. Auger's prayer before bedtime demonstrates clearly the prominence of royal imagery: "Lord, who for the body's rest has so wisely ordered the night to follow the day, I beg you very humbly . . . not to abandon me now in these shadows of death. . . . For on all sides I am surrounded by my enemies . . . who give me no rest." The entire creation is God's kingdom; Auger encourages the reader to do homage to the highest lord, "ruler of all creatures."[39] René Benoist likewise employed an elaborate royal imagery to describe human relationships with God.[40] While Auger called saints "our brothers," his fellow Jesuit Pierre Coton, writing fifty years later, even gave them a state office, calling them "almoners" of the divine king.[41]

Although they preferred a paternal image, Protestant writers did not refrain completely from using contemporary political titles for heavenly persons. Calvin often refers to human beings as part of "the Lord's kingdom and his household."[42] And even though he did not call God a judge, Viret called Jesus the *maître des requêtes* in the royal court.[43] Political language probably came naturally. After all, Viret and Calvin were engaged for decades in the politics of religious and moral reform. Auger and Coton were chaplains in the French royal court, and in other writings both argued for a strong family and a strong monarchy as foundations for a reformed French Catholicism. All these reformers were deeply committed to the task of creating order out of what they saw as the religious and political chaos of their world. No wonder they saw the kind of prayer expressed in books of hours as disorderly, "foolish," and "harmful." What they called "superstition" they understood as uneducated and inappropriate appeals to God's servants or relatives—offensive to the King as well as ineffective business practices.

Protestants and reformed Catholics also shared a concern with discipline—specifically, in the matter of prayer, the effort to teach lay people how to pray. Within three years of Luther's ninety-five theses, he, his followers, and his imitators were composing and publishing devotional books explicitly designed as alternatives to the book of hours. All over western Europe reformed pastors were forming disciplinary institutions aimed at supervising lay devotional life. Christians must pray from the heart, and "the heart requires understanding,"

Calvin insisted.[44] Catholics also insisted on a higher standard of doctrinal instruction for lay people; the catechisms, catechism classes, missions, and sermons of the Tridentine church clearly demonstrate this concern. Protestant and Catholic churches alike claimed the authority to teach lay people how to pray—an authority undermined by such independent means of instruction as books of hours, parents, and popular healers. Catholic theologians such as the Lyons Franciscan Jean Benedicti insisted that the Church must endorse the formula and manner of lay people's prayer.[45] Testimony before the Genevan consistory shows clearly what the Genevan pastors saw was at stake in their educational efforts. In 1548 a surgeon was called before the consistory and disciplined for telling the pregnant women he cared for to pray to the Virgin Mary in their hour of need. And in one moving case—not at all unique—a woman explained that she prayed the Ave Maria and Apostles' Creed as her mother and father taught her, in Latin. The consistory members, properly horrified, ordered her to go to sermons and catechism classes so she could learn to pray—as they said, with what I am sure was unconscious irony—"in her maternal language."[46]

Sixteenth-century clerical reformers clearly were concerned about the transmission of prayer—not only from devotees to heaven, but also the circulation of knowledge about prayer among lay people. Calvinist consistories and Catholic educational manuals both betray anxiety about who teaches lay people how to pray. Catholic priests no less than Protestant ministers wished the church to be the teaching authority. To this end, reformers designed a new language of devotion, one focused on paternal and royal metaphors and relationships. They wished to eliminate the complex and disorderly language of late medieval patronage—with its complicated hierarchies, overlapping jurisdictions, private laws, and outside appeals. As they tried to clarify boundaries between the sacred and the worldly, and sometimes even denied that explicitly secular metaphors were appropriate in devotional dialogue, Protestant and Catholic reformers of the sixteenth century intended to replace a language of prayer rich and varied in its secular associations with one more compatible with the concerns of a reformed church, a centralizing monarchical state, and a paternalistic family. But at least during the sixteenth century, they probably failed to teach this new devotional language to the laity. For until at least 1600, printers continued to produce and sell large numbers of books of hours that differed little from earlier manuscripts.[47] The traditional cult of Mary and the saints endured among lay Catholics (and possibly among many living in Protestant regions).[48] Reforming clerics labeled "superstitious" and tried to eliminate devotional practices rooted in intercession, mediation, pluralism, and materiality. But they succeeded only in creating a new model of Christian practice, not in abolishing the old.

NOTES

Some of the ideas discussed in this article are explored more fully in my forthcoming book, *Popular Prayers in Late Medieval France.* I am grateful to Sherrill Cohen, Natalie Zemon Davis, Barbara Diefendorf, David Ferris, Thomas Head, Robert M. Kingdon, and Marc Venard for their questions and suggestions; and to the American Council of Learned Societies and Boston College for research support. I would also like to thank Natalie Davis for her enduring guidance and support.

1. Martin Luther, *Betbüchlein* (1522), trans. Martin H. Bertram, in *Luther's Works,* ed. J. Pelikan and H. Lehmann, 55 vols. to date (St. Louis/Philadelphia, 1955–), 43:11–12.

2. Guillaume Farel, *Le Pater Noster et le Credo en françoys publié d'après l'exemplaire unique,* ed. Francis Higman (Geneva, 1982), 36–37. Higman's introduction explains how heavily Farel borrowed from Luther's *Betbüchlein.*

3. Pierre Viret, *Exposition familiere de l'oraison de nostre Seigneur Jesus Christ, et des choses dignes de consyderer sur icelle, faite en forme de dialogue* (Geneva: Jean Gerard, 1551), 72–74. The dedicatory epistle is dated 1547.

4. Pierre Chaunu, *Le temps des Réformes: Histoire religieuse et système de civilisation,* 2 vols. (Brussels, 1984), 1:172 and 173.

5. Jacques Toussaert, *Le sentiment religieux en Flandre à la fin du Moyen Age* (Paris, 1963), 288. For a more recent statement of similar views, see Carlos M. N. Eire, *War Against the Idols: The Reformation of Worship from Erasmus to Calvin* (Cambridge, 1986), especially chapter 1.

6. Johan Huizinga, *The Waning of the Middle Ages: A Study of the Forms of Life, Thought, and Art in France and the Netherlands in the XIVth and XVth Centuries,* trans. F. Hopman (New York, 1954), 153–55. See Lucien Febvre's doubts about Huizinga's analysis in "Sensibility and History," in *A New Kind of History: From the Writings of Febvre,* ed. Peter Burke (London, 1973), 16–19.

Natalie Zemon Davis, Etienne Delaruelle, Marc Venard, and others have offered a more sympathetic view of popular piety, and moreover discussed it in ways largely free of sixteenth-century clerical standards. See Davis, "Some Tasks and Themes in the Study of Popular Religion," in *The Pursuit of Holiness in Late Medieval and Renaissance Religion,* ed. Charles Trinkaus and

Heiko A. Oberman (Leiden, 1974), 307–36; Davis, "From 'Popular Religion' to Religious Cultures," in *Reformation Europe: A Guide to Research,* ed. Steven Ozment (St. Louis, 1982), 321–41; Delaruelle, *La piété populaire au Moyen Age* (Turin, 1975); Venard, *L'église d'Avignon au XVIe siècle* (Lille, 1980); and *Histoire de la France religieuse,* ed. Jacques Le Goff and René Rémond, vol. 2: *Du christianisme flamboyant à l'aube des Lumières (XIVe–XVIIIe siècle),* ed. François Lebrun (Paris, 1988) (with articles by Lebrun, Jacques Chiffoleau, Elisabeth Labrousse, Robert Sauzet, and Marc Venard).

7. I elaborate on many of the points raised in the next three paragraphs in *Popular Prayers,* chapter 1. See also *Time Sanctified: The Book of Hours in Medieval Art and Life,* ed. Roger Wieck (Baltimore/New York, 1988), especially chapters by Wieck and Reinburg; and L. M. J. Delaissé, "The Importance of the Book of Hours for the History of the Medieval Book," in *Gatherings in Honor of Dorothy E. Miner,* ed. Ursula McCracken et al. (Baltimore, 1974), 203–25.

8. Such evidence includes direct testimony about several owners; prescriptive literature directing lay people to use books of hours; and, most important, the physical evidence remaining in manuscripts themselves, including textual evidence, owners' annotations, marks left by owners' hands. In *Popular Prayers,* chapter 1, I discuss the nature of this evidence and ways it can be used.

9. Jean Calvin, *Institutes of the Christian Religion,* trans. Ford Lewis Battles, ed. John T. McNeill (Philadelphia, 1960), 879.

10. Francis Oakley, *The Western Church in the Later Middle Ages* (Ithaca, 1979), 117.

11. Bibliothèque de l'Arsenal, Paris, MS. 576, fol. 58 (Hours, use of Rouen, fifteenth and sixteenth centuries). The prayer is written in a late sixteenth-century hand. I have added modern punctuation; no capital letters, punctuation, or spaces separate words in the original. An ownership note on the end page notes that the prayer book belonged to Anthoinette Desprez, wife of Philippe de la Vallée of Amiens, 1559.

12. Bibliothèque Municipale de Nancy, MS. 35 (245), fols. 122v–123v (Hours, use of Toul, fifteenth century). See Pierre Rézeau, *Les prières en français à la fin du Moyen Age: Prières à un saint particulier et aux anges* (Geneva, 1983), 75–77.

13. Bibliothèque Nationale, Paris (hereafter, BN), manuscrit latin (hereafter, MS. lat.) 10555, fol. 271 (Hours, use of Rome, early sixteenth century; produced in Flanders).

14. In the prayer entitled O Intemerata. André Wilmart has edited and commented on the text in "La prière *O intemerata*," in *Auteurs spirituels et textes dévots du Moyen Age latin* (Paris, 1932), 474–504.

15. Fitzwilliam Museum, Cambridge [England], MS. 105, fols. 87–88v (Hours, use of Rouen, 1530). On saints as godparents, see A. N. Galpern, "The Legacy of Late Medieval Religion in Sixteenth-Century Champagne," in *Pursuit of Holiness,* 154–55; and John Bossy, "Godparenthood: The For-

tunes of a Social Institution in Early Modern Christianity," in *Religion and Society in Early Modern Europe 1500–1800*, ed. Kaspar von Greyerz (London, 1984), 194–201.

16. *Heures en francoys et latin a lusaige de Romme . . .* (Lyons: Guillaume Rouillé, 1549), fol. T6v.

17. BN, MS. nouvelles acquisitions françaises (hereafter, nouv. acq. fr.) 4600, fol. 272 (Latin-French psalter, fourteenth century; calendar indicates region of Rouen). See Rézeau, *Les prières en français*, 452–53.

18. This is the prayer O Intemerata, as in note 14 above.

19. Walters Art Gallery, Baltimore, MS. W. 89, fol. 3v (Hours, use of Paris, ca. 1380; Hours of Isabelle de Coucy, wife of Raoul II de Raineval) (fig. 1); and Harvard Law School Library, MS. 12, fol. 33v (Statutes of England, 1326) (figure 2). On rituals of homage see J. Russell Major, "'Bastard Feudalism' and the Kiss: Changing Social Mores in Late Medieval and Early Modern France," *Journal of Interdisciplinary History* 17 (1987): 509–35; and more generally Marc Bloch, *Feudal Society*, trans. L. A. Manyon, 2 vols. (Chicago, 1961), 1:145–62. On patronage and its cultural expression see Kristen B. Neuschel, *Word of Honor: Interpreting Noble Culture in Sixteenth-Century France* (Ithaca, 1989).

20. "Voeu faict par la ville de Cervieres, en octobre 1628, à saint Roch, confesseur, prins pour patron." Bibliothèque Municipale de Lyon, MS. 1402, fol. 128 (Hours, use of Rome, sixteenth century with seventeenth-century additions). I have used the text edited in Rézeau, *Les prières en français*, 442–44. Rézeau notes that Cervières (Lyonnais) suffered through the plague in 1628 and erected a chapel honoring Saint Roch in that year. The vow was likely undertaken on the occasion of the chapel's dedication and added to this book of hours by the book's owner. The text resembles the vows to saints undertaken by the sixteenth-century Spanish villagers William Christian has discussed in *Local Religion in Sixteenth-Century Spain* (Princeton, 1981), especially chapters 2–3, and appendix A.

21. BN, MS. nouvelles acquisitions latines (hereafter, nouv. acq. lat.) 592, fols. 78–85v (Hours, use of Paris, fourteenth century). This is a French prayer translated and adapted from a Latin prayer composed by Anselm. Most of the latter-day feudal language was added by the translator. The prayer book belonged to a woman. I discuss this prayer at greater length in *Popular Prayers*, chapter 3.

22. The rich language of charity and almsgiving is evident in Brian Pullan, *Rich and Poor in Renaissance Venice: The Social Institutions of a Catholic State, to 1620* (Cambridge, Mass., 1971); and Michel Mollat, *The Poor in the Middle Ages: An Essay in Social History*, trans. Arthur Goldhammer (New Haven, 1986). An example of the explicit use of charitable language in devotional life is Jean Gerson's *La mendicité spirituelle* (1401), in Gerson, *Oeuvres complètes*, ed. P. Glorieux, 10 vols. (Paris, 1960–73), 7:220–80.

23. *Louenges des benoistz sainctz et sainctes de paradis* (Paris: n.d. [early sixteenth century]), fol. xx5v.

24. Bibliothèque Municipale de Dôle, MS. 45, pp. 157–60 (Hours, unde-

termined use, fifteenth century; region of Langres). See Rézeau, *Les prières en français,* 27–29.

25. Quoted in Pierre Odin, *Sensuit la fondation de la saincte eglise et singulier oratoire de Nostre Dame du Puy translate de latin en francoys . . .* (Paris: Jean Trepperel, ca. 1530), reprinted in Charles Rocher, *Les vieilles histoires de Notre-Dame du Puy, réimprimées d'après les manuscrits ou les éditions originales* (Le Puy, 1890), 28.

26. "C'est l'oraison que Nostre Dame du Puy tient en sa main," found in two Parisian manuscripts: BN, MS. nouv. acq. lat. 592, fol. 120v (Hours, use of Paris, fourteenth century); and Bibliothèque Mazarine, Paris, MS. 509, fols. 107v-108 (prayer book, sixteenth century; Paris; belonged to Susane de Gonod). Both books were owned by women. See also Virginia Reinburg, "Les pèlerins de Notre-Dame du Puy," *Revue d'Histoire de l'Eglise de France* 75 (1989): 297–313.

27. Neuschel, *Word of Honor.*

28. On the Virgin Mary as *avocat* or counsel for the defense in a court trial see BN, MS. français (hereafter, MS. fr.) 145 (*Chants royaux en l'honneur de la Vierge au Puy d'Amiens,* early sixteenth century); BN, MS. fr. 379 (Jacques Le Lieur, *Chants Royaux,* Rouen, early sixteenth century); Bibliothèque Municipale de Rouen, MS. Leber 145 (prayer book, possibly late fifteenth century); and BN, MS. fr. 13167, fols. 123v–124v (Hours [in French], use of Paris, late fifteenth or early sixteenth century). Other examples of extensive use of legal metaphors in religious literature are Jacobus de Teramo (d. 1417), *Sensuyt la consolation des pecheurs autrement dit Belial procureur infernal,* trans. Pierre Ferget (Paris, ca. 1526), and Ulrich Tengler, *Laijen Spiegel: Von rechtmaessigen und peinlichen regimenten mit allegationen und bewergungen aufz geschrinen rechten und gesatzen* (Strasbourg, 1510). Both of these last works were known in many editions during this period.

29. For a Latin text and English translation of the Obsecro Te, see *Time Sanctified,* 94–96.

30. For a Latin text of the Stabat Mater, see *The Oxford Book of Medieval Latin Verse,* ed. F. J. E. Raby (Oxford, 1959), 435–37. It is found in most books of hours.

31. BN, MS. lat. 1183, fol. 126v (Hours, use of Paris, early sixteenth century): "Pape Innocent et Pape Boniface ottroirent à tous ceulx qui diront ceste oroison trois cens jours de pardon. Et soit tout certain quy devottement le dira chascun jour accoustuméement, il verra en lenfermeté de la maladie de sa mort la glorieuse vierge Marie, mere de Dieu, quy luy sera aidans et confortans encontre les mauvais ennemis denfer. En sensieult la ditte oroison. Je te prie dame sainte Marie, mere de Dieu . . . ." See also Fitzwilliam Museum, MS. 3–1954, fols. 263–64v (Hours, use of Paris, 1380s; Hours of Philip the Bold, duke of Burgundy); Library of Congress, MS. 169, fols. 94v-96 (Hours, undetermined use, early fifteenth century; possibly Picardy); Walters Art Gallery, MS. W. 170, fol. 73 (Hours, use of Rome, ca. 1430–40; produced in Belgium); and BN, MS. nouv. acq. fr. 4412, fol. 156v (prayer book, fourteenth to sixteenth centuries; Tournai).

32. BN, MS. lat. 1164, fol. 24v (Hours, use of Paris, mid or late fifteenth century) (figure 3). The text of the Obsecro Te, which precedes the illustration, employs the feminine pronoun. A similar illustration may be found in BN, MS. nouv. acq. fr. 4412, fols. 155–56v. For an exemplum telling of a woman whose prayer was rewarded with a vision of the Virgin, see Bibliothèque Sainte-Geneviève, Paris, MS. 2694, fol. 118v (devotional miscellany, fifteenth to early seventeenth centuries; Rouen; by the early seventeenth century the manuscript belonged to the Douette-Penart families). A similar if not identical text appears in the same manuscript on fols. 222–23.

33. *Le miroir du penitent* (Lyons: Jean de Tournes, 1549), especially 5–6, 22–30, 42–43, 54.

34. Viret, *Exposition familiere,* especially 122–23, 155–81.

35. *Brefve exposition sur la treschrestienne et tresparfaicte oraison du Pater noster* (Alençon: Simon du Bois, ca. 1532), fol. A3v. The edition is identified and described in Francis Higman, "Theology for the Layman in the French Reformation, 1520–1550," *The Library,* series 6, 9 (1987): 113 and Appendix VIII.

As Barbara Diefendorf reveals so beautifully in her article in this collection, Calvin employed an extraordinary range of images to explain God's care for human beings. (See also Diefendorf, *Beneath the Cross: Catholics and Huguenots in Sixteenth-Century Paris* [New York, 1991], chapter 8.) In the *Institutes* and other writings concerned with the religious practices and beliefs of the ordinary faithful, I find Calvin's God to be a stern and demanding father who also provides necessary support and affection for his human children. As Diefendorf shows, however, Calvin and Huguenot writers could also portray a loving, protective parent whose nurturing qualities are not unlike those associated with the Virgin Mary in prayers like the Obsecro Te.

36. Emond Auger, S.J., *Formulaire de prieres catholiques* (Paris: Gabriel Buon, 1576).

37. Benoist, *Advertissement charitable aux femmes et filles, enseignant comme elles doivent aller aux Stations et lieux ordonnez pour gaigner le present Jubilé de ceste annee 1576 . . .* (Paris: Nicolas Chesneau, 1577), fols. E1v-F2v.

38. Pierre Coton, S.J., *Interieure occupation d'une ame devote,* 2d ed. (Paris: Claude Chappelet, 1609).

39. Auger, *Formulaire de prieres catholiques,* 11 and 10.

40. See especially Benoist, *Du sacrifice evangelique: Ou manifestement est prouvé, que la saincte Messe est le sacrifice eternel de la nouvelle Loy: Que Jesus Christ le premier l'a celebrée et commandée aux ministres de son Eglise . . .* (Paris: Nicolas Chesneau, 1564), fols. 29–45.

41. Auger, *Formulaire de prieres catholiques,* 48; Coton, *Institution catholique, Ou est declarée et confirmée la verite de la foy. Contre les heresies et superstitions de ce temps. Divisée en quatre livres, qui servent d'Antidote aux quatre de l'Institution de Jean Calvin* (Paris: Claude Chappelet, 1612), 101–2.

42. Calvin, *Institutes,* 901 (this section is an exposition of the Lord's Prayer). On this point see also Viret, *Exposition familiere,* 251–69.

43. Viret, *Exposition familiere,* 483.

44. Calvin, preface to *Pseaumes octantetrois de David mis en rime Francoise par Clement Marot et Theodore de Beze* (Geneva: Jean Crespin, 1551). Calvin's preface is dated 10 June 1543.

45. Jean Benedicti, *La somme des pechez et le remede d'iceux* . . . (Paris: Denis Binet, 1595), especially 43–44. The first edition of Benedicti's work was published in 1586.

46. A. Cramer, *Notes extraites des registres du Consistoire de l'église de Genève* (Geneva, 1853), 35 and 8. See also cases on 2–3, 4, 5. Robert M. Kingdon discusses a number of similar cases in the records of the Genevan consistory: "The Geneva Consistory as Established by John Calvin," *On the Way: Occasional Papers of the Wisconsin Conference of the United Church of Christ* 7 (1990): 30–44. See also Alfred Soman and Elisabeth Labrousse, "Le registre consistorial de Coutras, 1582–1584," *Bulletin de la Société d'Histoire du Protestantisme Français* 126 (1980): 193–228 (especially the interesting case discussed on 202); and Raymond A. Mentzer, Jr., "*Disciplina nervus ecclesiae:* The Calvinist Reform of Morals at Nîmes," *Sixteenth Century Journal* 18 (1987): 89–115 (especially 93–95).

47. Albert Labarre, *Le livre dans la vie amiénoise du seizième siècle: L'enseignement des inventaires après décès, 1503–1576* (Paris, 1971); and Paul Lacombe, *Livres d'heures imprimés au XVe et au XVIe siècle conservés dans les bibliothèques publiques de Paris* (Paris, 1907).

48. See studies cited in note 46 above, as well as Keith P. Luria, *Territories of Grace: Cultural Change in the Seventeenth-Century Diocese of Grenoble* (Berkeley, 1991); and A. N. Galpern, *The Religions of the People in Sixteenth-Century Champagne* (Cambridge, Mass., 1976). For Germany this issue has been amply discussed by Gerald Strauss, "Success and Failure in the German Reformation," *Past and Present* 67 (1975): 30–63; and Robert Scribner, "The Impact of the Reformation on Daily Life," in *Mensch und Objekt im Mittelalter und in der frühen Neuzeit: Leben—Alltag—Kultur* (Vienna, 1990), 315–43.

The Huguenot Psalter and the Faith
of French Protestants
in the Sixteenth Century

Barbara B. Diefendorf

It is well known that the Psalms had a special place in the spread of
the Protestant faith in France.[1] Natalie Davis has drawn our attention
to the printers' journeymen who, with their wives and other artisans,
marched through the streets of Lyons in 1551 "singing the Psalms in
French and even interspersing their Psalms with insults shouted at
the noble canon-counts at the Cathedral of Saint Jean."[2] Other historical accounts have shown us occasions on which psalms were used
to disrupt Catholic services, demonstrate the faith of convicted heretics, or muster the courage of Huguenot armies.[3] Minister Daniel
Toussain, ambushed by Catholic forces as he was leading a group of
nearly five hundred Protestants out of Montargis in 1569, knelt in the
road and called upon his flock to prepare for their "deliverance" by
singing with him the Thirty-first Psalm.[4] The Huguenots of Bourges
celebrated their seizure of the city in 1562 by singing Psalm 124. The
Huguenots of Orleans considered the same psalm their anthem and
used it to celebrate the special protection they believed God had
vouchsafed them.[5]

The psalter also had an important place in the rituals of congregational and family worship for French Protestants, especially for those
who were forced by the circumstances of persecution and civil war
to worship clandestinely. Unable to receive the sacraments or even
to hear sermons with any regularity, they nourished their faith in
private through the reading and singing of psalms and through meditation upon their texts. My purpose in this essay is to examine more
closely the nature of the attraction the Psalms held for the Hugue-

nots. In particular, I wish to explore their use of the Psalms as a means of explaining and coming to terms with the horrible violence of Saint Bartholomew's Day. I shall argue that the Huguenots' affinity for the Psalms was theological, but it was also emotional and aesthetic.

The Huguenots found in the Psalms a rich treasury of song with which to praise God and console themselves, but they also found there a militant faith and a God that sanctioned holy war. Most important, they found in the Psalms a means to transform their vulnerability into a source of strength. The belief that persecution was a sort of test that God imposed upon the elect helped the Huguenots to survive the trials of civil war. The massacre of Saint Bartholomew's Day posed a crucial challenge to this belief, and the abjurations that occurred in the wake of the massacre resulted not just from fear of the Catholics' strength but also from a profound and sincere crisis of faith on the part of those who searched but could not find the signs of God's providence in the bloody slaughter of their coreligionists.

Huguenot minister Jean de L'Espine wrote in 1582 that the French churches had lost more than two-thirds of their members in the "horrible and appalling revolt" that occurred after Saint Bartholomew's Day.[6] There is no way to know just how accurate this estimate may have been, but it is clear that the losses were great. The tattered remnant of the French Reformed churches that emerged from the massacre had to find a means to strengthen the faith of the survivors, to ward off further losses, and perhaps win back some of those who had bolted under stress. Predictably, they turned to the Psalms and sought there the means to reconcile the horrors they had experienced with their conviction of a just and loving God. Huguenot ministers quoted the Psalms prolifically in treatises addressed to the faithful to console them in their losses and cited them relentlessly in appeals to the apostate to return to the true faith. Memoirists recording their own escape from Saint Bartholomew's Day and poets memorializing these events for posterity likewise quoted the Psalms with great frequency; they consciously paraphrased them and unconsciously forged a language saturated with their rhythms, images, and metaphors.

To understand why this particular book of the Bible assumed such an important role for the Huguenots, we must first look briefly at the Huguenot psalter itself—at the French translation of the Psalms begun by Clément Marot and completed by Theodore Beza—and at

Calvin's intentions in fostering the use of the Psalms for congregational singing, then at the absorption of the language and theology of the Psalms into the very heart of the Huguenot faith. We can then examine how the Psalms were used in coming to terms with the crisis of Saint Bartholomew's Day in the writings of Huguenot ministers and in poetry, including the great Huguenot epic, the *Tragiques* of Agrippa d'Aubigné.

Psalms and Faith before Saint Bartholomew's Day

The use of vernacular psalms only gradually became associated with Protestant dissent. Indeed, vernacular translations of the Psalms knew a certain vogue in France during the first half of the sixteenth century. Even after John Calvin had Clément Marot's elegant verses set to music and adapted for use in Reformed church services, French Catholics continued to recite and sing psalms in their native tongue, often using the same translations as the Protestants. The doctors of the Sorbonne forbade the singing of French psalms in 1543, but little heed was paid to their prohibition. Only in the 1550s, when enlarged editions of the Genevan psalter incorporated not only translations by Theodore Beza but also such assertively Protestant materials as the Calvinist "Profession of Faith" did the use of a French psalter come to be irrevocably associated with Protestant worship.[7] As early as 1551, civil and ecclesiastical authorities in France, referring to the same incident that Natalie Davis cited in "Strikes and Salvation," complained that bands of "Lutherans and Calvinists" several hundred strong were parading through the streets of Lyons singing Marot's psalms. The authorities accused the psalm singers of both public scandal and blasphemy, but they failed to put a stop to the assemblies, which spread from town to town during the 1550s.[8] In 1558, following a violent clash between Catholic crowds and a group of psalm singers on Paris's Pré aux Clercs, Henri II firmly forbade the public singing of psalms.[9]

French Protestants reacted to the prohibitions with defiance; they continued to sing the forbidden songs both in private services and publicly. They sang them as they went about domestic chores and as they marched out of the city gates to hold prohibited religious services in nearby fields. The Psalms were instrumental to Huguenot fellowship and identity. Strangers meeting on the road hummed a bar or two of a well-known psalm as a mark of recognition; congregations adopted favorite psalms as their anthems. Songs celebrating Huguenot victories—or mourning defeats—were written to the tune of psalms; often much of the rhetoric of the Psalms was borrowed as well.[10]

John Calvin himself set out the theory behind the Huguenots' use of the Psalms. Music, Calvin wrote, in a preface to the 1543 edition of the French psalter, has a special power to pierce the heart and enter therein. The very power with which words accompanied by melody can act upon our hearts led Calvin to believe that we should shun all vulgar, secular song. He found the Psalms of David, however, to be the perfect texts to be set to music: "When we sing them, we are certain that God puts the words in our mouth, as if he himself sings in us, to exalt his glory."[11] The singing of psalms was thus a privileged form of communion with God; it was, in Calvin's words, a means of "associating oneself to the company of Angels." He believed, moreover, that a spiritual song, once understood and committed to memory, was imprinted on one's heart forever, "so that it would never cease to be sung."[12]

The crafting of songs that would well up from within—that would be sung from memory and from the heart—was a conscious aim of the poets and musicians who collaborated to produce the Huguenot psalter. As poets schooled in the humanist tradition, Marot and Beza deliberately borrowed the simple constructions, parallelisms and symmetries, the highly colored metaphors, and the concrete imagery characteristic of the Hebrew psalms.[13] They endeavored to be faithful to the original, and the reward for their fidelity was a powerful poetry, lyrical in its simplicity, didactic in its message, rich in its juxtapositions of antithetical images and emotions. The tunes to which the psalms were set were intended, moreover, to reinforce the meaning of the words. Each syllable was assigned a note, so that the words would be clearly intelligible when sung. Created in a day when polyphony was the musical norm, the Huguenot psalter stands out for its determined monody.[14] Finally, each psalm was set to a unique and distinctive melody, so that the melody alone would call forth the words.[15]

The account of Nicolas Pithou's conversion, related in his history of the Reformed Church of Troyes, illustrates the success of this effort. Long a secret believer who had maintained an outward obedience to the Catholic church out of fear of losing both social standing and property, Pithou was moved to examine his conscience by a serious illness. In the midst of his fever, he began to pray, and he promised God that if he recovered from his illness he would refrain forever from the "abominations of the papacy" and retire to a place where he could live according to the true faith. At that very moment, Pithou reported, the Thirtieth Psalm of David came into his head, like a voice singing in his ear. In the rhymed verses and familiar melody of the Huguenot psalter, the psalm repeated itself again and again, "and half dead and enfeebled as he was, he took it as a sign and an infallible omen that God, having taken pity on him, had ordered his health restored."[16] That very day his fever broke, and he began to get better. The following year he retired with his wife to Geneva, though he later returned to France to serve as a minister of the Reformed Church of his native Troyes.

It is significant that it was Beza's verse translation of the Thirtieth Psalm that sprang unbidden into Pithou's mind, but the affinity of French Calvinists for the Psalms also extended to other translations, in particular the terse prose translation of the noted Hebraist Louis Budé.[17] The language of the Psalms was too powerful to be confined to verse form. Calvin set the model for his French followers through his own frequent use of the words and imagery, the metaphors and metonymies, of the Psalms. He used direct quotations or allusions to the Psalms in many of the letters he sent to the French churches to encourage their members to bear up under the strains of persecution. For example, the advice to take shelter "in the shadow of the wings of God," in a letter written to the Paris church in March 1557, employs a metaphor that appears half a dozen times in the Book of Psalms but only in one other place in the Bible.[18] Calvin's followers also adopted the language of the Psalms to express their confidence in divine protection, their conviction of being a chosen people, and their sense of sin. Minister Pierre Merlin used the same reference to being sheltered "under the wings of God" that Calvin used in 1557 to describe the situation of the Paris church ten years later.[19] Like Calvin, he used it to express his confidence that a higher protection would see the church through the current wave of persecution.

French Protestants attached to the Psalms three levels of meaning. They understood them first within the Old Testament context of David's own sufferings and his eventual triumph over his enemies;

second, within the New Testament context of the sufferings and triumph of Christ; and third, as prophetic of the sufferings and triumph of the church. These three levels of meaning were traditional
in Biblical exegesis, but the Huguenots' use of them is in several
respects distinctive. The first and third levels of meaning predominate and are sometimes even fused, with the Old Testament context
being directly appropriated through identification with David and the
children of Israel. The christological interpretation, by contrast, retreats to a more distant plane.

Again, the source and model is Calvin's own use of the Psalms. If
you contrast Calvin's commentaries on the Psalms with lectures and
commentaries by Luther on the same subject, for example, the differences are striking. For Luther, the important meaning is always the
christological one, and if there is a fusion it is between Christ and his
church. Explicating the metaphor of the "shadow of the wings of
God," Luther refers only briefly to the "wings of God" as his "powers
and gifts" and then goes on to say that this should be interpreted
allegorically: "The church is the hen, just as Christ is." The wings are
the bishops and teachers; the shadow their teaching of the true
faith.[20] For Calvin, on the other hand, the metaphor refers quite
naturally to God the Father, who spreads out his wings to cherish and
cover his young. The "shadow of his wings" is the safety he offers to
those who seek him.[21] When Calvin does refer to Christ in his commentaries on the Psalms, moreover, it is most often to the obligation
of all Christians to bear his cross. It is the Father who nourishes and
comforts us, Christ who suffers on our behalf and whose suffering
we share. Both of these themes are central to Huguenot piety.

The Huguenots' use of the Psalms is also distinctive in the very
direct and immediate fashion in which both Calvin and his French
followers appropriated the third level of meaning in the Psalms—the
ecclesiological meaning—to their own situation. The application of
the Psalms to the current situation was not just implicit in the Huguenot psalter but was clearly set out in the prefatory "argument" or
caption attached to each psalm. To make this level of meaning still
more explicit, some editions of the Huguenot psalter included a list
directing the reader to the most appropriate psalm for each occasion
or state of mind. Psalms to use as prayers for a church that was
afflicted or enfeebled, oppressed by combat, or held captive by its
foes are prominent on the list.[22] Some psalters also included a prayer

after each psalm, and many of the prayers make direct reference to the enemies who were persecuting the faithful.[23]

The martial imagery of the Psalms had a special resonance for the Huguenots, and invocations of the "Lord God of Armies" or the "God of vengeance" are common in Huguenot prayers and poems.[24] Most important, however, the Psalms helped to teach the Huguenots to view persecution as a trial imposed by God and a special mark of his covenant. Antoine de la Roche Chandieu was one of many Huguenot ministers who paraphrased Psalm 119 to say that "the afflictions that God has sent us are so many marks and signs of his good will toward us and his adoption."[25] Jean de L'Espine, writing in 1565, urged his readers not to flee affliction or to try to escape it. He reminded them rather that "persecutions are inevitable to all who wish dutifully to follow Jesus Christ; . . . to be disciples and students of Jesus Christ, we must take his cross on our shoulders and follow him."[26]

Daniel Toussain elaborated on the same theme. In a meditation on Psalm 124 composed in Orleans during the interval between the first and second religious wars, he wrote that "affliction, among other uses, brings the faithful man a special zeal and affection to pray ardently to Him, . . . and so to experience the effects of his divine force."[27] Toussain expressed his certainty that, although "the church since its earliest days has suffered greatly, . . . nothing can destroy it," and he wrote with great confidence in God's deliverance.[28] Most striking, however, is the sense of joy that pervades his work:

Oh happy the man who . . . not seeing any help in the world, looks at God and is assured of being seen by him! The mother often looks at her child with pity, because she cannot help him. But your look, Lord, is efficacious for your children: it is medicine for their ills.[29]

For this generation of Huguenots at least, the terrible majesty of God was more than balanced by his healing love. To obey God's law was not just an obligation, it was, as Psalm 119 repeatedly tells us, a "delight."

Psalms and Faith after Saint Bartholomew's Day

Of course, there were always Huguenots whose faith could not stand up to the trials of persecution. Membership in the French Reformed churches appears to have reached its peak in 1562, at the very beginning of the religious wars. At every trial or crisis in the course of the wars, some Huguenots recanted. The greatest trial, however, was that posed by the events of Saint Bartholomew's Day. Minister Hugues Sureau du Rosier typifies the attitude of those who recanted in the wake of the massacre. Captured and imprisoned as he tried to flee from the small church that he was serving outside of Paris, du Rosier began to think over the heinousness of the events that had just occurred. He found them to be of an entirely different order of magnitude from the persecutions he had known before, and he could no longer believe that they were the "visitations and rods by which God purged his church." Rather, seeing in these events "the entire ruin of the Church, without any sign to which one could attach the slightest hope for reestablishment," he began to interpret them as the marks of God's wrath, "as if he had declared by this means that he detested and condemned the profession and exercise of our Religion, . . . as if he wished entirely to ruin this Church and favor instead the Roman."[30]

While it was a source of great strength, the Huguenots' confidence in being the chosen of God was at the same time a vulnerable point, which, skillfully exploited, could lead to abjuration. It is worth noting, moreover, that, initially at least, it was not his own election that du Rosier came to doubt but rather the validity of the whole Huguenot enterprise. This was true of others who recanted as well. They could not reconcile the violence they had experienced with their image of a loving God.

Still, after the initial shock and horror had passed, it was precisely as a scourging by God and a test of faith that Huguenots came to terms with the massacre. Even du Rosier, regretting his cowardly apostasy and returning to the Reformed faith, expressed his reversal in these terms. He had, he said, been justly punished by God for the doubts that he had harbored and his lack of constance in the true faith. God had abandoned him to his own wishes, just as he had since ancient times punished idolaters by abandoning them to their idolatry. Du Rosier hoped that the painful lesson of his fall would teach others to tremble at the "dreadful judgments of God," and he asked for their prayers, "that the heavenly Father might receive my return to him after this horrible debauchery."[31]

If du Rosier attributed his apostasy to God's just judgment, Huguenots who survived the massacre with their faith intact gave credit rather to God's great providence in caring for his own. Charlotte d'Arbaleste, for example, repeatedly interrupts her accounts of her own perilous escape from the massacre and that of the man she later married, Philippe du Plessis de Mornay, to point out how "God's goodness and his providence watch over us, and for us, against all human hope."[32] She tells how Mornay, when he first heard of the killing around him, "having raised his mind to God, felt a certain assurance of getting through it, and of one day seeing justice done."[33] A companion, by contrast, could foresee nothing but death, and this was indeed his fate. Pompée Diodati credits God with three specific interventions to preserve his life and that of his family in their escape from Luzarches, a small village just north of Paris.[34] He likewise attributes the escape of those members of the family who were in Paris at the time of the massacre to the "miraculous effects of the Providence of God."[35] Diodati's niece, who survived the massacre thanks to the shelter offered by the duc de Guise, wrote of her escape in similar terms.[36] These references to God's providence are neither commonplaces nor literary affectations. They represent a means of coping with adversity that grew from but also ultimately determined the character of the Huguenots' faith.

It is important to note, moreover, that the Huguenots did not just blame the tragedy of Saint Bartholomew's Day on external causes— on the unjust attack of their enemies. Rather they assimilated it to their broader notion of persecution as punishment for sins. The conviction that even the elect remain burdened by sin is, of course, a central tenet of Calvinist theology, and it is at least an implicit theme in the lines of Psalm 119 so often quoted by the Huguenots ("It is good for me that I have been afflicted; that I might learn thy statutes"). An explicit connection between persecution and sin does occasionally appear in Huguenot writings prior to Saint Bartholomew's Day. In Jean de L'Espine's *Traitté consolatoire,* for example, he writes of persecution as a "paternal correction" or "discipline" to purge our natures of the vice to which we only too easily succumb.[37] Only in the wake of the massacre, however, does the connection between persecution and human sinfulness become a major theme.

The struggle against the flesh that plays such an important part in Puritan conversion narratives, for example, has little place in the Huguenots' stories of their conversions.[38] The only sin that seems really to preoccupy them here is the sin of denying God by refusing to accept his gift of grace. This is not to say that Huguenots were indifferent to their own sins or those of others. They would not have set up consistories and tried to reform morals if this were the case. Still, the Huguenots' confidence in the power of God's redeeming love saved them from dwelling obsessively on the inevitability of sin. God is faithful, they assured themselves; he does not allow us to be tempted beyond what we can bear.[39]

In the case of Saint Bartholomew's Day, however, many Huguenots apparently were tempted beyond what they could bear. To save their lives, they recanted their faith. Those who remained faithful attributed the apostasy of their former coreligionists to their having placed the fear of man before the fear of God.[40] Angered but also saddened by the defections, Huguenot ministers began a campaign to bring the "strayed sheep" back to the flock. The theme of persecution as punishment for sin plays a central part in the treatises that were published as part of this campaign, as it does in other works of Huguenot spirituality written in the wake of Saint Bartholomew's Day. What is perhaps surprising in this literature, given the natural horror with which Huguenots reacted to the massacre, is the fact that Huguenot authors continued to describe God's chastisement in terms that emphasized the sweetness of his paternal love. What is *not* surprising is that, to make their case, they drew heavily upon the Psalms.

A pamphlet published in 1573 on "the duty of perseverance in persecution to those who have fallen" typifies the Huguenot argument. The pamphlet begins by asserting that no Christian can be exempt from taking up Christ's cross. It cites both Christ's warning to his apostles that they would be delivered over to their enemies and 2 Timothy 3:12: "Yea, and all that will live godly in Christ Jesus shall suffer persecution." But then it turns to the Old Testament and says that David, in his time, already knew this truth: "Many are the afflictions of the righteous: but the Lord delivereth him out of them all." (The reference is to Psalm 34:19.)[41] Citing Psalm 119:67 ("Before I was afflicted I went astray: but now have I kept thy word"), the anonymous pamphleteer goes on to explain that, if God seems to deal harshly with his children, it is because the signs of sin, "the old corruption," appear in even the most perfect, so that God must correct us, for fear that if we continue in the path of evil "we will perish with this evil world."[42] The pamphleteer's attitude toward sin is nonetheless important here. He sees it as natural and inescapable, but not as a cause for despair. God tests our faith so that we will retain our vital awareness of his gifts and not be deflected by the corruptions of the world, but above all, he wishes to "accomplish in us the truth of his promises," to reveal the truth of his providence and the care he has for us. "This experience of the love of God not only sweetens the most bitter sadnesses but also gives our hope a new confidence in the future, [one] that easily overcomes all fear."[43]

Daniel Toussain echoes the same sentiment in the preface to his *L'exercice de l'âme fidèle,* which is dedicated to the "poor remnants of the church of Orleans," where he had been a minister. Reminding his reader that the alliance that God established with his church does not rest on us, on our good works or our dignity, but rather on his beloved son, "to whom he has elected, loved, and blessed us," Toussain recalls God's "beautiful and certain" promise to David that "I will visit their transgression with the rod, and their iniquity with stripes. Nevertheless my lovingkindness will I not utterly take from him, nor suffer my faithfulness to fail" (Psalm 89:32–33).[44] Once again the Psalms deliver the message of a loving God, who chastises those he wishes to save. The text of Toussain's *L'âme fidèle* is likewise studded with passages from the Psalms, all cited with the purpose of reassuring the faithful that God will not abandon those whom he has called to share in the inheritance of Christ. Toussain cites passages from other books of the Bible as well, but the most numerous references are to the Book of Psalms, which delivers the reassuring message in familiar terms.[45]

Jean de L'Espine's *Traicté de l'apostasie* makes even more frequent use of the Psalms in an attempt to draw repentant apostates back to the Reformed church. Indeed, long passages of this book are tissued entirely of verses from the Huguenot psalter, and they are quoted not in the prose translation that Toussain most frequently employed but rather in the rhymed verses of Marot and Beza. The choice was clearly deliberate and was intended to tug at the heartstrings, as well as the consciences, of those who had shamefully abandoned the faith.[46] It would have been impossible for Huguenots, apostate or otherwise, to read de L'Espine's treatise without hearing the familiar verses echoing in their minds. Quoting extensively from verses his readers knew well, de L'Espine was trying to reactivate the inner voices that he believed the apostates had stifled, to renew the conviction that would make a return to the Reformed church not only possible but necessary for them. He was hoping that, like Nicolas Pithou, they would hear a voice singing, "O Lord my God, I cried unto thee, and thou hast healed me;...thou hast brought up my soul from the grave" and that, like Pithou, they would take this as a sign of God's healing love and a message of his grace.[47]

De L'Espine may also have hoped that the familiar verses would conjure up memories of the fellowship of the elect, gathered to sing these same hymns, thereby underscoring the gulf that separates apostates from the children of God. It is worth noting in this regard that, although de L'Espine's whole treatise is structured to emphasize this gulf between apostates and the elect, he does not dwell on the punishment of the reprobate but rather on the joys of the children of God. He announces in the preface to the book, first published in 1583, that he has given up waiting patiently for the return of those who abandoned the church in the wake of the massacre and intends to take up his obligation as minister to remind the obstinate of the punishment that awaits those who reject God's promises, but in fact he writes more to affirm the confident hopes of the faithful than to threaten those who have strayed from the path.[48] Chapter 3, for example, though entitled "The Unhappiness of Apostates," treats of the great happiness of the children of God. Chapter 4, entitled "God Abandons Apostates," is about God's intense presence in the life of those who choose him. De L'Espine's strategy was not to use the threat of damnation to move those who had abandoned the church but rather to attempt to provoke a renewal of the conviction that had led to their original conversion by recalling God's promise and his love.

In a letter written in 1586, in which he appeals to those who have left the church as a consequence of the fresh wave of persecution ushered in by the treaty of Nemours in 1585, Jean de L'Espine makes an even stronger statement than any in the *Traicté de l'apostasie* about the intensity with which the chosen of God experience God's presence in times of adversity. Do not think that God abandons us at such times, he writes, for that is when he stays closest to us "to support and sustain us through his word and spirit, from which we receive and feel in our hearts more joy and consolation in a month of affliction than we would experience in two or three years of peace and prosperity."[49]

De L'Espine recognized that even the faithful might be so conscious of their sins that they could not help but retain some fear of God's judgment, and he tried to ease this fear by reminding them of God's promise and of the consolation he sent in the person of Jesus Christ, his son. The metaphors that he used to express the relationship that binds God to the elect include the sort of seigneurial and paternal images that Virginia Reinburg has discussed in her contribution to this volume. He wrote in terms of lord and men, father and children, teacher and pupils; but he also included intensely organic and affective images. "We are members, flesh, and bone of his only and beloved son," he writes; "we are his heart and the apple of his eye" (literally, the "pupil of his eye"). "We are his dear spouse, that is to say, all his love and his delight."[50] God is a powerful father for Jean de L'Espine, but he is also "clement, mild, and full of grace" (*doux, benin & gracieux*). Do we need to fear his judgment? "On the contrary," de L'Espine writes, "we hope to judge the world with him."[51] God does not want to condemn us but rather to save us. "Thus, God's promises and threats, however diverse they may be, all lead to the same end, which is to show us the love that God bears us, and the care that he has for our salvation."[52]

De L'Espine hoped to call back apostates by the same means that he used to reassure the faithful, by convincing them that they were indeed the objects of God's love and that participating in the fellowship of the elect was the unique path to salvation. It is doubtful that this strategy met with much success. The political situation in France in the wake of Saint Bartholomew's Day did little to encourage apostates to return to the Reformed faith. Persecution continued; it was difficult for publishers to distribute Huguenot treatises in France, and there is little reason to think that those who had abandoned the faith would in any event have formed a ready audience for this literature. But even beyond the pragmatic problem of reaching a reluctant audience is the problem that de L'Espine's approach was premised on the assumption that one could in fact recapture a very elusive sort of confidence. The conviction that they were God's chosen people was both a strength and a weakness for the Huguenots. It forged a community from the "little flock" and helped them to build a militant church.[53] At the same time, it required a measure of faith that, once lost, could not easily be regained.

The Huguenots were assailed by Catholic commentators for the overweening pride with which they trumpeted their assurance of salvation. It was sinful, the Catholics claimed, to count oneself so brazenly among the elect.[54] And indeed, it was this same dangerous presumption that one's election was assured that was later to trouble Puritan theologians. It was the sin of pride that prompted Puritan ministers to lay so much stress on the examination of conscience, the uncertainty of salvation, and the inscrutable majesty of God. For the Huguenots, however, the belief in being a chosen people was part and parcel of a religion—of an identity—forged in adversity.

And the psalter, for its part, was the principal tool by which this identity was forged. The psalter allowed the Huguenots, scattered and isolated as they might be, to become a part of a larger community just by raising their voices in song. The Spanish philosopher Unamuno wrote of the Psalms that they were meant to be sung when alone. "When one sings them, he withdraws into himself; the voices of the others resound in his ears only as an accompaniment and reinforcement of his own voice."[55] But the contrary is also true, or so it seemed to Calvin and his followers. One sang the Psalms, from memory and from the heart, "as a kind of meditation to join oneself to the company of Angels."[56] One sang them to feel oneself in the company of the elect—the children of Israel, coheirs with Christ. We may feel that there is some dissonance here—children of Israel, coheirs with Christ—but the Huguenots, though grateful for the new covenant that Christ represented, were comfortable with their Old Testament God. They identified with David the prophet and praise singer, and with David the warrior—the stripling youth who, armed only with faith, defeated the giant Goliath. But most of all, they identified with David the anointed of God, who maintained his innocence and his trust despite the terrible persecutions inflicted upon him.

Saint Bartholomew's Day in Huguenot Poetry

The Huguenots' identification with the Old Testament story of David emerges clearly in their poetry. Michel Jeanneret has written an excellent account of the influence of the Psalms on the polemical and devotional poetry written by French Protestants during the religious wars. He shows how Huguenot poets repeatedly borrowed turns of phrase and rhythms characteristic of the Huguenot psalter and how they grounded their work in theological elements characteristic of the

Psalms. From Jeanneret's perspective, the most important elements here are the centrality of God's omnipotence, which contrasts with the weakness of humanity and yet offers hope for a total reversal of the current state of affairs, and God's intervention in human affairs, in particular his punishment of the wicked for the wrongs suffered by the elect.[57] These same elements are present in Huguenot poems about Saint Bartholomew's Day, but from my perspective, the key characteristics of this poetry are, first, the attribution of responsibility for the massacre to the Huguenots' own sinfulness and, second, the reaffirmation in spite of the horrors of the massacre of a total confidence in God's mercy. As with the Huguenot ministers, Huguenot poets used the very acknowledgment of their sinfulness to reconcile the horrors of Saint Bartholomew's Day with the essential goodness of God.

The notion that the events of Saint Bartholomew's Day were the consequence of the Huguenots' own sins is well expressed in the anonymous "Complainte et prière des fidèles persecutez en la France," published by Simon Goulart in his *Mémoires de l'estat* (1579). Addressing God directly, the poet deplores the blood shed by enemies of the church. He points to the sad remnant of the battered flock and asks God if he is not a "careless shepherd," too weak to defend his own. "Where, Eternal One, is the accustomed help / promised to your children?," the poet asks.

> Where is that goodness formerly so prized?
> Shall we now say that it is used up?
> Alas, the harm comes from elsewhere; it is our own iniquity
> Which has justly irritated you against us,
> So that quite rightly your vengeful right arm
> Pursues us, strikes us down by a long oppression,
> Which grows and becomes more acute, as all the more obstinately
> We distance ourselves from your holy commandments.[58]

It is, the poet concludes, "our own concupiscence" that is to blame for the evils we have experienced. He asks God, his "kindly father," not to destroy his "poor servants" and reaffirms his confidence in the "holy promises" that have been made to them.[59]

The same themes appear in the concluding section of Agrippa d'Aubigné's "Misères," the first book of the *Tragiques*. Acknowledging that God's enemies and his elect are "equal in vice" and that the difference between the two groups is due to grace and not to merit, the poet adds that "if you do us harm, it is our own fault."[60] In verses that recapitulate the larger argument of the *Tragiques,* d'Aubigné depicts the enemies of God as the tool used to chastise the elect but at the same time prophesies the enemies' eventual destruction. Addressing God directly, he asks rhetorically,

> This murderous band invites us to drink
> The wine of your wrath: will not *they* drink it to the dregs?
> These switches, which play upon us as in jest,
> Besmirched with our blood, will not *they* go into the fire?
> Chastise in your mildness, punish in your fury
> Escape for the lambs, the slaughterhouse for wolves;
> Distinguish between the two, as you have promised,
> The switch for your children; the iron rod for your enemies.[61]

The depiction of Saint Bartholomew's Day as divine punishment is explicit in the fifth book of the *Tragiques.* D'Aubigné begins his description of the massacre with a prophetic invitation: "Venez voir comme Dieu chastia son Eglise." These words, recalling Psalm 118:18 ("The Lord hath chastened me sore"), frame d'Aubigné's account of Saint Bartholomew's Day, which assumes the character of a classic tragedy brought about by the Huguenots' own besetting sins. D'Aubigné does not of course excuse the Parisians for the part they played in the violence of Saint Bartholomew's Day. In "Jugement," the final book of the *Tragiques,* he prophesies the city's destruction in terms borrowed from Psalm 137.[62]

D'Aubigné's interpretation of the massacre in terms of lessons of the Psalms is most clear, however, in an incident recounted in "Les Feux," the fourth book of the *Tragiques,* in which d'Aubigné tells the story of two sisters, identified as daughters of the minister Serpon. Separated from their parents in the course of Saint Bartholomew's Day, the girls sought shelter with a Catholic aunt and uncle. Rather than receiving the protection they sought, the girls were tortured in an attempt to force them to renounce their faith. For thirty days, they were beaten with sticks in order to get them to recant. Finally, the cruel aunt and uncle gave up and the sisters were cast out. The younger girl died of her wounds on the doorstep; the elder, who was nine years old, fled and eventually was taken to a hospital. The words d'Aubigné places in the child's mouth, as she lies in her hospital bed, amount to a naive paraphrase of Psalm 119:71 ("It is good for me that I have been afflicted; that I might learn thy statutes"):

> She cries from her bed, "Oh God, double my faith,
> It is by misfortunes as well that your own come to you,
> I will not forget you, but, my God, make it so that
> By force of misfortune I become stronger."[63]

The young girl's story does not end there, for the hospital personnel, hearing these words, suspected that she was a Huguenot. When, after several months, she showed signs of recovery, they began by threats and blows to attempt her conversion. Bloody and battered, she finally died, but not before a touching scene in which she asks God to take her by the hand, to lift her up into his breast, "that I may die in you as in you I have lived."[64] God answers her prayer, and her last breath is exhaled on his breast. His tears fall on her face, as, gently raising her chin, he closes "the mouth of praise" just finishing its prayer. The sky cracks with thunder, the rain pours down. But what is striking here is less the animation of nature to echo God's sorrow than the tenderness with which the Eternal Father is depicted lifting the child's broken body to his breast and showering tears on her face. For the believing Huguenot, the cruelest tortures of Saint Bartholomew's Day were not incompatible with a loving, merciful God.

NOTES

1. This essay has its origins in the discussion of Huguenot conversion and the use of the Psalms in my recent book on the religious conflicts in sixteenth-century Paris. I am grateful to Oxford University Press for permission to reuse certain passages from *Beneath the Cross: Catholics and Huguenots in Sixteenth-Century Paris* by Barbara B. Diefendorf. Copyright 1991 by Oxford University Press, Inc. Reprinted by permission.

2. Natalie Zemon Davis, "Strikes and Salvation at Lyons," in *Society and Culture in Early Modern France* (Stanford, 1975), 4–5.

3. Orentin Douen, *Clément Marot et le psautier. Etude historique, littéraire, musicale, et bibliographique*, 2 vols. (Amsterdam, 1967; reprint of edition of Paris, 1878), 2:4–11, cites examples of the singing of psalms by prisoners and on the field of battle. See also Theodore Beza's prefatory epistle to the *Psaumes mis en vers français*, for example, in the edition published by Pierre Pidoux in the series *Travaux d'humanisme et renaissance*, vol. 199 (Geneva, 1984). In this epistle Beza urges religious prisoners to sing the Psalms from

their funeral pyres. Jean Crespin, *Histoire des martyrs persecutez et mis à mort pour la verité de l'évangile*, new ed., ed. Daniel Benoît and Matthieu Lelièvre, 3 vols. (Toulouse, 1889), 2:702n, describes Anne du Bourg singing Psalms as he went to his death. On the disruption of Catholic services, see Jean de La Fosse, *Journal d'un curé ligueur de Paris sous les trois derniers Valois*, ed. Edouard de Barthélemy (Paris, 1866), 41.

4. Agrippa d'Aubigné, *Histoire universelle*, book 5, chap. 13, as cited in Jules Bonnet, "Les réfugiés de Montargis et l'exode de 1569," *Bulletin de la société de l'histoire du Protestantisme français* [hereafter, *BSHPF*] 38 (1889): 182. See also d'Aubigné's poetic rendering of these events in the *Tragiques*, book 5, "Les fers," lines 443–98. Lines 480–81 are a direct citation of Psalm 31 in Theodore Beza's translation. All citations of the *Tragiques* are from Agrippa d'Aubigné, *Oeuvres*, ed. Henri Weber et al. (Paris, 1969).

5. Nathanael Weiss, "La Réforme à Bourges au XVIe siècle," *BSHPF* 53 (1904): 350; Simon Goulart, *Mémoires de l'estat de France sous Charles IX* (Middleburg, 1578), 2:10; Daniel Toussain, *L'exercice de l'âme fidèle; assavoir, prières et méditations pour le consoler en toutes sortes d'afflictions. Avec une préface consolatoire aux pauvres résidus de l'Eglise d'Orléans, contenant un brief récit des afflictions qu'a souffert ladite Eglise* (Frankfurt, 1583), unpaginated fol. Avi.

6. Jean de L'Espine, *Traicté de l'apostasie faict par M. J. D. L., Ministre de la parole de Dieu en l'Eglise d'Angers* (n.p., 1583), fol. Aii.

7. On the popularity of the Psalms at the French court during this period, see Michel Jeanneret, *Poésie et tradition biblique au XVIe siècle. Recherches stylistiques sur les paraphrases des psaumes de Marot à Malherbe* (Paris, 1969), 107–8. See also Francis Higman, "Le levain de l'évangile," in *Histoire de l'édition française*, vol. 1: *Le livre conquérant. Du Moyen Age au milieu du XVIIe siècle*, ed. Henri-Jean Martin, Roger Chartier, and Jean-Pierre Vivet (Paris, 1982), 318.

8. Pierre Pidoux, ed., *Le psautier huguenot du XVIe siècle. Mélodies et documents*, 2 vols. (Basel, 1962), 2:51, citing Lyons, Archives de la Ville, BB 72 (proceedings of 22 June 1551); Déclaration du consul Hugues de la Porte (Lyons, 23 June 1551) and Chronique lyonnaise de Jean Guéraud, 1536–1562, as cited by Natalie Zemon Davis in "The Protestant Printing Workers of Lyons, 1551," in *Aspects de la propagande religieuse* (Geneva, 1957), 247 and 249.

9. Letter of Jean Macard to Jean Calvin, 22 May 1558, as reproduced in Athanase Coquerel, *Précis de l'histoire de l'Eglise réformée de Paris*, vol. 1: *Première époque, 1512–1594* (Paris, 1862), xxxvii-xli.

10. See, for example, the "Cantique solennel de l'Eglise d'Orléans sur la délivrance que Dieu feit de son peuple le 5e décembre 1560; sur le chant du pseaume 73: On peult bien dire Israel" and the "Chanson spirituelle sur le chant du Ps. 71 [composé à la mort du roi François II], par une Damoyselle françoise" reproduced in *Le chansonnier huguenot du XVIe siècle*, ed. Henri-Léonard Bordier (Geneva, 1969; reprint of Paris and Lyons edition, 1870–71), 201–7.

11. Jean Calvin, "A tous chrestiens et amateurs de la parole de Dieu, salut,"

(Geneva, 10 June 1543), as reproduced in Pidoux, ed., *Le psautier huguenot*, 2:20–21.

12. Ibid. See also Beza's comments on first hearing the Psalms sung in Geveva, cited in ibid., 2:38. Patrice Veit, "Le chant, la Réforme et la Bible," in *Le temps des Réformes et la Bible*, ed. Guy Bedouelle and Bernard Roussel (Paris, 1989), 662–64, notes the influence of Martin Bucer's reforms in Strasbourg on Calvin's conception of congregational singing.

13. Jeanneret, *Poésie et tradition biblique*, 51–105, especially 56–61.

14. Veit, "Le chant, la Réforme et la Bible," 662. Versions of the Psalms arranged for two, four, or five voices were also published, but these were not intended for congregational worship.

15. Pidoux, ed., *Le psautier huguenot*, vol. 1: *Les mélodies*.

16. Nicolas Pithou, sieur de Changobert, "Histoire ecclesiastique de l'eglise de la ville de Troyes, capitalle du conté et pays de Champagne, contenant sa renaissance et son accroissance, les troubles, persecutions et autres choses remarcables advenues in la dicte eglise, jusques en l'an mil cinq cent quatre vingt et quatorze" (unpublished manuscript, Bibliothèque Nationale (hereafter BN), MSS. Dupuy 698), fols. 131v–132r.

17. Beza relied heavily on Louis Budé's translation of the Psalms, and the two versions were often published side by side in French psalters. See Jeanneret, *Poésie et tradition biblique*, 92.

18. Jean Calvin, "A l'église de Paris," letter of 15 March 1557, as reproduced in *Lettres de Jean Calvin. Lettres françaises*, ed. Jules Bonnet (Paris, 1854), 2:122–26; similarly, 140–41: letter of 16 September 1557, citing Ps. 56:8; and 253–57: letter of 18 February 1559, citing Ps. 119:61. The metaphor of God's "wings" occurs in Pss. 17:8, 36:8, 57:2, 61:5, 63:8, and 91:4. It also occurs in Ps. 31:21 in some modern French translations, though not in the sixteenth-century versions of Beza or Louis Budé. See Louis Jacquet, *Les psaumes et le coeur de l'homme. Etude textuelle, littéraire et doctrinale* (Paris, 1975), 422–23. All Psalms are numbered as the Huguenots numbered them; this corresponds to the system used in the King James version. Moreover, when quoting from the Psalms in this article, I have, unless otherwise noted, used the King James translation on account of its poetic value and force of expression. I have, however, closely checked all English translations against the Huguenot psalter to be certain that they do not distort the meaning of the French version or otherwise differ in any significant way.

19. Merlin de l'Espérandière to Bèze (Longueville [Paris], 10 January 1567), as reproduced in Theodore Beza, *Correspondance*, ed. Hippolyte Aubert et al., 14 vols. to date (Geneva, 1960–90), 8:29. Beza borrows the same metaphor but applies it to Protestant princes in the letter dedicating his Psalms "A l'église de nostre seigneur." The allusion comes in line 25 of the poem as reproduced in Pidoux, *Le psautier huguenot*, 2:63.

20. Martin Luther, *Works*, ed. Hilton C. Oswald (Saint Louis, 1976), 11:214–15. Veit, "Le chant, la Réforme et la Bible," 667–73, has some interesting observations on the tendency of Luther and his followers to "pull" the

Psalms in a New Testament—and more particularly a Pauline—direction in the translations they set to music.

21. Jean Calvin, *Joannis Calvini Opera quae supersunt omnia* (hereafter, *CO*), ed. W. Baum, E. Cunitz, and E. Reuss, 59 vols. (Brunswick, Germany, 1863–1900), vol. 31, cols. 162–63: commentary on Ps. 17:8; 362–63: commentary on Ps. 36:8; 554–55: commentary on Ps. 57:2; 582: commentary on Ps. 61:5; 597: commentary on Ps. 63:8; vol. 32, col. 3: commentary on Ps. 91:4.

22. See, for example, Clément Marot and Théodore de Bèze, *Les pseaumes de David, mis en rime françoise. Avec une oraison à la fin d'un chacun pseaume faite par M. Augustin Marlorat* (Paris: pour Antoine Vincent, 1566) [BN, Réserve, A.6173].

23. Ibid.; see especially 39: Ps. 13; 149: Ps. 42; 304: Ps. 83; and 497–98: Ps. 137. Not all editions that included prayers, however, included those of Marlorat. See, for example, Clément Marot and Théodore de Bèze, *Les cent et cinquante psaumes de David, mis en rythme françoise* (n.p., 1562) [BN, Réserve, A.6170]. These prayers are a much closer paraphrase of the Psalms than are Marlorat's.

24. The metaphor of God as a shield occurs in Psalm 84, as does the invocation of the "God of armies." The metaphor of God as a fortress occurs in Psalms 27, 31, 91, and 144, among others. The "God of vengeance" occurs in the first line of Psalm 94. See Marlorat's prayer for Psalm 144, which begins "Lord God of Armies, who knows that our weakness is so great that we cannot stand up to our enemies unless we are sustained by your admirable force, show those who rise up against us that you are our shield and defender" (Marot and Beza, *Les psaumes de David . . . avec une oraison*, 519–20). For other examples of the use of these phrases in Huguenot writings, see the letter from Beaumont [Daniel Toussain] to Renée of Ferrara (Orleans, 27 August 1568), in "Lettres de divers à la duchesse de Ferrare (1564–1572)," *BSHPF* 30 (1881): 456; "Cantique sur le psaume XXXV," in Bordier, ed., *Chansonnier huguenot*, 207; and "Sur les misères des églises françoises," in ibid., 304.

25. Antoine de la Roche Chandieu, *Histoire des persecutions et martyrs de l'Eglise de Paris, depuis l'an 1557 jusques au temps du roy Charles neufviesme* (Lyons, 1563), viii.

26. [Jean de L'Espine], *Traitté consolatoire et fort utile contre toutes afflictions qui adviennent ordinairement aux fideles Chrestiens* (Lyons: Jean Saugrain, 1565), 6–7.

27. Daniel Toussain, *Prières et consolations prises de plusieurs passages de l'Escriture, & des livres des anciens. Le tout accommodé à l'usage des vrais Chrestiens, & au temps auquel nous sommes* (Geneva: Pour la veuve de Jean Durant, n.d.), 216–17. The dedicatory epistle, dated "1 octobre 1366 [sic: 1566]" shows the work to have been composed in Orleans between the wars.

28. Ibid., 220–21.

29. Ibid., 118–19: meditation on Psalm 34.

30. [Hugues Sureau du Rosier], *Confession et recognoissance de Hugues Sureau, dict du Rosier, touchant sa cheute en la Papauté & les horribles scandales par luy commis. Servant d'exemple à tout le monde de la fragilité & perversité de l'homme*

abandonné à soy, de l'infinie misericorde & ferme verité de Dieu envers ses esleus (Basel: Martin Cousin, 1574), 7–8. Robert M. Kingdon, *Myths about the Saint Bartholomew's Day Massacres, 1572–1576* (Cambridge, MA, and London, 1988), 120, also sees du Rosier's abjuration, though later recanted, as emblematic of a sincere loss of faith that many French Protestants experienced under the pressure of Saint Bartholomew's Day.

31. [Du Rosier], *Confession et recognoissance*, 25, 33, and 42–46.

32. Charlotte d'Arbaleste, *Mémoires de Charlotte Arbaleste sur la vie de Duplessis-Mornay, son mari*, in Philippe Duplessis-Mornay, *Mémoires et correspondance* (Paris, 1824), 1:43.

33. Ibid., 45–46.

34. Pompée Diodati, "Rélation," in Gilles-Denijs-Jacob Schotel, *Jean Diodati* (The Hague, 1844), 122–24.

35. Ibid., 124–25.

36. "Mémoires de Dlle Renée, fille de Michel Burlamaqui," in ibid., 85–90.

37. [De L'Espine], *Traitté consolatoire*, 33.

38. For a discussion of Huguenot conversion narratives, see Diefendorf, *Beneath the Cross*, 115–18.

39. See, for example, Arbaleste, *Mémoires*, 1:5–9. The introductory paragraphs of Arbaleste's memoir, which she addresses to her son, demonstrate well the importance of God's love in Huguenot thought and the confidence in election that resulted. The power, goodness, and wisdom of God, she wrote, "nous donne aussy à ung chacun tranquillité en noz consciences au milieu des vagues de ce monde, constance et magnanimité en la lutte ordinaire contre le diable, le monde et la chair, en certitude de victoire, d'autant que Dieu est fidelle, qui ne nous laisse jamais outrer à quelconques tentations, bon, qui ne faict consequemment rien que pour le bien des siens."

40. Agrippa d'Aubigné, for example, refers to "Ceux que la peur a revoltez" (*Tragiques*, preface: "L'autheur à son livre," verse 49). See also "Jugement," verses 85–98. D'Aubigné, *Oeuvres*, 12 and 217.

41. *Instruction du devoir de perseverance en la persecution à ceux qui sont tombez. Pour respondre aux scandales qu'on se propose; & confirmation qu'il n'est point permis de dissimuler la profession de l'Evangile & communiquer aux superstitions de la papauté* (n.p., 1573), 6.

42. Ibid., 10–11.

43. Ibid., 14.

44. Toussain, *L'exercice de l'âme fidèle*, fol. Biiii. A similar sentiment is expressed in the "Complainte et prière des fidèles persecutez en la France," an anonymous poem published in Goulart's *Mémoires de l'estat*, 1:429–31; and in Pierre Merlin, *XXVI sermons sur le livre d'Ester* (La Rochelle, 1591), 14–16.

45. The same technique of extensive quotation from the Psalms is used in Daniel Toussain, *Le vray guidon d'un homme chrestien. Assavoir, une salutaire meditation de la mort, & du dernier depart*, translated from the German and published as book 2 of Jean Tassin, *Traicté de l'amendement de la vie comprins en quatre livres* (Geneva, 1610).

46. De L'Espine, *Traicté de l'apostasie*. See, for example, fol. 5, where a long passage from Psalm 16 is followed directly by a lengthy quotation from Psalm 73. Similarly, fol. 11, where he quotes a melange of Psalms 144, 33, and 73.

47. See above, n. 16.

48. De L'Espine, *Traicté de l'apostasie*, fols. Aii–Aiii.

49. *Lettres de M. Jean de l'Espine, Ministre de la parole de Dieu, & Jean le Mercier, ancien, à l'Eglise d'Angers* (n.p., n.d.), 329 [Bibliothèque de l'Histoire du Protestantisme Français, R.8411]. The letter itself is dated 25 February 1586.

50. Jean de L'Espine, *Excellens discours de J. de L'Espine, angevin, touchant le repos & contentement de l'esprit* (Basel, 1587), 632.

51. Ibid. De L'Espine and other Huguenot ministers do appear to depart here from Calvin's teachings, in terms of emphasis if not of theology. In the first of a series of sermons on Psalm 119 delivered in 1553, for example, Calvin set out the terms for a very affirmative interpretation of "the law." He pointed out that "the law" should not be taken just to mean a list of God's commandments about what he wants us to do, but rather that it includes much more. The assurance of his grace and the certainty of salvation, the love shown through the sacraments set out in his law, and the refuge we have in Christ, who alone can save us—these too are a part of God's "law." (*CO*, vol. 32, cols. 485–86.) Nowhere in the sermons that follow, however, do we find the confident, joyful acceptance of God's covenant that appears in Huguenot references to the same psalm. Each time that Calvin comments on one of the many references in the psalm to David "delighting" in God's law, it is to tell us that we *should* feel this pleasure, rather than to rejoice in it. Even when commenting on David's exclamation, "How sweet are thy words unto my taste! yea, sweeter than honey to my mouth!" (Ps. 119:103), Calvin reminds us first of the great majesty of God and the humility with which we should "tremble" before him. Only afterwards does he add that not only should we approach the word of God with "reverence" and "fear" but also we should find it "sweet" and "lovable," and even here his reason is a negative one: for if we do not find God's word "sweet," we may turn away from it and fail to listen or even rebel against it (ibid., col. 638).

52. [Jean de L'Espine], *Traicté des tentations et moyens d'y resister. Composé par un docte et excellent personnage de ce temps* (Lyons: Jean Saugrain, 1566), 59–60.

53. The term "little flock" ("petit troupeau") comes from Beza's preface to the Huguenot psalter.

54. See, for example, Simon Vigor, *Sermons catholiques pour tous les jours de Caresme et feriés de Pasques, faits en l'Eglise S. Estienne du Mont à Paris* (Paris: Gabriel Buon, 1588), fol. 106a.

55. Miguel de Unamuno, *Soledad*, trans. John Upton, *The Centennial Review* (Summer 1958), as quoted by Erik H. Erikson, *Young Man Luther: A Study in Psychoanalysis and History* (New York and London, 1958), 132.

56. See above, n. 12.

57. Jeanneret, *Poésie et tradition biblique*, 117–24.

58. "Complainte et prière des fidèles persecutez en la France," in Goulart, *Mémoires de l'estat,* fols. 429v–431v.

59. Ibid.

60. "Misères," verse 1282. D'Aubigné, *Oeuvres,* 51.

61. Cette bande meurtriere à boire nous convie
Le vin de ton courroux: boiront-ils point la lie?
Ces verges, qui sur nous s'esgayent comm'au jeu,
Sales de nostre sang, vont-elles pas au feu?
Chastie en ta douceur, punis en ta furie
L'escapade aux aigneaux, des loups la boucherie;
Distingue pour les deux, comme tu l'as promis,
La verge à tes enfans, la barre aux ennemis.

"Misères," verses 1285–92. Ibid., 51. The line that begins "Chastie en ta douceur,..." is taken from Ps. 6:2.

62. "Jugement," verses 251–64. Ibid., 221 and 1083, n.1. Similarly, in "La Chambre dorée," verses 1011–54, he paraphrases Psalm 58 to prophesy the divine retribution God will one day exact from the corrupt judges of the Parlement of Paris (ibid., 115–16 and 965–86, nn. 2–12).

63. Elle crie en son lict: "O Dieu, double ma foy,
C'est par les maux aussi que les tiens vont à toy:
Je ne t'oublierai point, mais, mon Dieu, fay en sorte
Qu'à la force du mal je devienne plus forte."

"Les feux," verses 1031–34. D'Aubigné, *Oeuvres,* 141.

64. "Les feux," verse 1075. Ibid., 142.

Rituals of Conversion:
Catholics and Protestants
in Seventeenth-Century Poitou

Keith P. Luria

Historians have most often recounted the fate of French Protestantism in the seventeenth century through the history of royal policy and
legislation provoked by the lobbying and polemics of the Catholic
clergy. The combined efforts of the church and the state led to the
Protestants' defeat as a political/military party, their decline under
persecution, their suffering after the revocation of the Edict of
Nantes, and their clandestine survival in the "Desert." As yet we do
not have a clear picture of how the campaign to convert Protestants
transmitted edicts and polemics into the daily lives of Catholics and
Protestants throughout France. In particular, scholars of the seventeenth century have not pursued the paths opened by Natalie Davis
and others in showing how rituals and symbols shaped the local
meaning of religion and religious rivalry. We know a good deal about
the use of ritual in the original spread of the Reformation, but far
less about its role in Protestantism's retreat.[1]

I would like to approach this issue by examining the beginnings
of the Catholic campaign to convert Protestants in the province of the
Poitou, where its initiation was most intensive. In particular, I will
examine how the missionaries who led the campaign constructed and
communicated to the local population a representation of conversion
that simultaneously pressured Huguenots to convert and enticed
them with the prospect of establishing a religiously defined community with their Catholic neighbors.

The Poitou had a large, socially complex, and politically powerful
Protestant population. At the beginning of the seventeenth century,

approximately one hundred thousand Protestants lived there, in congregations spread throughout the province.[2] Although in the capital city they accounted for no more than about 5 percent of the population, in towns like Niort, Saint-Maixent, Loudun, Chavigny, Saint-Savin, and Civray, they accounted for 20 to 40 percent. And in the region around Melle and in the Gâtine, they often composed 75 to 90 percent of rural parishes. In many areas, including those in which Catholics were the majority, the local elite of nobles, officers, professionals, and merchants—*les plus apparents*—were Calvinists. Furthermore, at the top of Poitevin society sat the great Huguenot clans of Rohan, La Trémoille, and Vérac. The eight local *places de sûreté* guaranteed in the Edict of Nantes protected the Protestants.[3] Saumur (with its important academy), Marans, Saint-Jean-d'Angély, and of course La Rochelle were nearby.

Reports to the Crown complained of the Huguenot domination of provincial society and politics.[4] But "domination" does not fully describe the Protestant-Catholic relationship in the early years of the century. Scholars such as Elisabeth Labrousse and Robert Sauzet have suggested that in other regions with both confessions, the two groups achieved a state of cooperative coexistence in the years following the promulgation of the Edict of Nantes.[5] Despite decades of religious warfare, deeply marked by (to use Natalie Davis's term) the "rites of violence" that defined and separated the two communities, and despite the Edict's close regulation of the Protestant corporate group, neighbors of different religions found ways to build bridges and place daily concerns ahead of confessional competition.[6]

The evidence for mutuality in the Poitou is varied, though I can only cite some very brief examples here. Local offices were often filled by means of patron-client ties that did not depend on religion. In 1619, the minister Nicolas de Marais of Montaigu complained to the Protestant duchesse de La Trémoille that she was not reserving the appointments she controlled for her fellow Huguenots. He deplored the lack of zeal that led those of the "true religion" to elevate papists to positions of responsibility.[7] In towns, civic obligations were frequently shared, though sometimes by a strict ordering designed to insure positions for each side. For instance, Niort's town militia consisted of twelve companies, of which six would have Catholic captains and ensigns with Protestant lieutenants and sergeants. Six others would have Protestant captains and ensigns with Catholic lieutenants and sergeants. The soldiers of the two religions would be mixed equally in each company.[8] Such militias could endure even in the face of religious hostilities. In Luçon, Protestants called to support Rohan's uprising in 1620 united instead with their Catholic neighbors in militia companies to "maintain and preserve" the community. Indeed, as Protestant nobles went to war in the 1620s, their coreligionists in Poitevin towns no doubt realized how much they had to gain by maintaining communal peace with their Catholic neighbors.[9]

Just as the two groups cooperated in civic office, so too they shared some parts of the sacred space in their communities, especially cemeteries. Protestantism and Catholicism had radically different conceptions of the sacred significance of burial grounds, but the awareness of this difference was slow to take root among local populations. Poitevins continued to prefer burial with their kin, even if they were of the rival faith. The conversion campaign would work hard to separate cemeteries and deny Huguenots the right to interment in their accustomed places. But Protestants would complain that conventions between the religious groups had established common cemeteries, and documents from the lawsuits over separation of burial grounds speak of communal consent to sharing and even to the *amitié ancienne* that had governed cemetery use.[10]

One last example of coexistence concerns family life. In many mixed-confessional areas, intermarriage was common.[11] Family interests, whether in strategic planning for the future or simply regarding the need to find spouses outside the prohibited degrees of kinship, could override religious rivalries. Regardless of the injunctions of Catholic clergy and Protestant consistories against such unions, those who took partners of the other faith were not punished harshly.[12] In 1618, an anonymous royal agent reporting to the court on the religious situation in the Poitou, complained that the young women of the province attached themselves to neither one religion nor the other. According to the women's mothers, they would adopt the faith of their future husbands.[13] This sort of casualness, though likely exaggerated, seems contrary to what we know about the distinctive role of women in constructing religious difference.[14] But Protestantism's elevation of matrimony, as well as women's Bible reading, psalm singing, and iconoclasm, never brought women equality in married life or in the marriage market.[15] They continued to be the currency of family alliance strategies, especially in aristocratic clans, even if that meant crossing religious boundaries. What is more to the point here is that such crossings, and the interconfessional kinships they produced, indicate the fluidity of these boundaries and the adaptability of religious identity to the service of other interests.

Indeed the *amitié ancienne* of religious groups may have been based not just on the calculation of family interests and on the need to preserve communities in the face of armed threats but also on the neighborly experience of toleration. Protestants and Catholics shared more than civic duty, sacred space, and kinship. Provincial notables of both confessions participated in common literary coteries and delightedly exchanged correspondence, books, and their own literary efforts.[16] And those who were not *érudits* still worked, feasted, and played together before—as was the case in Caen—"leaving each other freely, some to go to mass, others to go to the *prêche*, without any trouble from one side or the other."[17] Although it would require more demonstration than can be undertaken here, it is possible that under the provisions of the Edict of Nantes in the early decades of the century, Catholic and Protestant inhabitants of communities in the Poitou and elsewhere were transforming an uneasy coexistence into a more thoroughly tolerant society.

Nonetheless, such toleration, if it existed, was fragile and easily eclipsed by what divided the confessions. Historians such as Elisabeth Labrousse or Bernard Dompnier often describe religious discord and persecution as having been introduced into mixed-confessional areas by the clergy, by royal policy and legislation, or by the activities of local groups closely tied to religious and secular authority, such as the Company of the Blessed Sacrament. In Dompnier's words, "their enterprises of fanaticization" led to "escalations of violence" that disrupted "usually pacific relations."[18]

But pressures from church and state did not create divisions where they had not existed previously. Rather, in a fluid situation, religious bonds and oppositions crisscrossed kinship ties, family interests, communal alliances and rivalries, and patron-client networks. Religious boundaries could be transgressed in the pursuit of communal defense or advantageous marriages. Nevertheless, religious conflict was evident in disputes over practices and beliefs, such as in Huguenot resistance to observing Catholic holy days or in Catholic insistence that the Eucharist be paid proper reverence. Tensions over religious and social differences ran close enough to the surface that Protestants in

Parthenay feared a massacre after a 1618 debate between their minister and a Capuchin friar.[19] Shared ground could quickly become disputed territory, as happened in Poitiers in 1621 when Catholic students attacked the Protestant cemetery, breaking walls, destroying tombs, and violating graves.[20]

The conversion campaign, therefore, did not produce division where none had existed previously. Instead, it accentuated certain local differences and reinforced them with doctrinal and political authority, thus creating stricter boundaries between the religious groups. It defined the Huguenots as resolutely opposite and separate, the non-Catholic "Other" within local society. The campaign estranged the two groups and thereby excluded Protestants from full participation in the daily life of Poitevin communities. But once separated from their accustomed social bonds, Protestants could, through conversion, be reintegrated into the local and national, Catholic and monarchical society. In other words, the campaign of conversion took on the appearance of a vast, ongoing, Van-Gennepian rite of passage in which "potential converts" were separated from the normal order of their world, transformed, and then reintegrated into that world as changed people.[21]

The ritualistic aspects of the conversion campaign in the Poitou were conspicuous from its beginnings. In 1616, the Capuchin Father Joseph du Tremblay (the future "Gray Eminence," adviser to Cardinal Richelieu, and promoter of missions worldwide) requested papal approval to undertake a mission in the province.[22] The next year he received permission for six missionaries to travel the diocese of Poitiers, preaching "controverses," debating ministers, and instructing heretics. In 1620, the mission was extended to two other Poitevin bishoprics, Maillezais and Luçon.[23] In addition to having as its stated goal the converting of heretics (similar to that of overseas or "exterior" missions to pagan areas), the Poitou campaign was also an "interior" mission to the Catholic population of the province, seeking to instruct the Catholics in proper doctrine and to invigorate their zeal and devotion in the face of the Protestant community.[24] In fact, the two goals were linked; by creating a stronger sense of Catholic identity, missionaries hoped to break the intimate ties between religious groups and pressure Protestants to convert.

On Christmas Day 1617, the mission began in Lusignan with a spectacular ceremony—an *oraison,* or prayer vigil of Forty Hours.

Central to the Forty Hours Devotion was a watch before the Host, exposed on an altar during three days. Making this devotion the hallmark of their missionary campaigns in France, Capuchins dramatized the rite and focused attention on the Host by decorating altars to resemble small stages with the Host in the center, surrounded by veils or drapes and bathed with hidden lights.[25] In the Poitou, the friars enhanced the devotion by adding public preaching and processions. Father Joseph also politicized the ritual by ordering his cohorts to add public prayers for the prosperity of their majesties. Those who marched in processions to the site of each ceremony were to chant litanies for the Blessed Virgin with a *Vive le Roi* added to each refrain.[26] The call to political loyalty followed upon the Catholic accusation, heard frequently from the 1620s on, that Huguenots were mired not only in religious error but also in disobedience to the king.[27] Capuchins often used the Forty Hours Devotion as a counterpoint to Protestantism by performing it at the same time and place as Huguenot synods. But they also opened their missions among Catholics with *oraisons* of Forty Hours and found them especially useful as a means of drawing the faithful away from carnival celebrations or other such "popular" festivities.[28] As the accounts of the Poitou mission show, it was precisely by directing the Forty Hours Devotions toward Catholics that the Capuchins reinforced the boundaries between the Catholics and their Protestant neighbors, boundaries that Protestants could only cross by conversion and reintegration into the Catholic community.

According to the chronicle of the mission, the Lusignan Forty Hours Devotion attracted four thousand people from Poitiers, who came in a procession led by forty Capuchins. From Saint-Maixent, Niort, Parthenay, and Châtellerault arrived groups of similar sizes; and from lesser towns and rural parishes came smaller companies, until those attending numbered more than fifty thousand. The Forty Hours Devotion staged in Latilly in 1620 drew as many as seven thousand from the surrounding area, and that in Poitiers had ten thousand at just one of the public preaching sessions (the total for the celebration is not reported).

We need not accept these figures at face value, but it is clear that the devotions had a large impact. The Capuchins made a point of recording that the *trouppes et processions* included *hérétiques* as well as Catholics. But the baroque ceremony seems designed to appeal primarily to a Catholic sensibility. The first one in Lusignan took place on the already holy day of Christmas (the celebration of which Calvinism discouraged). Later ones sanctified days that were not otherwise festivals, creating sacred time out of ordinary time, a notion that Calvinism found antipathetic. The marchers arrived chanting and bearing banners, standards, and candles.[29] The ritual objects and gestures central to the celebration—the vigils for the Eucharist, sacred songs sung to popular tunes, litanies for the Virgin, processions that paraded the Blessed Sacrament from church to church led by cross-carrying and torch-bearing Capuchins—combined to produce an impressive spectacle of Catholic devotion, and one quite foreign to Calvinist beliefs and modes of worship. And the overriding purposes of the event—to hear Capuchin preaching and to proclaim the real presence—rallied the Catholic faithful. The ritual gestures, the preaching, the crowds, the sense of exhilaration, all contributed to what the Capuchins described as the "extraordinary fervor," or what the anthropologist Victor Turner would label the "catharsis" of the ritual. The catharsis intensified the consciousness of the moment and the awareness of a need for action, which, in turn, helped generate the new sense of Catholic community separate from the larger mixed community that had characterized Poitevin political and social life.[30] As Bernard Dompnier has pointed out in discussing Capuchin manuals on missions, the regeneration of community became as much of an acknowledged goal of the campaigns as the revival of individual devotion or the winning of converts. And the reconstruction of community required a rupture with local Protestants, provoked by collective devotions that championed Catholic dogma.[31]

As for the Protestants at the Forty Hours celebrations, for whose conversion the events were ostensibly organized, they appear at first glance to have been marginalized. They could not participate in vigils acclaiming the real presence, and they would have had no place in processions carrying the Blessed Sacrament. Indeed, the marginalization could be painfully evident, as in the case of a Huguenot converted by a missionary who found him alone in a village. His Catholic neighbors had left him in order to attend the Forty Hours in Latilly.[32] However, other Protestants were present at the ceremonies, and the Capuchin staging of the ritual provided them with a role. Those who converted during the Forty Hours were illustrative examples of how, after separation or disaggregation, the former heretic could be reintegrated into the majority community through the ritual experience. The chronicle of the mission reported that Protestants stood at the edge of the audiences that pressed around the preachers. Those who wished to approach the missionaries to make their profession of faith could not easily do so. They had to "squeeze" their way into the crowd of Catholics, force their way through the throng, and then they had to "oblige" the preachers to "interrupt their sermons and receive them." In the chronicle's description, not only was an act of faith necessary for would-be converts, it was also an act of will to put themselves back into the midst of a community that had relegated them to the margins. Converts are portrayed as joyfully taking on a role that made clear their reintegration, as did one from Parthenay who insisted on marching first in a procession to give "public witness of his profession of faith."[33]

Turner's notion of catharsis is appropriate to the conversion experience reported by Catholics during "interior" missionary campaigns. "Immersion in the ritual experience," "intensification of consciousness," "loss of ego," and "awareness of the need for action that feeds back into self-evaluation" are apt modern terms for what Capuchins sought to provoke in those who listened to the emotional preaching and participated in the spectacular ceremonies of the Forty Hours Devotions. Capuchin manuals instructed missionaries to appeal to the hearts of Catholic listeners, to "ravish" and "carry them away," or rather to carry them toward a reawakened faith and repentance. With "hearts inflamed by divine love," they would be led to a general confession, an outward sign of their inner transformation.[34] Conversion in this sense meant not a change in religion but a change in life, a determination to live according to proper doctrine and moral strictures. It led to an amendment of behavior, but, first and foremost, it was a movement of conscience, frequently revealed in the flowing of tears. Capuchin preachers were themselves moved to tears by their efforts in calling listeners to repent. And the converts cried. One Forty Hours Devotion provoked so many Catholics to make full confessions, which some of them had not done in as many as twenty-five years, that they could not all reach the platform on which the Capuchin preachers stood. In their "passion" to confess, and with "tears in the eyes," they publicly cried out their sins and "opened their consciences before everyone." The Protestants present "stretched out their hands to the truth," recognizing that only in the Catholic church could they find "remission of their sins, reconciliation with God, and repose for their souls."[35]

The Capuchins may have drawn on literary models in their descriptions of such conversions. Contemporary poets wrote of the tears shed by the Magdalen, the classic illustration of penitence and the change of life. Her tears of repentance, in the words of Pierre Le Moyne, washed eyes that had formerly burned with quite a different passion.[36] But the example most familiar to poets and preachers of the seventeenth century was Saint Augustine's transformation in the garden in Milan. In "torment" he "twisted and turned in [his] chain." He "probed the hidden depths of [his] soul" and "mustered [its pitiful secrets] before the eyes of [his] heart." A great storm broke within him. Fighting back tears, he collapsed under a fig tree. He could hold back no longer. The "tears . . . streamed from his eyes," and he cried out, "why not now," until the voice of a child told him to read. Opening his Scriptures, he read Paul's warning against reveling, drunkenness, lust, and wantonness, as well as "quarrels and rivalries." He became quite calm, and his friend Alypius then read the admonition to "find room among you for a man of over-delicate conscience."[37]

The flood of Augustine's tears shaped the rhetoric of preachers seeking to move their Catholic audiences to contrition, and it fashioned the way Capuchins and others (such as Pascal) described the conversion experience. But did Protestants who converted during the Forty Hours Devotions or, more generally, during a mission such as that in the Poitou, undergo the same emotional experience? Did the Capuchins, in their reports on missions or in the polemical writing used to encourage Protestant transformations during these campaigns, record sudden outpourings of repentance and transformation? At first glance, the answer would seem to be no. Pierre Dumonceaux has shown that, in the seventeenth century, the terms *conversion* and *to convert* could carry a variety of connotations, from emotional Augustinian repentance to a passage from one religion to another without deep emotional stirrings of the heart.[38] Emile Kappler has suggested that the polemical literature, which was employed in and grew out of conversion campaigns, contains little on the psychology of former Huguenots, on their struggles of conscience, or on the spiritual steps that led them to convert. According to him, conversion is described mostly as an intellectual decision based on a consideration of doctrinal differences.[39]

The chronicle of the Poitou mission and other polemical writings, especially by converts themselves, give us a sense of the Protestant conversion experience that, at first, seems to bear Kappler out. The Protestant pastor of Lusignan, Jacques Métayer, who converted after the mission there, depicted his transformation in an account addressed to Protestant ministers as a return to political loyalty. Métayer described himself as appalled by his seditious former colleagues, who were stirring up opposition to the king.[40] Political motives for conversion were buttressed by the "rational" recognition of truth. The Capuchin chronicle of the mission described the conversion of the minister of Parthenay, Guillemard, as following upon the clarification of "all his difficulties" and the acknowledgment of "all his errors." He had been too "opinionated" (a common characterization of heretics), but now he recognized the fallacies in his previous beliefs.[41] Similarly, although the duc de La Trémoille was impressed by the devotion of the large crowds coming in procession to the mission at Thouars, he converted only after long conferences with missionaries in Brittany and Paris resolved all of his doubts.[42] Converts of lesser social and political importance underwent comparable long, analytical processes. The Sieur de la Verdure, a "hôtellier" of Parthenay, described as "one of the firmest Huguenots of the region," converted on his sickbed after a series of encounters between a Capuchin and a local minister who debated whether Paul had praised (and thereby validated) the Roman church. The first meeting lasted almost five hours. The missionary pushed his opponent to support his position with formal scriptural texts, but the minister could only respond with "gross solecisms, equipollences, obscure arguments, and Aristotelian subtleties of logic." Convinced that the minister could not base his faith on Scripture, la Verdure converted and made a general confession.[43]

A closer reading of this literature suggests, however, that the emotions that drove Catholic hearts to change were not absent from the path the campaigners offered to Protestants. Protestant converts did not always shed tears, but they did experience a catharsis before their reintegration into the bosom of the Church. Father Joseph, in a letter to his mother, described the conversions as "coming like a bolt of lightning, rather than following upon polemical debates [*controverses*]. We see many heretics who, after hearing our preaching, throw themselves at the feet of the speaker and demand absolution."[44] One "gentleman of quality" converted during the *oraison* of Forty Hours at Coulonges-sur-l'Autize in 1620 because he was "tormented (*bourrelé*) in his conscience."[45] The dame de la Poste of Sanxay, formerly "very firm in her religion," fell ill and called a Capuchin to her side. The chronicler compared her plight to those whom the word of God had "delivered from anguish" when "their hearts were humiliated with illness and sadness." The missionary arrived, but seeing her surrounded by Huguenots and "tormented by sadness," he left so as not to provoke more "violence in her soul." After his return, God's grace "open[ed] her eyes"; she repented her errors with "all her heart"; and she received the Eucharist.[46] Métayer, in urging his former colleagues to convert, did not cite Augustine's case. But for these men steeped in Scripture, he did recall one tearful Old Testament example, that of King Hezekiah, who, prompted by the prophet Isaiah, converted on his sickbed after weeping bitterly for his past transgressions. Isaiah reported that the Lord had heard Hezekiah's prayers and had seen his tears.[47] Thus even those "men of erudition," the converted ministers, though they might stress the acknowledgment of correct doctrine or political obedience, could feel, as Métayer did, "violent movements of conscience," or as Guillemard did, "violent interior reproaches that prick[ed] at the depths of the heart."[48]

Therefore, the distinction between the emotional interior conversion of repentant Catholics and the intellectualized passage of Protestants to the rival faith does not entirely hold, either in the writings of the Capuchins or in those of former Huguenots. In all the cases cited above, doctrinal debate, usually over the interpretation of Scripture, coupled with an acknowledgment of error, led Huguenots to the point of conversion. But at the moment of transformation, they felt their own "swords (with which they had opposed God's church) enter their hearts" until suddenly they were replaced there with the "charity of God."[49] Then they might cry out, as did the Huguenot moved by a Capuchin preaching in the Protestant cemetery of Saint-Jean-d'Angély, "I want to be a Catholic from this moment on."[50]

The duality emerged from the central Christian quandary over acts of faith. Could the rational intellect recognize truth and hence bring about the conversion? Or was the only necessity God's grace, independent of and superior to human reason, and best felt at work in the heart? Of course, given the unresolvable problem, seventeenth-century Catholic missionaries and moralists answered that both were needed. Emphasizing only grace would have made them sound too much like their Calvinist opponents. Yet with their Augustinian heritage, they would hardly have seen the intellect as primary. Different writers combined the Augustinian, Scholastic, and Humanist traditions in different fashions; Francis de Sales leaned toward reason while Jansenists leaned the other way.[51] In constructing an effective model of conversion, the Capuchin missionaries in the Poitou incorporated both the intellectual and emotional approaches in their campaign. They sought to *persuade* Huguenots of the truth, and so they attacked the reasonability of the Protestant faith by debating ministers, questioning the accuracy of Huguenot Bibles, and challenging Calvinist doctrine. But the appeal to the intellect was insufficient for the Catholic understanding of conversion, and so the Capuchins included emotional appeals in sermons and rituals that would provide a rite of passage to transform the heretics into full members of the revivified Catholic community.

While Protestant converts thus shared the emotional experience of Augustine, their Catholic neighbors paid heed to the admonition Alypius took from Paul: "Find room among you for a man of over-delicate conscience." And find room they did, in ritualized ways that reintegrated those now transformed by the rite of passage. The conversions that the texts report in the most detail were never private affairs. Protestants and Catholics were present, each side hoping for victory. When the Sieur de la Verdure converted, on the festival of Charles Borromeo, the Capuchin missionary led the entire company of Catholics at the bedside in a prayer for the saint whose intercession had helped work the miracle. Those present to welcome the new believer were the cream of Parthenay's Catholic community: ecclesiastics, nobles, and judicial officers. When news of the conversion spread throughout the town, the canons of the chapter of Sainte Croix chanted a Te Deum in a church filled with a great crowd that had assembled in Parthenay for a market day. The heresy that had so "chilled" Catholic piety in the area seemed in retreat; Catholicism was resurgent. After dinner that day, the convert's reception into his new community was completed, as the "majority of Catholics" came to visit him and watch him hand over his copy of Marot's Psalms. Two days later, after "a grand and exemplary contrition," he received the viaticum and died.[52]

The day after the conversion of the dame de la Poste in Sanxay, her Capuchin missionary celebrated mass in the parish church with a number of local nobles present. Afterwards, two Capuchins, the curé, and all those present went in procession to her house, carrying the Blessed Sacrament, the cross, and holy water ("arms that horrified demons and Huguenots equally"). The friars, each carrying a torch in one hand and a cross in the other, marched alongside the priest. Nobles followed them, and then came other Catholics, all chanting praises to God, psalms, and hymns. En route they passed numerous Protestant inhabitants of Sanxay, whom the nobles forced either to retire or to get on their knees before the Blessed Sacrament—acts in accordance with royal edicts but rarely enforced in this area. When they entered the convert's house, she accepted the Sacrament, professed that it was the true body of her Savior, and proclaimed her willingness to die in that belief. The threshold was crossed, the reintegration accomplished. The ritual had transformed both the convert and the community she had joined. Now "tears of joy . . . bathe[d] the eyes of all those present, as they thank[ed] God for so perfect a conversion."[53]

The mission, then, mustered the rituals and symbols necessary for overcoming crosscutting political, social, and religious interests and for creating a clear sense of not just different but opposing communities. The ritual spawned a new social reality by selecting and emphasizing certain identities and differences. Missionaries also provided—again through ritual—a means through which the new outsiders could join, a means that stripped them of one identity and gave them another. The mission was only one part of the conversion campaign, but it would provoke the rupture that made other aspects locally meaningful and gave them their force. These other aspects—political pressure, the attractions of royal honors and largesse, the legislation that struck at all areas of coexistence—could not succeed without the creation of opposing local identities.[54] The response of Protestants, as a community, remains to be explored. They had a very different sense of symbol and ritualization. The bonds they eventually formed in reaction to the increasing isolation and inwardness forced upon them might well have given them the strength to survive in the "Desert." But more immediately, French Protestants found their world defined for them by the success of a conversion campaign that turned the permeable frontier between them and their Catholic neighbors into a strict, sacred boundary.

NOTES

1. Robert W. Scribner's work, for example, has been informative about the place of ritual in the development of Lutheranism. See, in particular, "Ritual and Reformation," in *The German People and the Reformation,* ed. R. Po-Chia Hsia (Ithaca, 1988), 122–44.

2. For this figure and for the following information, see Louis Pérouas, "La 'Mission de Poitou' des capucins pendant le premier quart du XVIIe siècle," *Bulletin et mémoires de la Société des antiquaires de l'ouest et des musées de Poitiers* (1964): 349–62; and Robert Favreau, ed., *Le diocèse de Poitiers* (Paris, 1988), 132–34 and 144–45.

3. They were Loudun, Châtelleraut, Saint-Maixent, Thouars, Maillezais, Fontenay-le-Comte, Talmont, and Beauvoir-sur-Mers.

4. "Estat de la religion en Poictou," Archives Nationales, Paris (hereafter, AN), TT. 262 (8), 232–35.

5. Elisabeth Labrousse, *Une foi, une loi, un roi? Essai sur la révocation de l'Édit de Nantes* (Paris, 1985), 81–89, and "Conversion dans les deux sens," in Roger Duchêne, ed., *La conversion au XVIIe siècle: Actes du XIIe colloque de Marseille* (Marseilles, 1983), 161–77. Robert Sauzet, *Contre-réforme et réforme catholique en Bas-Languedoc: Le diocèse de Nîmes au XVIIe siècle* (Louvain, 1979), 165–78. For a summary of their findings, see Bernard Dompnier, *Le venin de l'hérésie: Image du protestantisme et combat catholique au XVIIe siècle* (Paris, 1985), chapter 6.

6. Natalie Zemon Davis, "The Rites of Violence," in *Society and Culture in Early Modern France* (Stanford, 1975), 152–87.

7. Letter of 11 April 1619 cited in Pierre Dez, *Histoire des protestants et des églises réformées du Poitou* (La Rochelle, 1936), 256 n.1.

8. "Establissement des gardes de la ville de Niort au service du roi" (30 June 1621), Fonds Fonteneau, Bibliothèque Municipale de Poitiers (hereafter, BMP), 68:357–61.

9. "Acte" (21 July 1620), Fonds Fonteneau, 14:213, cited in Dez, *Histoire des protestants,* 253.

10. "Sommaire des raisons que ceux qui font profession de la religion refformée ont de se plaindre de l'arrest du seiziesme septembre 1634..." (1634), Archives Départmentales de Vienne (hereafter, ADV) C. 49. For discussion of the issue and a partial list of the rural communities that shared cemeteries, see André Benoist, "Catholiques et protestants en 'Moyen-Poitou' jusqu'à la révocation de l'Édit de Nantes, 1534–1685," *Bulletin de la Société historique et scientifique des Deux-Sevres,* 2d series, 16 (1983): 235–439, especially 343–44.

11. Labrousse, *Une foi,* 83–84; Sauzet, *Nîmes,* 165–68; Dompnier, *Le venin,* 154–57. The statistical frequency of intermarriage has, however, been challenged. Philip Benedict, personal communication, 12 December 1990.

12. For Protestants, a public penance with an expression of regret before the consistory usually led to a reconciliation with the congregation, and, according to Bernard Dompnier, Catholic spouses of Huguenots

suffered no greater trouble. Dompnier, *Le venin*, 155; Labrousse, *Une foi*, 83.

13. "Estat de la religion en Poictou," 234. For a similar complaint by Christophe Authier, a Catholic missionary in the diocese of Die, see Dompnier, *Le venin*, 154.

14. Natalie Zemon Davis, "City Women and Religious Change," in *Society and Culture*, 65–95; Nancy L. Roelker, "The Appeal of Calvinism to French Noblewomen in the Sixteenth Century," *The Journal of Interdisciplinary History* 2 (1972): 391–418.

15. Davis, "City Women and Religious Change," 94.

16. There has been, thus far, little description of such a situation in the Poitou, but see Odile Martin's discussion of the coterie in Lyons. *La conversion protestante à Lyon (1659–1687)* (Geneva, 1986), 72–76.

17. Description in C.-C. de Rulhière, *Eclaircissements historiques sur les causes de la Révocation* (Geneva, 1788), 1:38, cited in Martin, *La conversion*, 78.

18. Dompnier, *Le venin*, 154; Labrousse, *Une foi*, 91–93.

19. "Procès-verbal de l'émotion," AN, TT. 235 cited in Dez, *Histoire des protestants*, 259.

20. Ibid., 266; Auguste Lièvre, *Histoire des protestants et des églises réformées du Poitou* (Paris, 1856), 1:296.

21. Arnold Van Gennep, *The Rites of Passage*, trans. Monika B. Vizedom and Gabrielle L. Caffee (Chicago, 1960).

22. Pérouas, "La Mission," 352–53.

23. For a Capuchin account of the mission, see *Recueils pour l'histoire generalle en abbregé de touttes les missions des capucins depuis le commencement de la reforme jusques l'an 1673*, Bibliothèque Municipale d'Orléans, MS. 916, pp. 51–70.

24. For the distinctions between interior missions among Catholic populations and exterior ones among non-Catholics, see Louis Pérouas, "Missions intérieures et missions extérieures françaises pendant les premières décennies du XVIIe siècle," *Parole et mission*, 7ème année, 27 (15 octobre 1964): 644–59.

25. Keith P. Luria, "The Counter-Reformation and Popular Spirituality," in *Christian Spirituality: Post-Reformation and Modern*, ed. Louis Dupré and Don E. Saliers (New York, 1989), 93–120, especially 115–16; Bernard Dompnier, "Un aspect de la dévotion eucharistique dans la France du XVIIe siècle: Les prières des Quarante-Heures," *Revue d'Histoire de l'Eglise de France* 67 (1981): 5–31; Ronald F. E. Weissman, *Ritual Brotherhood in Renaissance Florence* (New York, 1982), 229–33.

26. Louis Dedouvres, *Politique et apôtre: Le Père Joseph de Paris, Capucin: L'eminence grise* (Paris, 1894), 2:161.

27. Dompnier, *Le venin*, 85–87. The minister Métayer, who would convert during the mission at Lusignan, would explain his change to a large degree as a return to political obedience. Jacques Métayer, *Conversions signalées depuis peu de iours par l'entremise des pères capucins de la mission du Poictou...* (Paris, 1620), 18–31.

28. Raoul de Sceaux, "Le Père Honoré de Cannes, capucin missionaire," *XVIIe siècle*, no. 41, 4 (1958): 349–74; Bernard Dompnier, "Pastoral de la peur et pastorale de la séduction: La méthode de conversion des missionaires capucins," in Duchêne, ed., *La conversion au XVIIe siècle*, 262–63.

29. *Recueils*, 52–58; Pérouas, "La mission," 357. For a detailed description of another Forty Hours Devotion during the mission, see *Le nouveau restablissement de la ville de Sainct Jean d'Angély, avec la conversion de plus de huict mille personnes à la religion catholique, apostolique et romaine. Faict par les pères capucins de la mission, le jour et feste de la pentecoste dernière 1623* (Paris, 1623).

30. Victor Turner, *Dramas, Fields, and Metaphors: Symbolic Action in Human Society* (Ithaca, NY, 1974), chap. 1, especially p. 56. For a later refinement of Turner's ideas, see his *On the Edge of the Bush: Anthropology as Experience* (Tucson, AZ, 1985), especially the epilogue entitled, "Are There Universals of Performance in Myth, Ritual, and Drama?," 291–301. See also Scribner's discussion of Turner's ideas on ritual catharsis in "Ritual and Reformation," 142–44.

31. Dompnier, "Pastorale de la peur," 269–70. Even the locales were significant. Lusignan was where Calvin had once lived. Poitiers was the diocesan seat. Latilly was described as a savage and deserted place where heresy had literally destroyed the local church and in which only two or three Catholic families now lived.

32. *Recueils*, 56–57.

33. Ibid.

34. The quoted words are from various Capuchin missionary manuals cited by Dompnier, "Pastorale de la peur," 263–67. I have discussed this sort of conversion experience in "Constructing Moral Order in a Socially-Stratified Society: The Role of Catholic Missions in Seventeenth- and Eighteenth-Century France," unpublished paper presented to the International Congress on the History of the French Revolution, Washington, D.C., May 1989.

35. *Recueils*, 62. The location of the ceremony is unclear in the text but seems to be La Rochelle.

36. See Sheila Bayne, "Le rôle des larmes dans le discours sur la conversion," in Duchêne, ed., *La conversion au XVIIe siècle*, 417–27. Tears as marks of sincerity were also important in other contexts. *The Malleus Maleficarium* suggests their use in trials of suspected witches. The accused, if innocent, will be able to shed real tears in the presence of the judge or while being tortured; a witch will not, though she might fake tears with spittle. In trying to conjure tears in the accused, the judge was to refer to those shed by Christ, Mary, and the saints. Heinrich Kramer and James Sprenger, *The Malleus Maleficarum*, trans. Reverend Montague Summers (New York, 1971), 227.

37. Saint Augustine, *Confessions*, trans. R. S. Pine-Coffin (Harmondsworth, 1961), 175–78.

38. Pierre Dumonceaux, "Conversion, convertir: Etude comparative d'après les lexicographies du XVIIe siècle," in Duchêne, ed., *La conversion au XVIIe siècle*, 7–17. Dumonceaux suggests that the sense of conversion

emphasizing an amendment of life became increasingly secularized across the century, but the accounts of missions in the later part of the century still stress the religious conversion experience as leading to a change of life.

39. See Kappler's comments on the article by Louis Desgraves, "Un aspect des controverses entre catholiques et protestants: Les récits de conversion (1598–1628)," in Duchêne, ed., *La conversion au XVIIe siècle*, 108.

40. *La conversion du Sieur Mestayer cy-devant ministre du Lusignan, faicte en la ville de Poictiers le 23 jour de mars 1617* (Poitiers, 1617), 3–9.

41. *Recueils*, 58.

42. Ibid., 59–60. The Capuchin chronicle neglects to mention, however, that La Trémoille's conversion had less to do with the missionaries' work and more with the campaign against La Rochelle. His conversion, for which Richelieu took credit, came in July of 1628 in the camp of the royal army besieging the city. David Parker, *La Rochelle and the French Monarchy: Conflict and Order in Seventeenth-Century France* (London, 1980), 118 and 144.

43. Métayer, *Conversions signalées*, 18–31.

44. Gustave Fagniez, *Le Père Joseph et Richelieu (1579–1638)* (Paris, 1894), 1:291.

45. *Recueils*, 57.

46. Indeed because her repentance was of the heart, she was truly able "to attach herself to the breasts of that good mother, which are the sacraments" of the church. Métayer, *Conversions signalées*, 47–53.

47. Ibid., 19, 51. Isa. 38:3–5.

48. Métayer, *Conversions signalées*, 13–16. Métayer reports Guillemard's feelings as well as his own.

49. Ibid., 22 and 23.

50. *Recueils*, 61, 62, 68.

51. A. H. T. Levi, "La psychologie de la conversion au XVIIe siècle: de François de Sales à Nicole," in Duchêne, ed., *La conversion au XVIIe siècle*, 19–28.

52. Métayer, *Conversions signalées*, 27–32. Métayer reports that the Catholics present at Verdure's home had already taken great "consolation" from the earlier conversion of the pastor Guillemard.

53. Ibid., 52–54.

54. On these aspects of the conversion campaign, see, for example, Dez, *Histoire des protestants;* Benoist, "Catholiques et protestants," 336; and Labrousse, *Une foi*, chapters 5–8.

Confessors, Penitents, and the Construction of Identities in Early Modern Avila

Jodi Bilinkoff

A striking feature of religious life in Catholic Europe during the sixteenth and seventeenth centuries was the frequency with which priests established deep and lasting relationships with women known for their piety and spiritual gifts.[1] These relationships often found expression in the genre of spiritual biography, a literary form that had earlier roots but gained immense popularity in the Counter-Reformation era. Typically, the confessors would become the biographers of the holy women after their deaths. The numerous biographical texts from Spain, Italy, and France make fascinating reading for what they reveal about the male confessor/biographers as well as about the female penitents who are their ostensible subjects.[2]

That male clerics would involve themselves so deeply in the inner lives of women may at first seem surprising. Some scholars suggest that the confessor-penitent relationship was a rather simple and fundamentally repressive one: confessors exercised complete authority, penitents displayed total obedience. Recent studies have stressed the elements of control, domination, and censorship in confessors' treatment of women, particularly in the aftermath of the Council of Trent.[3]

However, close examination reveals that in practice, relations between male confessors and female penitents were frequently more complex, more nuanced, and more reciprocal than conventional wisdom might have us believe. In this essay, I analyze five cases of holy women and their spiritual directors who lived in the diocese of Avila, in central Castile, between 1500 and 1650. These cases demonstrate that, despite official disapproval and considerable risks for members of both sexes, confessors and penitents could forge profound spiritual relationships. Far from occupying positions of unqualified control, male confessors were strongly attracted to the idea of directing spiritually advanced women and, in turn, became deeply influenced by them, identified with them, and even became dependent upon them. The experience of dealing with and writing about extraordinary women aided clerics in formulating and articulating their own sense of identity. And the position of spiritual director provided priests with an acceptable channel for discussing controversial, even dangerous, theological topics. The most common vehicle for exploring these religious and personal issues was the biography of a female penitent by a male confessor, a classic genre of baroque spirituality that insured a place in posterity for both subject and biographer.

Before turning to how and why some male clerics became so involved with women, I will briefly survey the cases of five holy women from the diocese of Avila in the sixteenth and seventeenth centuries. Considering them in chronological order, the first was María de Santo Domingo, a peasant *beata* (holy woman) born around 1485 in the southwest of the diocese. She joined the Dominican order as a tertiary but soon became the subject of a bitter dispute among its members. Some admired her for her ecstatic trances and prophetic utterances, while others denounced her as a fraud. Preeminent among her defenders were María's confessors Diego de Vitoria (dates unknown) and Antonio de la Peña (d. 1512), both Dominican friars.[4]

Another peasant woman, Mari Díaz, was born around 1500 in the village of Vita, near the city of Avila, and moved to the capital in the 1540s. From then until her death in 1572 this humble *beata*, who never attached herself to a religious order, was widely revered by members of Avila's urban community. We know about most details of her life through the beatification proceedings initiated (but not completed) by several bishops of Avila in the early seventeenth century and through a biography of her confessor, the prominent Jesuit Baltasar Alvarez (1533–80).[5]

By far the best known of the five was Teresa of Jesus, the future Saint Teresa of Avila. This brilliant mystic, monastic reformer and writer—one of Spain's greatest—was born to a middle-class merchant family in Avila in 1515. She initiated a reform of the Carmelite order

in 1562 and spent the next twenty years founding Discalced Carmelite houses in Castile and Andalusia. She died in 1582 and was canon-
ized in 1622. Teresa of Jesus had many confessors during her life-
time, several of whom wrote biographies. In this study I focus upon
Julián de Avila, a secular priest and native of Avila (1527–1605).[6]

Of the five holy women, only one belonged to Avila's aristocracy.
She was Doña María Vela, born in 1561 in the town of Cardeñosa and
raised in the capital. Doña María's intense and often eccentric spiritual experiences scandalized the highborn nuns of her Cistercian convent. During the fifteen years preceding her death in 1617, the controversial María developed an exceptionally close relationship with
her confessor (and later biographer), the secular priest Miguel
González Vaquero (1565–1636).[7]

The last woman, and the one about whom we have the least information, was Isabel de Jesús. Like María de Santo Domingo and Mari
Díaz, Isabel came from peasant stock. She was born in 1586 in the
mountain village of Navalcán. Forced to marry at an early age, Isabel
nevertheless maintained a vivid inner, visionary life and a passionate
desire for a religious vocation. After the death of her husband she
finally succeeded in entering an Augustinian convent in the town of
Arenas. Just before her death in 1648, the illiterate Isabel dictated
her life to a fellow nun. Many years later, in 1675, one of Isabel's
confessors, the Augustinian Francisco Ignacio (dates unknown) published the manuscript autobiography, appending to it his own biographical account of the holy woman's life, death, and miracles.[8]

Thus, for four generations priests in the diocese of Avila sought
out spiritual relationships with extraordinary women and recorded
their lives for posterity. This, in spite of the fact that members of
Spain's clerical hierarchy actively discouraged such close encounters
with the opposite sex. In a highly misogynistic age, writers warned
of women's intellectual and moral weaknesses. They were thought to
be more gullible than men, more likely to fall prey to the deceptions
of heretics, charlatans, and the devil. The prominent role of women
in the sect of the *Alumbrados,* or "Enlightened Ones," which first came
to the attention of authorities in the 1520s, only seemed to confirm
this gloomy assessment.[9]

By the end of the sixteenth century the situation had gotten worse.
Sensational cases of women revered as visionaries and stigmatics, only
to be revealed as frauds, cast aspersions on all female claims to mysti-

cal experience. The Inquisition clamped down on women perceived as purveyors of dangerous ideas, as well as the male confessors who aided and abetted them.[10] Several of the spiritual directors of holy women from Avila encountered firsthand the biases of their contemporaries. Among them was Baltasar Alvarez, who was admonished by a Jesuit official "not to waste time with women, especially Carmelite nuns" but rather to "apply himself more to the treatment of men, where there is less danger and greater advantage."[11]

But in spite of the warnings, the sanctions, and the threat of punishment, priests in Avila persisted in treating advanced religious women. What motivated these clerics?

On a very basic level, confessors associated themselves with holy women because doing so fulfilled their own emotional and spiritual needs. Their penitents, after all, were not ordinary women, but "handmaids of the Lord" (*siervas de Dios*), who experienced visions, voices, and other phenomena that early modern Catholics recognized as gifts from God. Virtually every confessor from Avila acknowledged undergoing some kind of personal transformation or renewal of spirit as a result of dealing with these exceptional women.

For example, Diego de Vitoria testified at the religious-fraud trial of María de Santo Domingo held in 1509 and 1510 that he had met the *beata* about three years earlier, on a trip to Toledo. He begged the holy woman to pray for him and to ask God to send him contrition for his sins. During that journey, Vitoria recalled, he felt "a degree of fervor and repentance that he had never felt before." Later, when Dominican authorities ordered him to break off his overly "familiar" relations with María, Vitoria attempted to comply, succeeding for a few days. But then, he recounted, "seeing the insistent needs that presented themselves to the witness to communicate with [María] he renewed his dealings, believing in all conscience that by doing so he was serving God and not offending anyone." Vitoria apparently tried to justify his disobedience to monastic superiors by claiming an almost addictive compulsion to visit his charismatic penitent.[12]

Francisco Ignacio, the biographer of the seventeenth-century *beata* Isabel de Jesús, related an intriguing incident. Once, when Isabel was still a laywoman, she traveled to confess with a Franciscan named Francisco de Cogolludo. As the pious woman approached, the friar dismounted and threw himself on his knees before her, asking for her blessing. According to Ignacio, the confused Isabel, "shedding many tears, prostrated herself on the ground and asked him rather to bless her; after all, he was one of the Lord's priests and her father confessor and she but a miserable woman." They argued back and forth this way for a while, but finally Isabel won "this holy debate" (*esta santa contienda*) and received the priest's blessing, as her biographer noted with obvious satisfaction. The story continues, however. When an astonished passerby asked Cogolludo why he would beg on his knees for a woman's blessing, the priest reportedly replied, "Don't be amazed, brother, for this is a soul who keeps God, as it were, in a state of passionate love."[13]

By the end of this anecdote of role reversals, hierarchy is restored and the actors have literally regained their socially sanctioned positions: priest on his feet, penitent on her knees. But neither Cogolludo nor, by extension, Ignacio questioned the notion that priests could reap spiritual benefits by interacting with divinely enlightened women. In a similar vein, one of Teresa of Jesus's early confessor/ biographers, Diego de Yepes, claimed that the nun, "while she lived on the earth," had granted him "many favors." And Miguel González Vaquero, describing his first meeting with María Vela, recalled his emotions: "confusion," followed by "consolation," and finally the conviction that, by taking her on as a penitent, "many advantages were to come to my soul."[14]

Perhaps even more significantly, by associating themselves with spiritually endowed women, confessors in early modern Avila bolstered their positions as priests. For example, mature religious women helped young or newly arrived priests to establish themselves. In the 1550s Teresa of Jesus promoted a group of young Jesuits, most of whom were twenty to thirty years younger than herself, at Avila's new College of Saint Giles. Later, as a monastic reformer, she actively recruited young men to serve as Discalced Carmelite priests. Notable examples such as John of the Cross and Jerome Gratian of the Mother of God were, in a very real sense, both her father/confessors and protégé/sons.[15]

One of the most interesting descriptions of the relationship between a young confessor and a mature penitent comes from the biography of Baltasar Alvarez, published in 1615 by his Jesuit disciple Luis de la Puente. De la Puente discussed at some length Alvarez's spiritual direction of the *beata* Mari Díaz. When Alvarez first arrived in Avila in 1559, Mari Díaz was approximately sixty years old and already enjoyed renown for her piety. Her new confessor was twenty-six and had just been ordained a priest. De la Puente pointed out that "this holy woman had good fortune in meeting Father Baltasar, who helped her a great deal in her [spiritual] ascent." But he acknowledged that Alvarez likewise had good fortune in meeting the *beata,* "because she helped him very much by her fine example and, for what she did, he came to be very well-known and esteemed by everyone in [Avila]." Clearly Alvarez owed much of his reputation as a sensitive and effective confessor to the promotional efforts of his illiterate but well-connected penitent.[16]

Holy women underscored the sacramental function of the priest by their profound devotion to the Eucharist. The five women from Avila all exhibited what Miguel González Vaquero called "a thirst for communion," a thirst that only a priest, invested with the power to consecrate the Host, could satisfy. Perhaps for this reason male confessors stressed this aspect of their female penitents' spiritual lives in their biographical accounts.[17]

Antonio de la Peña depicted María de Santo Domingo as "a follower of the Church and of the divine offices" who was "accustomed to confess and receive communion very often at the times specified by the Church and even more [frequently]." Writing to Cardinal Cisneros in 1512, his colleague Diego de Vitoria excused himself from visiting the prelate as commanded, protesting that "this handmaid of God now receives communion every day and would suffer greatly were I to discontinue it." Vitoria managed to convey at once María's reverence for the Eucharist, her dependence upon him as provider of spiritual nourishment, and his own sense of obligation to his penitent, an obligation that outweighed a summons from Spain's highest ecclesiastical authority.[18]

The desire of religious women to gaze upon, meditate on, and ingest the consecrated Host intensified during the course of the sixteenth and seventeenth centuries. Mari Díaz received permission to live at the Church of San Millán (an institution she later helped to convert into a seminary for priests) where "she placed herself continuously before the Most Blessed Sacrament."[19]

María Vela's obsession with receiving the Eucharist and her anguish over whether or not she should fast beforehand was accompanied by severe illnesses, bizarre bodily contortions, and widespread disapproval. The almost thaumaturgic ability of Miguel González Vaquero to control María's fits and trances by imposing obedience upon her formed the basis of a lasting relationship between spiritual director and penitent. As the nun wrote to him around 1600, "For a whole year now, it has always been necessary for you to impose obedience upon me in order to enable me to confess, . . . [the] same thing has happened with regard to communion; . . . when you were not at hand, I have seldom been able to receive."[20] All five holy women from Avila were reported to have experienced mystical phenomena—ecstasies, visions, locutions, and the like—just before, after, or at the moment of receiving the Host. Their spirituality was thus closely linked to the sacramental authority of the priest, as well as to the doctrine of transubstantiation, two articles of the faith under attack by Protestants during this period.[21]

Confessors also used their acquaintance with exceptional religious women to affirm their apostolic roles as preachers and teachers. Many clerics strove to edify the faithful by portraying their female penitents as exemplars of holiness in sermons, lessons, doctrinal treatises, and, of course, spiritual biographies. For instance, Luis de la Puente used the word "example" (*exemplo*) no fewer than four times in the first paragraph of his biographical sketch of Mari Díaz. The Jesuit also recalled how his teacher, Baltasar Alvarez, had used the words of his humble penitent to instruct seminarians in the spiritual benefits of suffering. On another occasion Alvarez invoked the memory of Mari Díaz in a contemplation on the reverence due the saints and their shrines. Preachers in Avila made reference to Mari Díaz and other holy women in their sermons, holding them up as models of Christian devotion and behavior. For spiritual directors this practice provided an excellent opportunity to remind listeners of their proximity to persons of exceptional virtue, to exhort others to imitate those persons, and to claim at least partial credit for their penitents' saintly status.[22]

The biographies of holy women written by spiritual directors also suggest that the confessional enterprise helped these men to define themselves, as priests and as human beings. Their close association with advanced female penitents contributed in significant ways to the construction of identities: for themselves, for contemporaries, and for posterity.

Nearly all the confessors and penitents from Avila portrayed their relationships as divinely ordained and sanctioned and suggested that

God had especially chosen them to direct or be directed by this particular person. The resulting sense of destiny expressed by priests, and of relief and gratitude expressed by penitents, is understandable considering that all five women went through long periods with inadequate or even hostile confessors before meeting a genuine "soulmate." Teresa of Jesus detailed this painful process in her autobiography, charging at one point that poorly educated and insensitive confessors had "done my soul great harm." Later, as a monastic reformer, she devoted many pages to this problem and insisted that her nuns have the freedom to choose and change their spiritual directors.[23] María Vela and Isabel de Jesús, forced to reveal themselves to priests who ignored, humiliated, or denounced them, also spent many years searching for the right confessor.[24]

But what was seen as a test or trial for women could serve as a source of validation for men. The relationship between María Vela and Miguel González Vaquero offers a poignant example. In his biography of Doña María, González Vaquero recalled how he had heard stories about an extraordinary Cistercian nun who experienced visions and trances and who had already gone through a long string of confessors. Mutual acquaintances arranged a meeting. He was left astounded by her humble and earnest manner of speaking, "so filled with the love of God."

For her part, María later wrote to her director that, from that first meeting, "your spirit and mine seemed in such complete accord, and I felt so deeply satisfied and so encouraged, that I hardly recognized myself." Her impressions were dramatically confirmed by the voice of God, which assured her that, "even when I seem to leave thee, I am with thee; because I have given thee into the care of another who can guide thee." When she asked the Lord whether or not she should offer González Vaquero her special obedience, María heard in reply a quotation from Scripture: "This is my beloved Son, in whom I am well pleased: hear ye him" (Matthew 17:5). She understood these words to refer to her new confessor. Thus, for the long-suffering María, the sympathetic González Vaquero was not only divinely chosen but explicitly Christlike in his role as director of her soul.[25]

Not surprisingly, this kind of regard added immeasurably to his self-esteem. Discernible in his biography of María Vela is the subtle yet steady transformation of Miguel González Vaquero from a rather insecure cleric who constantly sought advice and approval from older, more experienced confessors, to a supremely confident, even arrogant priest with whom others consulted as an expert in the spiritual direction of women.[26]

Nor was González Vaquero the only confessor in early modern Avila to gain a reputation among contemporaries as an expert in this field. Baltasar Alvarez and Julián de Avila also established themselves as specialists in the confession of women. The Jesuit Francisco de Ribera, a student of Alvarez's and the first biographer of Teresa of Jesus, told a revealing anecdote about his mentor. "Although Father Baltasar Alvarez had knowledge and experience of spiritual matters," he recalled, "Mother Teresa of Jesus flew so high that he had to really hurry to keep up with her." "I remember," he continued, "that once in Salamanca I discussed with [him] various devotional books and the value of each one of them and he replied: 'I read every one of those books in order to understand Teresa of Jesus.'"[27]

Alvarez also tried out various methods of confession on Teresa, as well as several other women in Avila, including Mari Díaz and the younger *beata* Ana Reyes. His biographer, Luis de la Puente, discussed how the priest worked at Ana Reyes "like a hammer" in order to mortify her passions and once deliberately insulted Mari Díaz by calling her "an old lazybones" (*vieja harona*). Yet, on other occasions, Alvarez treated these women with great kindness and respect, apparently attempting to strike a balance between encouraging holiness and discouraging pride. Miguel González Vaquero and Diego de Vitoria also made "experiments" (the word is María Vela's) on their penitents, testing their obedience, their veracity, and the genuineness of their mystical experiences.[28]

Over time these clerics, recognized for their skill at treating challenging religious women, became the teachers of new spiritual directors. Baltasar Alvarez trained a whole generation of Jesuit priests in Avila and elsewhere, including Luis de la Puente, Francisco de Ribera, Alvarez's nephew Francisco Salcedo, Diego de Villena, and also Miguel González Vaquero (who did not actually join the Society of Jesus). These men all came to be regarded as effective confessors of women.[29] Toward the end of his life, Julián de Avila instructed and counseled his younger colleague, Miguel González Vaquero. The latter devoted many pages of his biography of María Vela to extolling the virtues of his now-departed master. González Vaquero also described how Julián guided his initial direction of the troubled nun, offering what might be called an "internship" in the treatment of souls.[30]

The case of Julián de Avila also demonstrates how involvement with an exceptional woman during her life could provide a male confessor with an unshakable "claim to fame" after her death. Thanks to his close association with Teresa of Jesus, this otherwise obscure figure became known to contemporaries and to posterity. Clearly, for Julián, aiding Teresa in the foundation of a reformed convent in Avila and, especially, accompanying her on many journeys across Spain to establish religious houses represented the great adventure of his life. Teresa expressed sincere gratitude for his loyalty and steadfastness, although she also complained about his stodginess and a certain carelessness in his direction of her nuns during her absences.[31]

But, after Teresa's death, the priest was free to construct his identity around his relationship with her. Julián frequently alluded to his acquaintance with the Holy Mother and to the closeness of their friendship. Certainly he did nothing to correct the growing impression that he had been her constant companion. At beatification hearings held in 1596, Julián made the rather ambiguous statement that "it was I who accompanied her and came and stayed at the locations where they founded houses all the time that it was necessary to stay until she sent me back to Avila." In fact, the priest aided Teresa with about half of her foundations and had relatively little contact with her during the last ten years of her life.[32]

Nevertheless, Julián de Avila became something of a cult figure in Avila, a sort of "saint by association." A seventeenth-century Carmelite chronicler reported that "gentlemen and well-known people" made their way to Avila to see the humble priest who had been the "secretary of Saint Teresa's heart." At his death in 1605, large crowds turned out to grab pieces of his clothing as relics, attend his burial, and listen to funeral sermons preached in his honor.[33]

Within one generation, writers came to identify Julián de Avila the way he had attempted to present himself. His protégé Miguel González Vaquero praised him as "confessor of the Saint and inseparable companion through all her troubles." Another commentator made reference to Teresa's "confessor and companion in her foundations." At last, around 1646, the historian Gil González Dávila categorically described Julián de Avila as a "priest of exemplary life [and]

confessor of Saint Teresa, who accompanied her on all her foundations"—an assessment that has seeped into the collective memory of
those times and events.[34]

The genre of spiritual biography provided confessors with a useful
vehicle, not only for presenting the lives of their female penitents,
but also for representing themselves. As the biographers of holy
women, male clerics exercised the prerogatives of authorship—
including or excluding information, emphasizing and deemphasizing
details of their subjects' lives as they saw fit. Francisco Ignacio, for
example, lauded Isabel de Jesús for her gift of prophecy, an issue she
herself never discussed, and one which may have held greater
significance for the priest than for the *beata*.[35]

While ostensibly writing about a female subject, male writers frequently interjected themselves into the text of their biographies. Julián de Avila introduced his *Life* of Teresa of Jesus as the story of a
modern-day saint, "whom I knew, treated, confessed, and to whom I
gave communion for twenty years." Throughout the book, he highlighted his role as Teresa's "squire" (*escudero*) and eyewitness of
events.[36]

This tendency is even more pronounced in Miguel González Vaquero's biography of María Vela. The priest constantly used the first
person *I* or *me*, stressing María's dependence on him, his responsibility for curing her erratic fits, and the hardships and tribulations to
which he was subjected, along with her. Writing his penitent's biography must have satisfied some deep-rooted literary aspiration, for
González Vaquero carefully collected his predecessors' notes on
María, kept written records during his tenure as her spiritual director, and published her biography a mere five months after her
death.[37]

Confessors even made their presence felt in the autobiographies
written by women by functioning, in effect, as coauthors, editors, and
publishing agents. These autobiographies came about precisely because priests ordered their female penitents to record their lives and
submit them for scrutiny. As several recent studies of Teresa of Jesus
have illuminated, this instrument of clerical surveillance also gave
women an unparalleled opportunity for self-expression, providing
them with the convenient explanation that they were merely writing
out of obedience.[38] The promptings of confessors may have also
helped women to become more self-reflective. After the holy women's

deaths, their spiritual directors often took control of the texts, deciding what parts to include or delete, and when or whether to publish the books at all. We can only speculate as to why Francisco Ignacio published the *Life* of Isabel de Jesús nearly thirty years after her death, or why Miguel González Vaquero declined to publish María Vela's autobiography, which remained in manuscript form until 1960.[39]

It is worth emphasizing, however, that for all the power that male confessors could exercise over women's texts, they were still as dependent upon their female penitents in the biographical enterprise as the women were upon them. The women, after all, provided the subject matter and the point of reference. Male biographers certainly managed to talk about themselves, but always in relation to the holy woman who was crucial to their own sense of identity—"the chaplain of Saint Teresa," "the confidant of María Vela," and so on. Thus the presentation of selves in early modern Avila involved a reciprocal exchange, a process of negotiation between subject and biographer, female and male. Without the authority and authorization of male clerics these women would have been unable to record their lives, but if not for their exceptional female penitents these men would have lacked the literary means, the self-confidence, and the sense of mission that allowed them to assume the role of biographer.

Finally, responding to the confessional urge to direct spiritually advanced women provided priests with an acceptable channel for treating controversial religious issues. In the charged atmosphere of mid-sixteenth-century Spain, amid fears of Protestant and Illuminist heresies, ecclesiastical authorities strongly discouraged mystical contemplation and other forms of interiorized, and therefore unmonitored, spirituality. In 1559 officials placed on the Index of Prohibited Books virtually all devotional literature written in the vernacular, including works that had profoundly influenced Teresa of Jesus and previous generations of religious women.[40]

Interestingly, just as these devotional works were being suppressed, spiritual biographies of holy women emerged as a popular form of religious literature. And, while the authors of these biographies did not offer systematic instruction in prayer and meditation as earlier writers had, they did treat these now-taboo topics by describing and, at least implicitly, endorsing the spiritual paths taken by their penitents.

For example, as we have seen, all five holy women from Avila longed for and received the Eucharist on a frequent, even daily, basis. The issue of how often to receive Communion provoked lively debate in late sixteenth- and seventeenth-century Spain, as it had in other parts of Europe in earlier periods. The confessor/biographers praised their penitents for their eucharistic devotion and also detailed how they themselves participated in the system of frequent Communion as spiritual directors. Confessors routinely denied their penitents the Sacrament at first, as a means of testing their consciences or controlling their passions, then slowly increased their access to the consecrated Host. By promoting this use of the Eucharist as a penitential tool, these confessors effectively cast their lots with the pro-frequent Communion party among clerics.[41]

In similar ways, confessors expressed positive opinions on other issues regarded as highly controversial, and gendered as "feminine": the spiritual benefits of overcoming suffering caused by illness and demonic attacks,[42] the preference for interior, mental prayer as opposed to chanted vocal prayer,[43] and the superiority of the knowledge derived from direct, mystical experience to that gleaned from formal theological education.[44] At a time of intense distrust of the mystical and the supernatural, these priests insisted on the exceptional nature of "their" penitents. Their presentation of female religious experience, as mediated by men, rendered this experience acceptable to ecclesiastical authorities, while keeping open the possibility that future generations of women could draw inspiration from their accounts. Their biographies of holy women thus contributed to the articulation of a generalized "baroque" spirituality heavily linked to gender.

In conclusion, between 1500 and 1650, priests in the diocese of Avila, as in other parts of Catholic Europe, found that the advantages of directing female penitents outweighed the risks. Their acquaintances with holy women transformed them personally, bringing them into contact with a direct and ecstatic form of religious experience beyond anything they had learned at seminary or university. In a variety of ways their relationships with exceptional female penitents enhanced their roles as priests and authorized them to preach, teach, and write on even controversial matters. And the confessional enterprise deeply informed these clerics' sense of self and helped them to construct meaningful identities. Men gained all these benefits and more from female penitents who, in theory, owed them nothing more than complete obedience. Perhaps they realized that, in the final analysis, these extraordinary women looked to a higher authority for the direction of their inner lives.

NOTES

1. I am interested here in the relationships between confessors and women penitents regarded as extraordinarily holy or spiritually advanced. For a study that begins to explore the issue of how confessors dealt with the most common type of female penitent, the married lay woman, see Rudolph M. Bell, "Telling Her Sins: Male Confessors and Female Penitents in Catholic Reformation Italy," in *That Gentle Strength: Historical Perspectives on Women in Christianity*, ed. Lynda L. Coon et al. (Charlottesville, 1990), 118–33.

2. On the genre of spiritual biography in the sixteenth and seventeenth centuries see, for example, on Spain: José Luis Sánchez Lora, *Mujeres, conventos y formas de la religiosidad barroca* (Madrid, 1988), especially 359–453 and bibliography. On Italy: Gabriella Zarri, "Le sante vive: Per una tipologia della santità femminile nel primo cinquecento," *Annali dell'Istituto Storico Italo-Germanico in Trento* 6 (1980): 371–445. On France: Henri Bremond, *A Literary History of Religious Thought in France*, 3 vols. (London, 1928–36) 1:193–204 and 2:3–54.

3. See, for example: Darcy Donohue, "Writing Lives: Nuns and Confessors as Auto/Biographers in Early Modern Spain," *Journal of Hispanic Philology* 13 (1989): 230–39. Claire Guilhem, "La Inquisición y la devaluación del verbo femenino," in *Inquisición española: Poder político y control social*, ed. Bartolomé Bennassar (Barcelona, 1981), 171–207. Ottavia Niccoli, "The End of Prophecy," *Journal of Modern History* 61 (1989): 667–82.

4. María probably died in 1524. Jodi Bilinkoff, "Charisma and Controversy: The Case of María de Santo Domingo," *Archivo Dominicano* 10 (1989): 55–66. Ibid., "A Spanish Prophetess and Her Patrons: The Case of María de Santo Domingo," *Sixteenth Century Journal* 23 (1992): 17–30. Mary E. Giles, *The Book of Prayer of Sor María of Santo Domingo* (Albany, 1990), 7–20. Sections of trial proceedings of 1509–10, during which the *beata* was exonerated of all charges, have been published in Vicente Beltrán de Heredia, *Historia de la Provincia de España (1450–1550)* (Rome, 1939), 78–142, and Jesús G. Lunas Almeida, *La Historia del Señorío de Valdecorneja en la parte referente a Piedrahita* (Avila, 1930), 123–215.

5. Jodi Bilinkoff, *The Avila of Saint Teresa: Religious Reform in a Sixteenth-Century City* (Ithaca, 1989), 96–107. Archivo Diocesano, Avila, Códice 3.345, "Información de la Vida, muerte, y milagros de la Venerable María Díaz." Luis de la Puente, *Vida del Padre Baltasar Alvarez* (Madrid, 1615), fols. 39v–43v.

6. The literature on Teresa of Jesus is vast. I have used as basic references Efrén de la Madre de Dios and Otger Steggink, *Santa Teresa y Su Tiempo*, 2

vols. (Salamanca, 1982–84), and *The Collected Works of St. Teresa of Avila*, 3 vols., trans. Kieran Kavanaugh and Otilio Rodríguez (Washington, D.C., 1976–85). A reliable biography in English is Stephen Clissold, *St. Teresa of Avila* (New York, 1982). For the urban setting of Teresa's reform movement, Bilinkoff, *Avila*, 108–51. Julián de Avila, *Vida de Santa Teresa de Jesús*, ed. Vicente de la Fuente (Madrid, 1888) (orig. 1603).

7. Bilinkoff, *Avila*, 184–99. María Vela y Cueto, *Autobiografía y Libro de las Mercedes*, ed. Olegario González Hernández (Barcelona, 1961). Quotes taken from the English edition: *The Third Mystic of Avila: The Self-Revelation of María Vela, a Sixteenth Century Spanish Nun*, trans. Frances Parkinson Keyes (New York, 1960). Miguel González Vaquero, *La muger fuerte: Por otro título, la vida de Doña María Vela*. This biography, first published in 1618, underwent several editions during the seventeenth century. I have used, as indicated, the editions of Barcelona, 1627, and Madrid, 1674. See Donohue, "Writing Lives," for a fascinating, but rather different, analysis from the one I offer here.

8. *Vida de la Venerable Madre Isabel de Iesus . . . Dictada por ella misma y Añadido lo que falto de su Dichosa Muerte el P. Fr. Francisco Ignacio* (Madrid, 1675). This work is discussed and excerpted in Electa Arenal and Stacey Schlau, *Untold Sisters: Hispanic Nuns in Their Own Works* (Albuquerque, 1989) 191–227. See also the penetrating essay by Electa Arenal, "The Convent as Catalyst for Autonomy: Two Hispanic Nuns of the Seventeenth Century," in *Women in Hispanic Literature: Icons and Fallen Idols*, ed. Beth Miller (Berkeley, 1983), 147–83.

9. For a good overview of these attitudes see Alison Weber, *Teresa of Avila and the Rhetoric of Femininity* (Princeton, 1990), 17–41.

10. Jesús Imirizaldu, *Monjas y beatas embaucadoras* (Madrid, 1977). For Inquisitorial activity against both a woman and her confessors, see Richard L. Kagan, *Lucrecia's Dreams: Politics and Prophecy in Sixteenth Century Spain* (Berkeley, 1990).

11. Baltasar Alvarez, *Escritos Espirituales*, eds. Camilo María Abad and Faustino Boado (Barcelona, 1961), 151, "No gastar tiempo con mujeres, especialmente monjas carmelitas, en visitas y por carta; sed suaviter et efficaciter irse soltando de ellas. Sí, aplicarse más al trato de hombres, donde hay menos peligro y más fructo; y éste más durable." Teresa of Avila, *The Book of Her Life* 28:14, in vol. 1 of *Collected Works*. For attempts to reduce the level of "familiarity" certain friars (especially Diego de Vitoria) maintained with María de Santo Domingo, see Lunas, *Historia*, 166–67, 175, and 188–89; and Beltrán, *Historia*, 86, 109, and 117–19. Miguel González Vaquero had to begin directing María Vela in secret, for fear of causing scandal. *La muger fuerte* (1627), fols. 193v–194v; 14v–15v and 139v–142v (1674). *Third Mystic*, 191–93.

12. Lunas, *Historia*, 175.

13. *Vida de . . . Isabel de Iesus*, 411–12, "no se admire hermano, que esta es una alma que trae a Dios como perdido de amores . . ." There is also the hint of spiritual healing in this story, as Ignacio mentions that Cogolludo was ill

at the time. For the suggestion of healing powers shared between María Vela and Miguel González Vaquero, see *Third Mystic*, 106–7.

14. Tomás Alvarez, "El ideal religioso de Santa Teresa de Jesús y el drama de su segundo biógrafo," *El Monte Carmelo* 86 (1978): 205–7. While Yepes may not have actually composed the biography attributed to him, he did apparently write the prologue from which this quote is taken. *La muger fuerte* (1627), fols. 193v–194r.

15. J. Mary Luti, "Teresa of Avila: Maestra Espiritual" (Ph.D. dissertation, Boston College, 1987), 260–71. *Su Tiempo* 2-2:143–51. On College of St. Giles, Bilinkoff, *Avila*, 87–95.

16. De la Puente, *Vida*, fol. 39v.

17. *La muger fuerte* (1627), fols. 28v–30r. For eucharistic piety as a characteristic of late medieval female spirituality, see Caroline W. Bynum, *Holy Feast and Holy Fast: The Religious Significance of Food to Medieval Women* (Berkeley, 1987). This trend began later in the Iberian peninsula, around the midfifteenth century, and lasted into the eighteenth century.

18. Lunas, *Historia*, 151, "seguidora de las iglesias y de los divinos oficios y acostumbro a confesar y a comulgar muchas veces en los tiempos ordenados por la iglesia y aun mas y allende." See also 152–53, 158, and 177. Beltrán, *Historia*, 258–59, "Yo, Señor, no voy alla, como vuestra Señoria reverendisima manda . . . porque esta sierva de Dios comulga agora cada dia, e recibia pena que lo dejase. . . . "

19. De la Puente, *Vida*, fol. 40r. "Información," testimony of Ana Reyes, for Mari Díaz's reception of daily Communion and reference to the Host as her "neighbor" (*vecino*).

20. *Third Mystic*, 103–4.

21. For María de Santo Domingo: Bilinkoff "Charisma." For Teresa of Jesus: *Su Vida*, 2-1:40–41 and 198–99; *Life* 32:11 and 39:22–23. (But see also *The Book of Her Foundations* 6:9–14, in vol. 3 of *Collected Works*, where she cautions against excessive dependence on the sacrament.) For Isabel de Jesús: *Vida* 58, 123, and 202.

22. De la Puente, *Vida*, fols. 39v–40r and 42r–43v. Alvarez, *Escritos*, 262 and 404–6. On the exemplarity of María de Santo Domingo: Lunas, *Historia*, 151–58, 177, and 201–9.

23. *Life*, 5:3. See also *Life*, 23:13–18, 24:1–5, 25:14–18, 26:3–4, 29:4–6, and 30:13. *Spiritual Testimonies*, nos. 58, 60, in vol. 1 of *Collected Works*. *The Way Of Perfection* 4:13–16, 5:1–7, in vol. 2 of *Collected Works*. Antonio Comas, "Espirituales, letrados y confesores en Santa Teresa de Jesús," in *Homenaje a Jaime Vicens Vives*, vol. 2, ed. J. Maluquer de Motes (Barcelona, 1967), 85–99.

24. *Third Mystic*, 86, 139–40, and 145. Isabel de Jesús, *Vida*, 27, 58, 157, and 174. While the mistreatment of penitents by confessors may represent something of a literary convention in the lives of religious women, there is no reason to call into question the pain each one actually experienced.

25. *La muger fuerte* (1627), fols. 191r–194r, and (1674), fols. 139v–141r. *Third Mystic*, 91–93.

26. For expressions of self-doubt, consultations with other priests, etc.: *La*

muger fuerte (1674), fols. 84v, 142r–v, and 171v. For others coming to consult him: Ibid. (1627), 261r, and the many instances cited by Donohue in "Writing Lives," 232–35.

27. Francisco de Ribera, *Vida de Santa Teresa de Jesús*, ed. Jaime Pons (Barcelona, 1908), 136 (orig. 1590).

28. De la Puente, *Vida*, fols. 39r–42r. Bartolomé Fernández Valencia, *Historia y grandezas del insigne templo . . . de . . . San Vicente* (Avila, 1676), 282–89. *Third Mystic*, 115. Lunas, *Historia*, 176, 203–4, and 210–11.

29. On Baltasar Alvarez as charismatic teacher and novice master, see introduction by Camilo María Abad and Faustino Boado to his *Escritos*, 128–33. On Salcedo, an earlier confessor of María Vela, see introduction by Olegario González Hernández to her *Autobiografía*, 67–77. Diego de Villena preached at the funerals of Mari Díaz and Ana Reyes, and also of Julián de Avila.

30. *La muger fuerte* (1627), for example, fols. 89v and 136r-139v. The local historian Bartolomé Fernández Valencia reported that Julián de Avila had written a manual on the cure of souls for use by other priests. The book does not seem to have survived.

31. See, for example *Su Vida*, 2-1:385 and 404–5; 2-2:722–23 and 725. Interestingly, Teresa often referred to Julián as an "old priest," although he was actually some twelve years younger than herself.

32. *Procesos de Beatificación y Canonización de Santa Teresa de Jesús*, 3 vols., ed. Silverio de Santa Teresa (Burgos, 1935). Julián de Avila, *Vida de Santa Teresa*, 2:249–86. He brought up his relationship with Teresa during testimony on the saintliness of Mari Díaz, "Información" (7 April 1603).

33. See introduction by Vicente de la Fuente to Julián's *Vida de Santa Teresa*, xvi–xvii. Gerardo de San Juan de la Cruz, *Vida del Maestro Julián de Avila . . .* (Toledo, 1915), 320–25. *La muger fuerte* (1627), fols. 137v–139v and 210v–211v; (1674), 153. Fernández Valencia, *Historia*, 296–311. For elaborate funerals, burials, and reburials in late sixteenth- and seventeenth-century Avila, Bilinkoff, *Avila*, 166–84.

34. *La muger fuerte* (1627), fols. 136v–139v. Julián de Avila, *Vida de Santa Teresa*, viii. Gil González Dávila, *Teatro eclesiástico de la S. Iglesia apostólica de Avila y vidas de sus hombres ilustres* (Avila, 1985), 202. (This is a facsimile edition; the original dates from the midseventeenth century.)

35. See his prologue to *Vida de . . . Isabel de Iesus* (no pagination) and 399–470.

36. Julián de Avila, *Vida de Santa Teresa*, 2–4, 188, 212, 216, and 249–86.

37. Donohue, "Writing Lives." Olegario González Hernández, in his introduction to María's *Autobiografía*, makes some very astute points along these lines; see 109, 116, and 120–21. *La muger fuerte* (1627), fols. 116r, 136r–139v, 191r–194v, 240r, and 261r–v; (1674), fols. 6r, 26r, 49v, 56v, 99v–11v, 114r, and 173r.

38. Rosa Rossi, *Teresa de Avila: Biografía de una escritora* (Barcelona, 1984). Francisco Marquéz Villanueva, "La vocación literaria de Santa Teresa," *Nueva Revista de Filología Hispánica* 32 (1983): 355–79. Weber, *Teresa of Avila*, 42–76. Luti, "Teresa of Avila," 57–77 and 212–20.

39. For publication histories of the works of Teresa of Jesus, see Enrique Llamas Martínez, *Santa Teresa de Jesús y la Inquisión española* (Madrid, 1972), 221–488. Alberto Barrientos, ed., *Introducción a la lectura de Santa Teresa* (Madrid, 1978). For the extraordinary story of how the American writer Frances Parkinson Keyes discovered the autobiography of María Vela and published it for the first time, in English, see *Third Mystic*, 3–14. The Spanish edition followed one year later, in 1961.

40. See, for example, Ricardo García-Villoslada, "Felipe II y la Contrareforma Católica," *Historia de la Iglesia en España*, 3 vols., ed. José Luis González Novalín (Madrid, 1979), 3-2:5–106.

41. Donald H. Marshall, "Frequent and Daily Communion in the Catholic Church of Spain in the Sixteenth and Seventeenth Centuries" (Ph.D. dissertation, Harvard University 1952). For earlier periods see Bynum, *Holy Feast and Holy Fast*, 48–69, and Yngve Briloth, *Eucharistic Faith and Practice* (London, 1939), 70–93. María de Santo Domingo: Lunas, *Historia*, 151 and 177; Beltrán, *Historia*, 258–59. Mari Díaz: de la Puente, *Vida*, fols. 40v–42r. Teresa of Jesus: *Su Vida*, 2-2:746. María Vela: *Third Mystic*, 103–4. Isabel de Jesús: *Vida*, 58 and 123.

42. On spiritual meanings of illness, see Elizabeth A. Petroff, ed., *Medieval Women's Visionary Literature* (New York and Oxford, 1986), 37–44. María de Santo Domingo: Lunas, *Historia*, 155, 157, 160, and 202. Mari Díaz: "Información," testimony of Ana Reyes; de la Puente, *Vida*, fols. 42r–43v. Teresa of Jesus: *Su Vida*, 2-1:50. María Vela: *La muger fuerte* (1627), fols. 205v and 244r–v; *Third Mystic*, 102 and 106–7. Isabel de Jesús: *Vida*, 13.

43. Bilinkoff, *Avila*, 140–45. Teresa of Jesus: Luti, "Teresa of Avila," 38–41 and 304–11. María Vela: *Third Mystic*, 86–90. Isabel de Jesús: *Vida*, 32.

44. Luti, "Teresa of Avila," 94–157. María de Santo Domingo: Lunas, *Historia*, 151–58 and 160–61. Mari Díaz: de la Puente, *Vida*, fol. 40r. Teresa of Jesus: *Su Vida*, 2-1:40–41 and 199. María Vela: *La muger fuerte* (1674), fols. 14v–15v. Isabel de Jesús: *Vida*, 399–470.

Part 2
Social Identities

Writing and the Power of Speech:
Notaries and Artisans in Baroque Rome

Laurie Nussdorfer

In seventeenth-century Rome even artisans and tradesmen who could not write operated in a world in which they had to deal with writing. Whether it was an excommunication threat posted on the door of the fishmongers' church or a notice from the masons' officers to report for plague duty at the city gate, men of the laboring classes regularly encountered information in written form and had to respond to it.[1] In these two examples, writing conveyed the warnings or wishes of those in authority, but writing was not just a repressive instrument to be wielded by those higher up in the political hierarchy. Ordinary artisans often sought to put their own warnings and wishes into written form, and they had a variety of ways at their disposal to do so. It had long been the custom in Italy for craftsmen who married, formed business partnerships, or left a will to seek out notaries to draft their agreements and testaments. They might also convince acquaintances to record a payment or read a letter, or they would pay a public writer for his services. Some Roman tradesmen, perhaps a growing number of them, made the effort to learn to write themselves, by studying with a workshop companion or family member, or by attending the new vernacular schools set up in the sixteenth century.[2] We do not know precisely how many Romans of the artisanal milieu knew how to write, but it is clear that writers and nonwriters alike had to confront the power and possibilities of writing and that they did so with habits and assumptions that we still know little about.

One of the ways writing figured in the world of Roman craftsmen was as a record of their meetings with men in the same trade. When working men—and occasionally women—who shared common professional interests gathered together, they sometimes hired a notary to take down their proceedings. Usually the notary filed these reports with the other contracts he had drawn up for his vast clientele, although sometimes he bound them in a volume for the artisans to keep.[3] These documents stand at the intersection of several important social and cultural relationships in the early modern city. Socially, they are the result of a common, but not much studied, interaction between a ubiquitous professional in southern Europe, the notary, and his lower-class clients. Culturally, they reflect an intriguing double relationship between the oral and the written: the transformation into writing of the words spoken by the artisans in their gathering and the representation of certain moments of speaking during the meeting in written form.[4]

The meeting minutes raise questions about the power of speech and the power of writing and about why and how the minutes were acquired and used. They allow us to explore some of the historically specific ways in which speech and writing functioned for men who could certainly speak, but who may or may not have been able to write. They also shed light on how social groups who were denied a formal political role in an absolutist regime, like artisans, understood and used other kinds of power, especially the power of collective organization and the power of a legal system based on Roman law. The relationship between notaries and tradesmen offers clues to some neglected cultural and political resources for men of the artisanal milieu.

I will begin by briefly describing the relations between craft guilds and notaries so as to situate the speakers and writers of the meeting minutes. Then I will examine the notary's representation of the spoken word in his accounts of tradesmen's gatherings. Finally, I will look at the uses of the notary's writing for his artisan clients.

Guilds and Notaries

Guilds, a robust feature of medieval town life, were supposed to be moldering in the dustbin of history during the early modern period; yet it did not happen quite that way in Rome. The sixteenth and seventeenth centuries actually saw the number of trade corporations reach their highest peak. Although the reasons for this growth are still somewhat obscure, the associational creativity of the Counter-

Reformation may well have had something to do with it. There was a real organizational effervescence in baroque Rome, as men in a whole variety of trades formed both new religious sodalities and new craft guilds.[5] The civic and papal governments seem to have supported the formation of new guilds, although they kept them under tight surveillance. Guild statutes had to be approved by both civic and papal officials. Artisan corporations had to receive written permission from the municipal administration to hold a meeting, and a city employee attended most meetings so as to be able to give a personal report, if needed, to the magistrates. Yet these restrictions reflect efforts to control, not suppress, organizations among laboring men, and such bodies could also serve various interests of state. Guilds were a regular source of taxes for the papal treasury, a good way to raise manpower during civic emergencies, and a potential means to enforce discipline in urban trades.[6]

The notary figured importantly in the process of creating a new corporation and in many of its subsequent activities, as we shall see. But the notarial records provide a picture of artisans acting collectively that embraces more than the deeds of formally sanctioned guilds. Guilds represent only the very top of the associational "food chain," so to speak: they were the bodies with written statutes that had received the approval of the civic and papal authorities. There could be a whole range of degrees of organization among men in a common trade; artisans who had not yet secured formal privileges, and who did not have official guild status, still came together for joint action and hired notaries to do their business. In a sample of registers for the year 1630 from the largest Roman notarial college, the Thirty Capitoline Notaries, over two dozen trades left some trace of their corporate life; in eighteen cases this included minutes from a meeting. Guilds with approved statutes predominate, but more shadowy associations, of muleteers, rosary makers, and apprentice stocking knitters, for example, also emerge from the notaries' volumes.[7]

What did notaries do for these clients? Obviously they drew up the legal instruments that they, like any other client, needed. These might include a receipt from the master mason who had just put a new roof on the guild church, a surety from the husband of a young woman who had received a cash grant from the guild to subsidize her dowry, or the rental agreement for a house that belonged to the guild's patrimony.[8]

The notary also produced for artisans' corporations certain kinds of instruments that ordinary private clients would not need. These might include a record of the oath taken by new officers and the transfer to them of symbolic authority in the form of guild statutes, coffers, or keys; a record of the audit of the guild treasurer's accounts at the end of his annual term in office; or a record of the list of men (and sometimes women) in the corporation and how much they owed in taxes to the papal government.[9] Most relevant to the purposes of this essay were the records notaries made of artisans' meetings.

Men of the artisanal milieu knew that their associations, like their shops and families, often needed notarial services, and many guild statutes required the group to designate a guild notary. This notary sometimes bore the formal title of secretary to the guild. Notaries charged specified fees for drawing up different types of instruments, but meetings and audits and tax lists were not among these canonical types.[10] Instead of paying "by the piece," as it were, many guilds may well have done what the hotelkeepers did and paid their official notary a yearly retainer, augmented by gifts of pepper and wax and the promise of a monopoly on members' business. Not all of the notaries had guild clients, of course, and some, like the Capitoline notary Taddeo Raimondo, worked for several guilds at once. Nor did a guild necessarily stick to one notary. Sometimes two notaries even worked together, each formally designated as *connotarius* (co-notaries). But it was not unusual for enduring bonds to develop between a tradesmen's association and a particular notarial office, ties that sometimes lasted for decades and were passed down from father to son within notarial dynasties.[11]

Since notaries themselves are the window through which we peer into craftsmen's gatherings, and because their role was to transcribe discussions accurately rather than to participate in them, it is not easy to discern the feelings of artisans about the notaries they hired. When the guild notary was given the responsibility of insuring that a particular tax was collected from members of the wool guild, he was clearly a figure trusted to execute delicate internal matters.[12] That the guild notary could be regarded with suspicion, however, is also revealed in several cases. Dissident masons who opposed a dues increase by their officers mounted a protest through the pen of a notary who was deliberately *not* the man the guild regularly employed for its business.[13]

The officials of the vegetable sellers' (*ortolani*) corporation used a similar tactic in a conflict over the choice of the guild's notary. Flavio Paradisi, who had been serving the vegetable sellers, was in prison, and at a meeting on 1 January 1630, complaints were raised by two individuals about the way guild business was being handled during his incarceration. Paradisi's substitute, who was reporting this rather distasteful discussion, offered to serve the *ortolani* himself, "according to their taste," for a portion of Paradisi's income. He had to record, however, that, despite his efforts, "various people" (*diversi*) resolved to take a vote on whether to stay with Paradisi or transfer their business to the office of Leonardo Bonanni.[14] The vote, a landslide victory (46 to 16) for the unfortunate Paradisi, showed the strength of the vegetable sellers' loyalty to their familiar notary. But Paradisi's reprieve, it turned out, was not to the liking of the guild leadership. Two weeks later they hired a different notary, Taddeo Raimondo, to record a second meeting to which they summoned their members. When the ensuing discussion still did not produce the result they were hoping for, the fourteen guild officers simply went off by themselves and voted 10 to 4 to make Bonanni the guild notary.[15]

Although we would like to know more about the webs of patronage and information networks around these competing notaries, the sparse evidence we do have tells us that the notary's role in guild affairs did not go entirely unnoticed. The notary might sometimes be an interested party to a discussion, or he might be allied with one faction in the guild and thus seem a partisan presence rather than a neutral one. This was not the image notaries themselves wanted to show the world, of course, and they strove to leave few clues of their commitments in the record. However, the fact that guilds would change notaries might be an indication of their assessment of a particular notary's impartiality.[16]

To sum up, groups of artisans and tradesmen in early modern Rome were accustomed to seek out notarial services for a wide range of purposes. Although it is difficult to plot how and when this practice developed, notaries were recording meetings of the wool merchants from at least the early fifteenth century.[17] As new artisan collectivities quickened in the sixteenth and seventeenth centuries, the notary emerged as an intimate part of the process by which tradesmen acted in concert. We will now look more closely at the implications of these encounters between notaries and tradesmen for understanding some of the social meanings of speaking and writing in baroque Rome.

The Spoken Word

Contemporary notarial handbooks are largely silent about the proper forms to employ in making a record of a meeting, but Roman notaries followed a standard format.[18] The notary's account of a meeting, usually entitled *adunantia* or *congregatio*, began with the date, location, and names of the officers, if there were any, and men and women in attendance. Often the notary also noted that the artisans had the required written permit from the civic authorities to hold their gathering and that a servant of the civic magistrates, or occasionally the sacristan or parish priest of the church in which they were meeting, was also present. What followed these regular features varied greatly from guild to guild and from notary to notary, but the report usually summarized at least what was decided (*decretato*) by the members and sometimes what was attempted or discussed without any resolution.

Regardless of their specific content, the notaries' reports abound with representations of the spoken word. Although direct quotation was rare,[19] the oral element was present at every turn. Relatively impersonal or collective speaking prevailed; the notary usually represented the oral not as highly individualized but as the voice of a guild officer or of the group as a whole. He preferred to indicate that talking had occurred "after long argument and discussion" rather than to detail the debate. At times the notary briefly characterized the style of conversation, telling us that an issue was "reasonably discussed" (*maturamente discorso*) or that the men "listened intently" (*benissimo ascoltata*).[20] More commonly, decisions were simply "decreed" or "approved *viva voce*" (by oral vote) by the members, the notary sometimes adding "with no one objecting." Harmony was preferred, and unanimous *viva voce* resolutions were favored in the record.

With his laconic syntheses of sometimes lengthy and disputatious gatherings, the notary clearly imposed verbal order on speakers who had not produced it themselves. Though he did not banish difference of opinion from his account, he did not dwell on it, tending instead to listen for a result he could summarize in a few words. Significantly, however, he took pains to convey that speech had taken place. The fact that discussion had taken place was a recurring element in the notarial record, though it was speaking rendered in its most generalized and abstract form.

The one particular voice to which the notary paid close attention in his text was his own. References to his actions and his words were frequent. One notary wrote that money would be paid from the butchers' account "with a receipt from the secretary," but he then crossed out "secretary" and identified himself more prominently: "with a receipt from me notary and secretary of said company."[21] At the sortition of new officers of the masons' guild, "the sack was opened by me notary" before the altar of the guild church. A petition to the barbers with a message from the pope on it was "handed to me notary to read and ... then given back by me notary to the guild officers [*signori consoli*]."[22]

Indeed the notary figures himself most often as a reader—of permits, petitions, names of new officers, previous meeting minutes, and, above all, guild statutes. The sheep dealers' (*affidati e pecorari*) meeting was recorded by two notaries:

> In the presence of the aforementioned [members] the articles made and established in years past were read aloud by us notaries beginning at the first page of the guild of sheepdealers' statutes ... these articles read aloud by us were by all the aforementioned approved *viva voce* with no one disagreeing.[23]

To the tailors, the notary read the decision of a previous meeting: "That delegation and decree made [at the earlier meeting] and read by me notary to the present meeting in a loud and intelligible voice [was] ratified and approved by all those attending *viva voce* with no one disagreeing."[24]

It is possible, but unlikely, that the notary was the only person at a meeting who could read. Impressionistic evidence suggests that the ability to read and write was common among men of the artisanal milieu, and many guild statutes required that officers be able to read and write.[25] The notary may well have been a *better* reader, with a smoother style or louder voice, but I suspect this is irrelevant. What was more important about him was that he was in some way an authoritative reader, and, of course, an authoritative writer. This authority in turn demanded that he be personally present in his text.

The notary's authority was particularly related to words, of course; since his acquisition in the High Middle Ages of "public faith" (*publica fides*), a document attested by a notary had the force of absolute truth.[26] Because he possessed this quality of "public faith," the notary circulated the spoken word back to his clients in the form of writing that had a special legal status. It was thus essential to establish his textual presence: "me notary." And it may well have been the case, though this is speculative, that an informal seepage of authority to his physical presence, utterance, and gesture in meetings had also occurred. It certainly had occurred in *his* version of the story.

In each of the foregoing examples of notarial self-reference, a collective decision, swift and unanimous, followed the notary's reading. He read "in his loud and intelligible voice" and the group approved *viva voce* in theirs. Clearly the spoken word was not unimportant; it made things happen in this particular institutional setting. The oral enabled, effected, and empowered group action.

But the notary's inscription of these moments of orality—both his and theirs—increased the weight of what was spoken by giving it a legal resonance of a particular kind. In these examples the notary was conveying the fact of publicity, the fact that everyone listening to his reading now shared the same knowledge and that their common agreement was based on equal access to that knowledge. The ensuing commitments, one could claim, were made by people who understood what they were doing. Without this publicity and informed approval—and written record thereof—the group's actions would have no legal validity. With this documented approval the group's actions acquired special power. Of course, the notary's way of formulating the proceedings was potentially coercive too. The notary was paid to produce a document that made those present (all carefully named) responsible for their own words, and his report was a testament to agreement that could be used against those who did not go along.[27]

It is interesting to speculate on how the notarial practice of reading important writings aloud at meetings came about and whether it represented a moment when access to texts was *un*equal because not all members could read. Such conditions certainly still prevailed in the seventeenth century, but I think by then the oral reading was also an expected procedure, both in the meeting and in the document, and that people would not have felt a legitimate decision had taken place, nor report of it been produced, without this convention. Unanimous voice votes, which from one point of view are saying something aloud simply so that it can be written down, are another example of the mutual dependence of the oral and the written in the meeting minutes. In these cases, speaking and writing were intertwined in a collective ritual that helped the group get a sense that it was acting *as* a group—and that left a charged text to attest to it.

The Uses of Writing

Meeting minutes were produced at the initiative of a group of artisans, who hired a notary for this purpose. Why? To what uses might they put those "charged texts" he wrote for them? To give an idea of the kind of power made available to Roman artisans in the seventeenth century by the notary's record of a meeting, we will look closely at two examples, one from the wholesale wine merchants and one from the masons. As it happens, neither of these meetings was an official guild meeting—one was a meeting to form a guild and one was a meeting to fight guild officers—but they were both perfectly official notarial instruments.

In 1631 the wholesale wine merchants (*magazzinieri di vino*) wanted to form their own guild. Writing played a crucial role in this process of organization at two distinct moments. First, prior to the notary's involvement someone wrote out a document, signed by forty men, setting forth the reasons for which the winesellers wanted their own guild. In "step two," twenty-seven winesellers, with a permit from civic officials, met in the presence of a notary.[28] The notary copied over in his own hand the statement the wine merchants had previously produced. But his report also showed how he worked his notarial alchemy upon the gathered assembly of men and upon their document: he states that he read their statement aloud ("from beginning to end"); that all the men present listened to it carefully "and understood it"; that they then decided to petition the political authorities for permission to form a guild; that they deputized three men to start this process; and that both the deputies and the rest of the men backed up the promises to which they had affixed their names with a sworn oath before the notary.

In trying to figure out the uses of writing for tradesmen we need to ask what "step two"—the notarial record of the meeting—gave to the winesellers that they did not already have. They already had a written statement of their purpose, and some of them clearly had already met, since someone must have decided to solicit those forty signatures. What the notarial inscription made of their actions was to formulate a text with a special legal status that could be read by a judge if anything the winesellers had done or decided that day was ever challenged. The decision to have a notary record a meeting (and we know nothing about the meetings at which notaries were not present) was a decision informed by some awareness of the legal importance of writing in a judicial culture based on Roman law.

The masons offer another example, one in which the legal implications of the notarial instrument are more explicit. The officers of the masons' guild set annual dues in 1634 that seemed much too high to some of their members, and an internal revolt ensued, which made canny use of the notary's particularly powerful brand of writing. Thirty-five dissenting masons held a meeting, at which a notary whom they had hired for the occasion, rather than the guild's regular notary, was present. He recorded their resolution to appeal to the pope and/or a competent judge and to hire an attorney to bring suit against their officers. This "act" then went into the notary's files without the guild officers being able to do or say anything to stop it. Over the next few weeks many other masons contributed written testimony to help build the dossier for the lawsuit. More than three hundred of them checked in at the notary's office, each man formally declaring his "protest" against the dues hike or his refusal to pay it.[29] The masons seemed to have had quite a sophisticated understanding of how the legal system could serve them, how they could get access to it, and what role the notary and the written record played in that process. Since vernacular legal or notarial handbooks were lacking in Italy, they must have acquired this knowledge via oral sources and their experiences in guilds, commerce, and family life.[30] The notaries themselves may have played an important, if undocumented, educational role as informal legal consultants to their clients.

Although the masons were somewhat unusual in producing written evidence with the conscious intent of going to law, other artisans "thought legally" too. Even a brief survey of business at meetings of other trades reinforces the impression that these documents were crafted with an eye to possible legal uses. Admittedly, the "crafting" of the text was the specific responsibility of the notary, but the men who hired him could not have been unaware of the legal impact of his presence on their words. I would argue that the habit of speaking as a group before a notary shows an appreciation for the legal potential of written evidence, even when there was no specific judicial action in mind.

What potential "legal" messages did meeting reports convey? The guild officers had let everyone know the business at hand. ("There is no secrecy here and these will be valid decisions.") The election was held in full accord with the procedures laid down in the statutes. ("No one can accuse us of not following the rules.") These vegetable sellers had agreed to make a contribution to the new roof of the guild hospital. ("So when the time comes, they are obliged to come up with the money.") All of these carpenters' names were drawn by lot for guild offices and had refused to serve. ("They will have to pay the fine.") The following butchers said they would slaughter this many lambs at Easter. ("The papal food supply office wants to be able to enforce these promises.") These masons protest the dues increase. ("And they hereby serve notice that they will sue their officers for imposing it.") These winesellers want to form a guild and have taken an oath to show they are ready to pay the extra taxes that will entail. ("Their petition to receive guild privileges should be granted.")[31]

These examples suggest the many circumstances, foreseen and unforeseen, in which meeting minutes might come in handy. This uncertainty made these documents somewhat different from the notary's ordinary fare. Unlike most of the legal instruments the notaries routinely drafted for clients, it was not clear how these records would eventually be used, nor how they should look. As we have noted, printed formularies did not give much guidance, and the notary had a good deal of leeway in shaping his representation of the group's actions. In other kinds of notarial writing, *how* he put his words was crucial; here what was most consistently important was the fact that they were his words. Thus, again, we understand the need to hear the notary's voice. By adding his character of public faithfulness to the scribal function of recording what would otherwise be forgotten, he gave his clients a written artifact of great flexibility, capable of being activated, should need arise, in litigation of every conceivable kind.[32] This threat alone had consequences. The verbal commitments set down by the notary could be used as a way of exerting group pressure, or fending it off, even if the document was never produced in a court of law.

To conclude, the notarial reports of artisan meetings show that craftsmen, who may or may not have been able to write themselves, appreciated the power of writing for purposes of collective action and had a ready means of getting access to it. They used the notary to acquire kinds of writing that maintained the discipline of the guild, empowered group decision making, protected its autonomy, and advanced its interests. He was their means for tapping into the potentialities of the legal system, especially through that great early modern stimulus to political negotiation: the threat of a lawsuit.

Moreover, tradesmen and artisans, whose associations were regarded with suspicion by government authorities and were closely monitored by them, had a remarkable degree of autonomy when it came to hiring a notary. They did not need permission to go to a notary, and what they received from the notary for their money was a document with a legal "punch" to it that was pretty much theirs to use as they saw fit. Of course, their freedom was conditioned by the need for funds to pay the notary, *and* the lawyer, if they were serious about litigation. But short of fully actualizing the potential of a notarial instrument before a magistrate, there were many other defensive, coercive, or creative uses to which the written record could be put. The notary gave tradesmen, talking together in a group, an avenue to legal and political resources that were important forms of cultural power.

And yet the artisans' dependence upon the notary attests to the ultimate triumph of the written word over the power of speech. The oral played through the texts of their meetings, giving them authority, but the invisible pen was what inscribed and gave potency to the voice. Whatever the reality of "oral culture" in their personal lives, when Roman tradesmen acted collectively they functioned as "textual communities,"[33] groups whose associational lives were shaped by the use of writing and who had grown skilled in its manipulation.

NOTES

I am indebted to Richard Landes and Paul Gehl for their suggestions; I am also grateful for comments on earlier versions of this essay from Nicholas Adams, Katherine Gill, Orsola Gori, Renato Pasta, and Fred Travisano. I would particularly like to acknowledge the contribution of Daniel Rosenberg, whose senior honors thesis at Wesleyan University first stimulated my interest in the wider meanings of literacy.
1. Archivio di Stato di Roma (hereafter, ASR), 30 Notai Capitolini (here-

after, 30 N.C.), uff. 2 (Bonanni) 1633, pt. 2, 154v; 30 N.C., uff. 25 (Raymundus) 1630, pt. 1, 156r. See also Peter Burke, "The Uses of Literacy in Early Modern Italy," in *The Historical Anthropology of Early Modern Italy* (Cambridge, 1987), 110–31.

2. Armando Petrucci, "Scrittura, alfabetismo ed educazione grafica nella Roma del primo Cinquecento," *Scrittura e Civilta'* 2 (1978): 170–71, 184, 188; idem, "Pouvoir de l'ecriture, pouvoir sur l'écriture dans la Renaissance italienne," *Annales E.S.C.* 43 (1988): 831–33, 837. On the formal teaching of writing see Guerrino Pelliccia, *La scuola primaria a Roma dal secolo XVI al XIX* (Rome, 1985), 323–27, and Paul F. Grendler, *Schooling in Renaissance Italy* (Baltimore, 1989), 323–29. For examples of artisanal handwriting, see the exhibition catalogue edited by Armando Petrucci, *Scrittura e popolo nella Roma barocca 1585–1721* (Rome, 1982). William V. Harris distinguishes among three levels of literacy, "scribal literacy," "craftsman's literacy," and "mass literacy." Reading and writing skills in early modern Rome would probably fall in the category of "craftsman's literacy," that is, "the condition in which the majority, or a near-majority, of skilled craftsmen are literate, while women and unskilled labourers and peasants are mainly not." *Ancient Literacy* (Cambridge, Mass., 1989), 8.

3. A good source, though not the only one, for these reports, which are full versions in generally fair copies, is the series of the 30 Notai Capitolini in the Archivio di Stato di Roma. Although this group of thirty civic notaries was the most active in Rome, smaller bodies of notaries connected with the papal government also occasionally had guild clients. The goldbeaters, for example, who were closely supervised by the officials of the papal mint, used the papal notaries known as the Segretari e Cancellieri of the Reverenda Camera Apostolica, whose records are also in the ASR; see Antinori (1611–13), vol. 77. On the public notaries of Rome, see Giovanni Battista De Luca, *Il dottor volgare* (Rome, 1673), bk. 15, pt. 3, ch. 43.

When the notary's minutes of meetings were separately bound, they sometimes ended up in individual guild archives; few of these survive in Rome, but some volumes of meetings from the 1640s can be found in ASR, Universita' di Arti e Mestieri, vol. 14 (carpenters); vol. 26 (millers). A few others have turned up in confraternity archives; see the useful inventory of these archives in the journal *Ricerche per la storia religiosa di Roma* 6 (1985): 175–413.

The only guild meetings attended by women were those of the hotelkeepers, although a woman was appointed as one of the glassmakers' dues collectors.

4. Marino Berengo pointed out the importance of investigating the social relations of notaries and their clients almost two decades ago. "Lo studio degli atti notarili dal XIV al XVI secolo," in *Fonti medioevali e problematica storiografica* (Rome, 1976), 1:161. Armando Petrucci pioneered the use of notarial records to illuminate the history of literacy; see "I documenti privati come fonte per lo studio dell'alfabetismo e della cultura scritta," in *Sources of Social History: Private Acts of the Late Middle Ages*, eds. Paolo Brezzi and Egmont Lee (Toronto, 1984), 251–66.

5. Estimates of the number of guilds and craft-based confraternities vary. Antonio Martini reproduces figures showing that 47 new guilds were founded in sixteenth- and seventeenth-century Rome for a total in 1700 of 79; *Arti, mestieri e fede nella Roma dei papi* (Bologna, 1965), 40. Emmanuel Rodocanachi lists 96 guilds in *Les corporations ouvrières à Rome depuis la chute de l'empire romain* (Paris, 1894), 2:58. A census of workshops in Rome, probably dating to the 1620s, counts 71 guilds; it was published by Vincenzo Paglia in *La Pieta' dei carcerati: Confraternite e societa'a Roma nei secoli XVI–XVIII* (Rome, 1980), 283–84. For the chronology of new confraternities see Matizia Maroni Lumbroso and Antonio Martini, *Le confraternite romane nelle loro chiese* (Rome, 1963), 441–45.

6. Meeting permits are often attached to the notaries' meeting reports. On guilds and government authorities see Laurie Nussdorfer, *Civic Politics in the Rome of Urban VIII* (Princeton, 1992), 128–35.

7. Meetings in 1630 of the following trades were found in ASR, 30 N.C.: barbers, butchers, butchers' apprentices, carpenters, clogmakers, fishmongers, hotelkeepers, masons, mattress makers, merchants, secondhand-goods dealers, sheep merchants, shoemakers, soapmakers, apprentice stocking knitters, tailors, taverners, and vegetable sellers. The best source for locating guild statutes is the bibliography in Martini, *Arti*, 267–302.

8. ASR, 30 N.C., uff. 2 (Bonanni) 1633, pt. 3, 333r–34v (vegetable sellers); uff. 25 (Raymundus) 1630, pt. 3, 399r–401r (butchers' apprentices); uff. 20 (Camillus) 1630, pt. 1, 208r (carpenters).

9. ASR, 30 N.C., uff. 26 (Scoloccio) 1630, pt. 1, 319r–v, 322r (mattress makers); uff. 7 (Paradisi) 1630, pt. 1, 260r–61v (vegetable sellers); uff. 25 (Raymundus) 1630, pt. 1, 46r–47v, 80r–81r (butchers).

10. For a sample list of fees see *Notarii*, ed. Armando Petrucci (Milan, 1958), plate 83. For the fees of civic notaries see *Statuta almae urbis Romae* (Rome, 1580), bk. 3, ch. 93.

11. ASR, 30 N.C., uff. 18 (Bonincontro) 1630, pt. 2, 138v (hotelkeepers); see also the 1609 statutes of the guild of secondhand-goods dealers (*regattieri*) in ASR, Biblioteca, Statuti, no. 600, 12, 20. Taddeo Raimondo (or Raymundus), who was active in one office from 1626 to 1641, retained many of the clients (butchers, soapmakers, masons, and shoemakers) of his predecessor, Giulio Raimondo, who worked between 1586 and 1621.

12. ASR, 30 N.C., uff. 2 (Bonanni) 1648, pt. 3, 580v.

13. See n. 29. This incident is discussed in more detail below.

14. ASR, 30 N.C., uff. 7 (Paradisi) 1630, pt. 1, 24r. The notary's decision to note that complaints came from (only) two individuals, as well as his choice of the word *diversi* to describe proponents of a vote (indicating how far from unanimous this desire was), may be signs of his disapproval of the proceedings.

15. ASR, 30 N.C., uff. 25 (Raymundus) 1630, pt. 1, 277r–v.

16. For a defense of the notary's rectitude, see Placido Puccinelli, *Della fede e nobilta' del notaio* (Milan, 1656), 2–3. For a more caustic view see Tommaso Garzoni, *La piazza universale di tutte le professioni del mondo* (Venice, 1585),

128–30. On occasion the notary was the scapegoat for a guild member who was angered at his treatment by guild officials. ASR, 30 N.C. (Camillus) 1630, pt. 2, 476v, 540r.

17. The statutes of the wool merchants' guild include copies of notarial reports of meetings beginning in 1416; ASR, Biblioteca, Statuti, no. 879, 81–112. The history of the practice in Rome is obscure because series of notarial registers date only from the midfourteenth century; see Anna Maria Corbo, "Relazione descrittiva degli archivi notarili Romani dei secoli XIV–XV nell'Archivio di Stato e nell'Archivio Capitolino," in Brezzi and Lee, *Sources*, 49–67.

18. Although Italian notaries had covered meetings of town councils since the Middle Ages, and in the seventeenth century they worked routinely as recorders for meetings of Roman confraternities, convents, chapters, and even urban districts, the formularies do not mention meetings as such. They are occasionally referred to, however, in the context of acts by corporate bodies. The form for a meeting of a rural community is described in Leo Speluncanus, *Artis notarie tempestatis huius speculum* (Venice, 1538), fols. 211r–212v. The grant of power of attorney by an abbot with the consent of a meeting of his monks is treated in Rolandinus de Passageriis, *Summa totius artis notariae* (Venice, 1546), fol. 225.

19. For an example see ASR, 30 N.C., uff. 25 (Raymundus) 1630, pt. 2, 355v.

20. ASR, 30 N.C., uff. 2 (Bonanni) 1634, pt. 1, 71r; uff. 18 (Bonincontro) 1630, pt. 2, 136v; uff. 25 (Raymundus) 1631, pt. 1, 695v, 700.

21. ASR, 30 N.C., uff. 25 (Raymundus) 1630, pt. 2, 289r.

22. ASR, 30 N.C., uff. 25 (Raymundus) 1630, pt. 2, 120r; uff. 15 (Salvatori) 1630, pt. 1, 360v, 363r.

23. ASR, 30 N.C., uff. 15 (Salvatori) 1630, pt. 2, 656r.

24. ASR, 30 N.C., uff. 1 (Ricci) 1630, pt. 2, 17v.

25. Petrucci, "Pouvoir," 831–32, 837. The statutes of the fishmongers (1636), masons (1639), and hotelkeepers (1595) are among those stipulating that guild officers, particularly treasurers, be literate. Fishmongers' statutes, ASR, Biblioteca, Statuti, no. 449/7, 4. Masons' statutes, Biblioteca Apostolica Vaticana, R. G. Storia IV 9253 (8), ch. 2. For the relevant article of the hotelkeepers' statutes, see Mario Romani, *Pellegrini e viaggiatori nell'economia di Roma dal xvi al xvii secolo* (Milan, 1948), 285. The carpenters required proof that a member did not know how to write, if he used that excuse to evade guild office; statements from two witnesses would suffice. ASR, 30 N.C., uff. 20 (Camillus) 1630, pt. 2, 540r.

26. Alessandro Pratesi, *Genesi e forma del documento medioevale* (Rome, 1979), 50. See also *Enciclopedia del diritto* (Milan, 1958–), s.v. "Notaio, diritto vigente," by Marcello di Fabio.

27. For a comparative view of the interpenetration of the oral and the written in legal transactions under the very different judicial regime of medieval England, see Michael T. Clanchy, *From Memory to Written Record: England, 1066–1307* (Cambridge, Mass., 1979). See also Petrucci's comment on

Clanchy that the existence of notaries gave a different inflection to the diffusion of writing in medieval Italy, "Documenti," 258.

28. ASR, 30 N.C., uff. 25 (Raymundus) 1631, pt. 1, 694r–95v, 700r–701v. Eight of the original forty signatories could not write their names.

29. ASR, 30 N.C., uff. 2 (Bonanni) 1634, pt. 2, 810, 837r, and pt. 3, 3r–9r, 26r–33r.

30. Legal procedures were made accessible to those literate in Italian in 1673, when Giovanni Battista De Luca published the translation of his multivolume legal treatise, *Il Dottor Volgare* (Rome, 1673). Although notarial handbooks existed in other European vernaculars, I have not yet located any sixteenth- or seventeenth-century Italian translations. That a workingman's daily life taught the importance of "having it in writing" finds support in countless articles of guild statutes. To take two examples, the masons (ch. 32) insisted that claims for back wages owed for more than six months be supported by a document, and the butchers (ch. 2, 34) demanded that those seeking justice before the guild tribunal supply written evidence of a broken agreement. Butchers' statutes, Biblioteca Angelica, MS. 1584.

31. ASR, 30 N.C., uff. 2 (Bonanni) 1633, pt. 2, 30v, 51 (vegetable sellers); uff. 20 (Camillus) 1630, pt. 2, 476, 501v (carpenters); uff. 25 (Raymundus) 1630, pt. 2, 354r–57v, 389r (butchers).

32. There has been little research as yet on civil litigation in early modern Rome, perhaps because the relevant judicial records have not been inventoried.

33. The notion of a textual community is elaborated to stimulating effect by Brian Stock, *The Implications of Literacy* (Princeton, 1983), 90–91.

People of the Ribera: Popular Politics and Neighborhood Identity in Early Modern Barcelona

James S. Amelang

On 10 October 1786, Johann Wolfgang Goethe returned to his hotel room in a decidedly un-Olympian mood. "At last I have seen a real comedy!" he wrote, fresh from having attended a performance at Venice's San Luca Theatre.[1] What so enthused this most objective of spirits was *Le Baruffe Chiozzotte,* one of the best known works by the contemporary Venetian dramatist Carlo Goldoni. Dismissed by his aristocratic rival, Carlo Gozzi, as a "plebeian" and "most trivial" play, the *Baruffe* (which Goethe translated as "The Scuffles and Brawls in Chioggia," a fishing village just south of Venice) has delighted audiences from the eighteenth century to the present.[2] While its appeal derives in part from its rich language and colorful setting, much of its success comes from the very familiarity of its plot. For the *Baruffe* is about a quarrel among neighbors, something Goldoni himself noted was most "frequent among the common people," especially in Chioggia, five sixths of whose population was *gente volgare.*[3]

Goethe's diary provides a concise synopsis of the play.

> The characters are all . . . fishermen and their wives, sisters and daughters. The habitual to-do made by these people, their quarrels, their outbursts of temper, their good nature, superficiality, wit, humor and natural behavior—all these were excellently imitated.

A trivial dispute among the villagers, who were notorious for their quick tempers and sharp tongues, set off a donnybrook of verbal

119

abuse; in Goethe's words, "all hell broke loose." This quickly provoked the intervention of an outside magistrate who, although
charged with rendering impartial justice, nevertheless became too
personally involved in the fray, which gave rise to a series of comic
mishaps. In the end, however, all turned out well, and the neighbors
who had been at each other's throats joined together to celebrate the
marriages that put an end to the brawl.

As the young judge learned, common sense warns against getting
involved in fights among neighbors. Historians, however, rush in
where angels fear to tread, and poke and pry into the conflicts (and
concords) among citizens in pasts both distant and near. Neighbors
and neighborhoods loom increasingly large as objects for study by
urban historians in particular. The neighborhood as a unit of political
organization, locus of economic and social relations, and source of
collective and personal identity now receives growing attention from
scholars interested in the wide variety of associations, institutions, and
patterns of sociability that mediated between the individual citizen
or household and the city as a whole.

To attempt to examine all the significant aspects of neighborhood
life within early modern Barcelona would clearly exceed the limits
of this brief essay. Instead, its purpose is a more modest one: to
explore the ways in which neighborhoods are defined. How does a
neighborhood come to be recognized as such? How are its boundaries
fixed, and who does the fixing? How do certain neighborhoods obtain
renown for specific characteristics, and what impact can this have
upon their inhabitants? Above all, what role do the latter play in the
process of definition? Despite the elementary nature of these questions, relatively little attention has been devoted to such issues. As one
historian has recently noted, most studies dealing with urban neighborhoods say little about the "changing nature of beliefs about neighborhoods, or about the changing nature of the relationship between
neighborhoods and the larger city."[4]

This essay explores definitions of neighborhood within a single
quarter in early modern Barcelona, the Ribera. It first examines the
construction of neighborhood identity by studying the influence of
administrative demarcations upon the creation and transformation
of social space within the city. It then considers some of the roles
other, less formal definitions play within the constitution of neighbor-

hoods. Throughout, emphasis will be placed on the relations among intramural geographic boundaries, representations of collective identity, and specific forms of social and political organization.

The Ribera

Few visitors to Barcelona neglect to frequent the Ribera. The earliest references to this singularly evocative district date from the eleventh century, when local population growth encouraged the proliferation of independent settlements between the city's nucleus and the Mediterranean. This area, immediately to the east of the original Roman walls, was first called *vilanova de la mar*, or "new town by the sea." Eventually known as the Ribera (literally "shore" or "riverbank"), it attracted growing numbers of merchants, sailors, and craftsmen and their families.[5] By the later Middle Ages, its population and wealth had begun to overtake that of the rest of Barcelona, thus commencing a preeminence which lasted well into the eighteenth century. While physically it was not the largest district in the city, it nevertheless became densely inhabited. In 1516 the Ribera contained 41 percent of the city's population, while occupying only 14 percent of its space. In 1787, the area still housed 38 percent of Barcelona's inhabitants, and this despite the massive recent growth of the rapidly industrializing Raval district on the opposite side of the city.[6]

Foremost among the topographical features of the quarter was the Church of Santa Maria del Mar, or Saint Mary's by the Sea.[7] Immediately following its construction in the fourteenth century on the site of an earlier paleo-Christian foundation, Santa Maria emerged as the city's largest and most sumptuous parish. Adjoining the basilica was the *Born*, or spacious plaza housing Barcelona's leading market. The stately avenue known as the Carrer de Montcada ran northwest from the square. By the fourteenth century this street had become a favored locus of residence of the city's wealthier merchants. On the other side of the Born stood the *marina*, a ramshackle cluster of tenements inhabited by a floating and impoverished populace of sailors, fishermen, and dockworkers. Finally, the Ribera also contained numerous streets named after individual guilds, especially in the cloth, leather, and glass sectors. Craftsmen sold their wares in shops huddled together for mutual aid and close supervision of production.

Taken together, these landmarks underscore the mixed character of the quarter. Within its confines, merchants, patricians, artisans, and wage earners mingled to a degree unmatched in the rest of the city.

What precisely were these confines? The Ribera straddled a broad range of internal boundaries within medieval and early modern Barcelona. Study of the different terms used to demarcate the area it enclosed illustrates considerable fluidity—as well as rivalry—among urban spatial designations. In particular, ecclesiastical and lay definitions of civic geography vied for preeminence in the formal drawing of the district's frontiers.

Boundaries

Beginning in the later Middle Ages, the Ribera was frequently regarded as coterminous with the parish of Santa Maria del Mar.[8] To be sure, the area did not lack other religious establishments, for it housed numerous convents, and even another parish church, the small *rectorat* of Sant Cugat. Yet in the eyes of many contemporaries, the Ribera was indistinguishable from its most treasured adornment. By far the most imposing edifice in the eastern half of the city, Santa Maria literally towered over the quarter, as an anonymous map from the later sixteenth century makes graphically clear (see fig. 1).[9] In similar fashion, the visible, albeit limited, role it played in Barcelona's devotional life and civic ritual enhanced its protagonism within the more circumscribed sphere of the Ribera. The prestige and wealth accruing to this powerful church did much to strengthen the neighborhood's identification with the basilica, thus extending the overlap between parish and quarter.

Yet the Ribera did not live only in the shadow of its parish church. The city's administrative jurisdictions provided rival definitions of the maritime district.[10] The earliest full census of Barcelona (1363) divided the city into four quarters, which were in turn broken down into *illes* or blocks. The *quarter del mar* was the standard bureaucratic designation of the Ribera until the reorganization of local government during the eighteenth century. The cadastre, or tax on real property imposed by the new Bourbon government in 1716, broke with tradition by dividing the city into ten *barrios*, each identified by number. This moreover proved to be merely the first of several shifts in interurban boundaries decreed during the eighteenth century.[11]

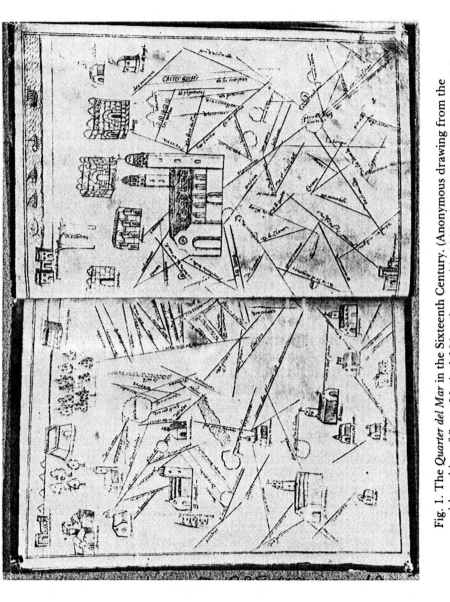

Fig. 1. The *Quarter del Mar* in the Sixteenth Century. (Anonymous drawing from the parish archive of Santa Maria del Mar, destroyed in 1936. Photo: Arxiu Històric Municipal, Barcelona.)

There were some exceptions to the use by lay authorities of nonparochial spatial divisions. Prior to the adoption in the nineteenth century of uniform municipal subdivisions throughout Spain, Barcelona's administrative boundaries drew upon both civil and ecclesiastical categories. For example, in the national census of 1787, the Ribera figured as the parish of Santa Maria del Mar, in clear recognition of the superiority of parish registers and paschal Communion lists as sources of vital statistics.[12] On several occasions, the overlap between lay and parochial designations was complete, as in the 1651 plague orders or the 1694 street cleaning ordinance, which referred to the "Quarter of Santa Maria del Mar."[13] Yet despite the persistent alternation of lay and religious boundaries, as an administrative entity the Ribera gradually lost its identification with the parish of Santa Maria del Mar. As a result, the quarter was referred to in increasingly impersonal terms. In fact, in the eighteenth century, bureaucratic procedure eventually replaced its name with a number.

There is reason to question whether either set of designations inspired deep loyalties among most of the Ribera's residents. To be sure, Santa Maria dwarfed Barcelona's other parishes. According to a panegyric published in 1589, it housed a community of 120 priests serving over five thousand of the city's forty thousand inhabitants. "It is well known," proclaimed the enthusiastic chronicler, "that there is no larger [parish] in all Christendom."[14] Despite such exaggeration, it is clear that Barcelona's other parishes were, with the single exception of Santa Maria del Pi in the far side of the city, miniscule and poorly endowed by comparison. Yet Santa Maria's very predominance distanced it from the concerns of many of the Ribera's citizens. It simply was too large to provide the sort of intimacy that contributes to the development of a strong sense of parochial identity. Its impersonality seems especially apparent when one contrasts its size with that of parishes elsewhere in the northern half of the peninsula. Fifteenth-century Saragossa contained a population smaller than that of Barcelona, yet it was served by fifteen such churches, in contrast with Barcelona's seven. In 1504, Salamanca, with a maximum total population of twenty thousand, housed 24 parishes; the largest, Saint Martin's, ministered to fewer than two thousand persons. In the same period Avila, one third the size of Barcelona, contained 8 parishes. And in 1639, Toledo's twenty five thousand inhabitants were distributed among 27 parish churches.[15] In short, the average number of parishioners in Barcelona was considerably larger than in comparable Iberian cities. Moreover, this problem was especially acute in the case of Santa Maria del Mar.

Perhaps the problem of scale could have been resolved had the parish assumed the sort of social and political functions that would have provided its inhabitants a focus for common activity. Some of these functions did exist; for example, charity in Barcelona tended to be distributed along parish lines, and Santa Maria's *bací de pobres vergonyants,* or collection plate for the shameful poor, was of sufficient importance for the church vestry to appoint a special board to oversee its operation. Yet on the whole, Barcelona's parishes housed a relatively narrow range of functions. This was especially true of their extramural activities, which were limited to occasional participation in citywide processions and other ritual acts. In particular, they played virtually no role in local politics, in contrast with other cities in the peninsula, where municipal officials were elected by (or chosen from among) parishioners.[16]

The relative weakness of the parish as a source of collective identity seems thus to have characterized the experience of the Ribera.[17] It is equally unlikely that the municipal government's definitions marked the outer boundaries of most of its inhabitants' sense of neighborhood. Both quarter and *barrio* were artificial constructions imposed from outside, and susceptible to changes suiting administrative convenience. The geographic entities delimited by tax lists, plague orders, and censuses, while demonstrating an impressive degree of flexibility, nevertheless lacked autonomy and an ongoing life of their own. As such, they differed from, say, the *gonfaloni* created by the guild regime of fourteenth-century Florence, which were permanent, semi-independent bodies charged with considerable responsibilities in local government. These districts played important political and fiscal roles in Florence, although they eventually atrophied (along with both major and minor guilds) following the establishment of the Medici *signoria*.[18]

Taken together, the weakness of parish ties and the absence of social and political organization along either geographic or parochial lines point to something corroborated by documentary conventions of the period. The identification of persons in public records habitually makes no reference to their status as parishioners or inhabitants of specific districts or streets. Instead, adult males and their dependents are invariably identified by their trades. For most early modern Barcelonans, theirs was a "corporate city," in that membership in a guild or confraternity was the most important means of establishing public identity. In addition to clearly defining social status, membership in corporations also delimited access to political office. For the majority of Barcelonans—in fact, for virtually all adult males not members of the urban elite—belonging to a guild was a prerequisite for service on the city council or as aldermen. Guilds moreover served as crucial links within the chain of municipal administration in both the key areas of defense and taxation. Significantly, the civic militia that had formerly been organized by streets gave way in the later Middle Ages to a new watch based upon guilds. And while most of the city's revenues derived from indirect imposts on consumer goods, whenever direct taxes were levied, their collection did not rest in the hands of geographic units like the Florentine *gonfaloni*, or parishes (which collected the royal *taille* in France), but it was the responsibility of the guilds, which were given leeway to decide how to apportion the burden among their members.[19]

Formal political activity in early modern Barcelona was thus fairly centralized, in the sense that decisions were made on a citywide basis, without the intervention of lesser administrative bodies constituted along geographic or parochial lines. There were, of course, exceptions to this rule. For example, the municipal government found that localized responses by street or neighborhood were more effective in dealing with catastrophes like famines or epidemics. Hence, during emergencies alternative forms of administration were adopted and then disbanded when the threat passed. Moreover, it was considered acceptable for informal coalitions, like groups of immediate neighbors, to petition the city government regarding specific reforms or needs. Thus, for example, the 1621 supplication by the "neighbors and inhabitants of the Pla d'en Llull" (a large square in the Ribera to the east of the Born) for aid in repairing the damage caused by flooding in their low-lying area.[20] Finally, it should be kept in mind that the practitioners of many trades tended to reside near each other. As a result, it could be argued that representation by guilds was not wholly incompatible with the notion of political participation by geographic areas.

Still, one must conclude that small-scale, geographically defined units played at best a minor and intermittent part in local governance.

Instead, Barcelona's numerous guilds mediated between the city at large and its inhabitants. What was true for the civic regime apparently held for important aspects of social life as well. Neighborhoods played little role in the public organization of productive activity and of sociability and leisure. In Barcelona, formal collective identity was rooted in trades, not in parishes or quarters.

Representations

Shifting attention away from official jurisdictions and toward more informal representations and venues quickly reveals that not all definitions derive from decrees. Governments and churches exercised no monopoly over the characterization of social space. The case of the Ribera suggests that where formal boundaries contributed little to the definition of neighborhood, informal representations stepped in to provide a firmer basis for local identity. The waterfront district provides a useful arena for examining not only how sociogeographical boundaries could be defined through reputation, but also how political mobilization outside official institutions could in turn influence, and be influenced by, local identity.

The neighborhood—or neighborhoods—of the Ribera evoked strong symbolic associations among the inhabitants of early modern Barcelona. Two images dominated representations of the maritime district. In a seeming paradox, the quarter was seen as housing both extremes in civic hierarchies of prestige, wealth, and power.

On the one hand, the Ribera sheltered a transient *lumpen* populace, especially the cluster of itinerant poor huddled in tenements between the Born and the sea. Beginning in the late sixteenth century, the expression *gent de la Ribera,* or "people of the Ribera," appeared with growing frequency in contemporary documents, ranging from the minutes of the civic council to private diaries. The inhabitants of this district garnered special notoriety through their penchant for political and economic violence. In 1604, some four thousand "women, children and men from the Ribera" protested bread shortages by setting fire to a house on the Born owned by the alderman in charge of food supplies.[21] In 1623, the *gent marítima* ("seafaring folk") occupied the bishop's palace in the city's center and treated the government building next door to a shower of stones. The following year, dockworkers, seamen, and their families attacked blackleg laborers from Mallorca. Amid shouts of "long live the Ribera!" a crowd led by a baker and a fisherwoman sacked the Carrer de Montcada palace of the Genoese banker who had employed the Mallorcans. Finally, similar mobs turned out to riot in 1629, 1640, and 1641 in defense of customary work rights and contracts.

One can hardly deny the protagonism of the inhabitants of the Ribera, and especially of its seaside tenements, in the frequent instances of popular violence in seventeenth-century Barcelona. To a certain degree, the "people of the Ribera" constituted a separate city within the city, an *imperium in imperio* of the mobile poor. Possessing little corporate organization, they lacked well-defined channels of access to political authority. Thanks to their precarious means, they also found themselves more exposed than other commoners to changes in the local economy. Equally evident was the group's willingness to defend traditional work policies and low bread prices—both issues of crucial importance to those living on the margin of survival.

At the same time the quarter also boasted an important symbol of the civic elite: the Carrer de Montcada, the imposing thoroughfare long preferred as a locus of residence, first by the city's merchants and later by urban patricians and nobles. References within elite sermons and other literary expositions placed overriding emphasis on the nobility of the street and the surrounding neighborhood. In 1691, for example, an effusive preacher gushed at length in praise of this "illustrious *barrio*," so full of "noble and ancient houses." And in 1720, a local chronicler hailed the *carrer* as the "most noble street in the city," and went on to paint a glittering canvas of opulence and display within its palaces.[22] These are but two of the many testimonies to the aristocratic character of the street, whose exclusivism was enhanced by its association with the increasingly privatized festive life of the civic elite. Indeed, few other loci within early modern Barcelona possessed a public *persona* as recognizable as the Carrer de Montcada's evocation of wealth, splendor, and social distinction.

The Ribera thus found representation as a mixture of high and low. Complexity and contradiction marked both the quarter and its images. Not surprisingly, this pattern was reproduced not only in the social composition of its inhabitants, but also in the ambivalence that characterized its leading symbols.

First, the district's residential patterns display this ambiguity. Admixture of popular classes and the elite was typical of many areas in

Barcelona, and the Ribera was no exception. The residential segregation by social class found in most modern cities had little counterpart in preindustrial urban society, where rich and poor often lived side by side. There was, to be sure, a tendency for certain craftsmen to be concentrated in areas. It is equally true that the wealthier members of local society could be found in much greater numbers in the center, instead of the periphery of the city. Still, from the later Middle Ages well into the nineteenth century, the population of the Ribera was decidedly mixed. Close proximity of different social classes, not segregation, was the norm governing local residential patterns.[23]

What seems to have characterized the Ribera in particular was the proximity of the *extremes* of high and low. It was not so much the mixture of rich and poor, but the mixture of the richest and the poorest, that lent such a distinctive cast to the neighborhood's reputation. The waterfront district was one of only two neighborhoods in early modern Barcelona with any specific identity as such, the other being the Raval, the large, if sparsely populated, former suburb on the other side of the city, which housed an almost exclusively working-class population. And of the two, the Ribera was the only quarter whose public image presented any degree of multivalence. The reason for this seems apparent: by the seventeenth century, two strong class identities had consolidated their presence within the same area of the city. In other words, at least two sets of neighbors inhabited the same space and competed over its definition.

The dominant symbols of the Ribera—the Carrer de Montcada, the Born marketplace, and the parish Church of Santa Maria del Mar—also partook of this ambivalence and sense of mixture. A closer look at the Carrer de Montcada reveals another side to its exclusively elite image. The list of its residents registered in the cadastre of 1716 would have surprised panegyrists who suggested that its inhabitants numbered only merchants and nobles. Of the fifty houses and shops on the street, fully one-half (twenty-four) were owned by patricians, ranging from titled aristocrats to "honored citizens," or ennobled rentiers.[24] Yet if one inspects the roster of tenants actually living in the buildings, over half (twenty-nine, or 58 percent) of which were leased, the street takes on a different complexion. Members of the civic elite made up only 10 percent of the *carrer*'s residents, in contrast to 43 percent artisans and shopkeepers. In fact, the single largest occupational group living on the street was not its nine patricians, but rather its eleven sailmakers. In short, the image of the Carrer de Montcada as a "noble" street was, while not inexact, certainly incomplete. While members of the elite predominated as owners of property on the *carrer,* the vast majority of its residents hailed from a far inferior social background.

Residential patterns moreover exhibited an impressive capacity for transformation, as another example from this street makes clear. Throughout the sixteenth and seventeenth centuries, the Meca Palace, one of the most imposing edifices on the *carrer,* remained in the hands of traditional Catalan aristocratic families. In the early eighteenth century, however, its owners leased the building out to tenants. According to the cadastre of 1716, some fifty-six inhabitants divided among eighteen different families occupied the palace.[25] The heads of these households—who paid one of the lowest annual rents in Barcelona—worked in some of the poorest paid trades in the city. They included fishermen, sailors, stevedores, and craft apprentices. To be sure, the "tenement" (or perhaps "charity") phase of the Meca Palace appears to have been short-lived, as the building passed into the hands of another noble family shortly thereafter. Still, it reminds us not only of the complex reality underlying certain images and representations but also that status distribution within residential patterns was neither fixed nor static. To the contrary, it proved susceptible to considerable change, especially in the short term.

The same tendency toward admixture characterized other landmarks of the quarter. Note, for example, the way in which the city's ritual calendar dictated an even more rapid (if regular) transformation of the sociogeographic image of the Born. During most of the year the area served as a fruit and vegetable market, replete with all the picaresque details attending "low life" in a port city (see fig. 2). Yet during Carnival, on 23 April (Saint George's Day, the patron of Catalonia-Aragon), and on Midsummer's Day, Catalan aristocrats took over the square for their colorful jousts and tourneys.[26] Local festive traditions thus endowed the square with an alternating cycle of high and low associations. By briefly, if persistently, superseding the prosaic rhythms of daily life, ritual time transformed the representation of space.

Finally, much the same can be said for the "cathedral of the Ribera," Santa Maria del Mar. While its parishioners may have included some of the city's wealthiest and most distinguished citizens, the

Fig. 2. The *Born* Marketplace in the Eighteenth Century. (Anonymous painting in the Museu d'Història de la Ciutat, Barcelona.)

trades represented in its parish brotherhood (the Confraternity of the Holy Sacrament, founded in 1523) included sailors, stevedores, fishermen, porters, and blanket and mattress makers.[27] Similarly, while Santa Maria boasted the most aristocratic vestry in the city, its composition nevertheless followed the local norm of representing *tots estaments,* or all estates. Thus its five posts were distributed among a noble, an honored citizen, a merchant, and one master each from the major and minor guilds.[28]

In short, social boundaries overlapped or blurred within even the most distinguished symbols of the quarter. One must, of course, take care to note the historical specificity of the representations of neighborhoods. To take but one example: like many waterfront areas, the Ribera appears to have been associated with poverty and overcrowding. However, it was only in the first half of the seventeenth century—more exactly, from around 1590 to the 1640s—that it gained notoriety for collective lower-class violence as well.

This linkage—in large measure a product of the downswing in urban economic conditions during the second half of the Mediterranean "long century"—not only suggests that representations of neighborhood experienced historical cycles of creation, diffusion, and decline. It also raises the possibility that insiders—the neighbors themselves—forged or adapted these informal definitions to suit their own purposes in specific circumstances.[29] One could argue that through their readiness to resort to violence, the "people of the Ribera" constituted themselves as an effective, if informal, pressure group within local politics. They may, in fact, have obtained more satisfaction than many guild members who, despite official representation within the organs of municipal government, nevertheless found it increasingly difficult to persuade the civic elite to adopt the protectionist policies that they hoped would resolve the crisis in local trade and production, a crisis whose signs were all too evident during the 1620s and 1630s. The Ribera's fame as a neighborhood of rough-and-ready street politics proved to be a potent weapon within the hands of workers denied a berth within the corporate city. Thanks to their efforts, neighborhood identity took shape more through the politics of reputation than by the drawing of formal boundaries. As we have seen, the neighborhood as an officially recognized alternative to the guild played virtually no role in Barcelona. Unofficially, however, the neighborhood provided a strong focus for social and political mobilization, especially for those who lacked other means of representation.[30]

Conclusion

The central emphasis of this essay has been on the links between neighborhood identity and diverse modes of social and political activity. In the first half, I argued that the absence of administrative and other functions based on territorially defined units both reflected and contributed to the existence of alternative forms of organization, most notably the guilds. In the second half, however, I went on to suggest that collective representations opened a different path to the development of a sense of place. Mobilization outside the confines of official politics derived from, as it simultaneously helped to strengthen, consciousness of neighborhood, especially for those living outside the corporate regime. Despite the divisive potential of conflict, riots and disputes did not threaten the collective identity of the "people of the Ribera." This identity was, in fact, nourished by conflict, which lent the social definition not provided by other, more formal boundaries.

This brings us back to our starting point, the violent fight and subsequent reconciliation among the fishing folk of Chioggia that so delighted Goethe. There too neighborhood identity, as well as the norms of proper neighborly behavior, came into clearer focus as conflict deepened. Moreover, it was outside political authority, in the person of the Venetian magistrate, that received the most chastening lesson about the ability of determined neighbors to achieve their ends. The inhabitants of Chioggia were all too aware of their reputation for brawling and colorful invective, and at the end of the play they asked the judge "not to let the word out that we Chioggians like to quarrel."[31] More than a little tongue met the cheek in this request, though. For after all, by artfully bringing into play their biting words and willingness to stand up to local authorities, these fishermen and their families found a way to manipulate the structures of power to suit their own ends. Like the "people of the Ribera," they turned an unflattering representation into some boundaries of their own.

NOTES

This essay had its distant origins in papers delivered at meetings of the American Anthropological Association (November 1984) and the American Historical Association (December 1985). I am grateful to my fellow panelists and commentators, and in particular to Gary McDonogh, Richard Kagan, and Sydel Silverman, for their helpful remarks and criticism. The National Endowment for the Humanities and the University of Florida provided funding for research for this project.

In the following notes, place of publication is Barcelona unless otherwise indicated.

1. J. W. Goethe, *Italian Journey, 1786–1788,* trans. W. H. Auden and E. Mayer (San Francisco, 1982), 85. The quotations within the following paragraph can be found on pp. 85–86.

2. C. Goldoni, *Le Baruffe Chiozzotte,* ed. G. D. Bonino (Turin, 1981); the Gozzi quotation appears on pp. 10–11 of this edition. This is the only play Goldoni wrote in Venetian language that is still regularly performed in Italy.

3. Ibid., 15. For a recent study of this area, see R. J. Goy, *Chioggia and the Villages of the Venetian Lagoon: Studies in Urban History* (Cambridge, 1985).

4. P. M. Melvin, "Changing Contexts: Neighborhood Definition and Urban Organization," *American Quarterly* 37 (1985): 357. However, D. M. Hummon's *Commonplaces: Community Ideology and Identity in American Culture* (Albany, 1990), especially 79–80, takes in account "images of neighborhoods."

5. For the early history of the Ribera, see C. Batlle, "Els Prohoms de la Ribera de Barcelona i llurs atribucions en matèria d'urbanisme, segona meitat del S. XII," in *El Pla de Barcelona i la seva història* (1984), 155–60; J. M. Font Rius, "La Universidad de Prohombres de Ribera de Barcelona y sus ordenanzas marítimas," *Estudios de Derecho Mercantil en homenaje al Profesor Antonio Polo* (Madrid, 1981), 199–240; and P. Banks, "*Burgus, suburbium* and *villanova:* The extramural growth of Barcelona before A.D. 1200," in *Història urbana del Pla de Barcelona* (1990), 2:107–34. I am indebted to Dr. Banks for answering various queries about the Ribera during the Middle Ages.

6. A. Garcia Espuche and M. Guàrdia Bassols, *Espai i societat a la Barcelona pre-industrial* (1986), fig. 19; J. Iglésies, *El Cens del Comte de Floridablanca* (1969), 2:496–99.

7. General works on the waterfront area include S. Sanpere i Miquel, *Topografía antigua de Barcelona: la Rodalía de Corbera* (1890–92), 3 vols., and A. Duran i Sanpere, *Barcelona i la seva història* (1973), passim.

8. Much of what follows on this parish derives from the standard two-volume history by B. Bassegoda, *Santa Maria del Mar* (1927).

9. M. Galera et al., *Atlas de Barcelona* (1982), 30–33.

10. The following summary is based upon the city censuses located in the A[rxiu] H[istòric] M[unicipal], B[arcelona] [AHMB]/Consell de Cent XIX, Fogatges, and the Cadastre series housed in the same archive. For background information on these documents and their uses for local history, see

A. Garcia Espuche and M. Guàrdia Bassols, "Els usos del plànol: la riquesa en la Barcelona del XIV," *L'Avenç* 64 (October 1983): 72–77, and their "L'Estudi de l'espai urbà de la Barcelona de principis del S. XVIII: el Cadastre de 1716," in *Actes del Primer Congrés d'Història Moderna de Catalunya* (1984), 1:643–80.

11. In 1769 local officials reformed the cadastre groupings by redistricting the urban population into five *quarteles,* which were then subdivided into eight *barrios.* In 1801, when another reform of the property register led to the creation of eight *barrios,* the Ribera became known as *Barrio One.*

12. Iglésies, *Cens,* 496–99. In 1631, a municipal ordinance regulating bread supply during a famine also called for subdividing the city's seven parishes into *centenes,* or units of 100 houses; B[iblioteca de] C[atalunya] [BC]/F. Bon. 5405.

13. The plague orders are located in AHMB/Consell de Cent, Deliberacions, II-160, 187r. [1 April 1651]; the 2 February 1694 street cleaning ordinance is reproduced in the *Manual de novells ardits; vulgarment apel.lat Dietari del antich consell barceloní* (1967), 21:127.

14. D. J. Jorba, *Descripción de las Excelencias de la muy Insigne Ciudad de Barcelona* (1589), fol. 10r. A 1594 episcopal visitation estimated Santa Maria's population at 5000 *domos sive familias:* Archivio Segreto Vaticano/Sac. Cong. Concilio, *Relat. Dioc. ad Liminam,* III A (Barcinon.), anno 1594.

15. I. Falcón Pérez, *Organización municipal de Zaragoza en el S. XV* (Saragossa, 1978), 37–42; C. I. López Benito, *Bandos nobiliarios en Salamanca al iniciarse la Edad Moderna* (Salamanca, 1983), 29; J. E. Bilinkoff, *The Avila of Santa Teresa: Religious Reform in a Sixteenth-Century City* (Ithaca, 1989), 8–9; and J. Montemayor, "Tolède en 1639," *Mélanges de la Casa de Velázquez* 18 (1982): 139.

16. For the election (and eventually selection) of municipal officials on the basis of parishes in Valencia, to cite but one instance, see L. Tramoyeres Blasco, *Instituciones gremiales: su origen y organización en Valencia* (Valencia, 1889), 309–34.

17. Similar conditions prevailed in other early modern cities, including Florence, Venice, and Lyons. See: R. Trexler, *Public Life in Renaissance Florence* (New York, 1980), 13, and R. Gaston, "Liturgy and Patronage in San Lorenzo, Florence, 1350–1650," in *Patronage, Art, and Society in Renaissance Italy,* ed. F. W. Kent et al. (Canberra and Oxford, 1987), 125; D. Romano, *Patricians and Popolani: The Social Foundations of the Venetian Renaissance State* (Baltimore, 1987), 152–53; and N. Z. Davis, "Religion in the Neighborhood: The Stones of Sainte-Croix Parish," unpublished paper presented at the American Historical Association meeting, December 1979.

18. D. V. Kent and F. W. Kent, *Neighbours and Neighbourhood in Florence: The District of the Red Lion in the Fifteenth Century* (Locust Valley, NY, 1982), especially chapter 1. Florence provides just one example of the important functions, administrative and otherwise, of local forms of sociopolitical organization within medieval and early modern cities. Other such units

included the *rioni* of Rome, the *contrade* of Siena, Genoa's *alberghi*, and the Neapolitan *seggi*.

19. Kent and Kent, *Neighbours*, 24–37; J. R. Farr, *Hands of Honor: Artisans and their World in Dijon, 1550–1650* (Ithaca, 1988), 86. For corporate participation in Barcelona's government, see J. S. Amelang, *Honored Citizens of Barcelona: Patrician Culture and Class Relations, 1490–1714* (Princeton, 1986), 28–32.

20. AHMB/Consell de Cent, Deliberacions, II-130, 32v. (17 February 1621). In turn, groups of neighbors could be obliged to pay special taxes for local improvements; see J. Mutgé i Vives, "Algunes millores urbanístiques a Barcelona durant el regnat d'Alfons el Benigne (1327–1336)," in *El Pla de Barcelona*, 163.

21. The alderman in question was Jaume Hernandez, an apothecary. His highly visible tombstone can still be seen behind the main altar in Santa Maria del Mar. The main sources for this paragraph are the *Dietari*, or daybook of the City Council (cited in note 13), and the contemporary diary accounts of the barrister Jeroni Pujades and the tanner Miquel Parets. I am presently preparing a study of popular revolts in seventeenth-century Barcelona, which will discuss each of these incidents in detail.

22. R. Costa, *El Príncipe verdadero en su propio Principado* (1691), 3; the 1720 poem can be found in Biblioteca Universitària de Barcelona/MS. 5, F. Tagell, "Obras de la Mussa Catalana Dessocupada."

23. Garcia and Guàrdia, "Usos del plànol," 77, and their *Espai i societat*, 29–40. Prior to the nineteenth century, segregation by social status in Barcelona seems to have taken place more by different floors within buildings than through differentiation by neighborhoods or streets. See M. Arranz, "De la casa artesana a la casa capitalista: l'habitatge a la Barcelona del S. XVIII," in *La Vida quotidiana desde la perspectiva històrica*, ed. I. Moll (Palma de Mallorca, 1985), 245–54, and M. Lopez Guallar, "Vivienda y segregación social en Barcelona, 1772–1791," *Cuadernos de Arquitectura y Urbanismo* 19 (1973): 73–75.

24. AHMB/Cadastre, vol. 13, 244v.–252r.

25. Ibid., 247v.–248r. Dennis Romano notes a Venetian example of popular tenants inhabiting a noble palace in his *Patricians*, 193; instances from early modern London are cited in M. J. Power, "John Stow and his London," *Journal of Historical Geography* 11 (1985): 17.

26. There are numerous references to aristocratic fêtes in the Born and the Carrer de Montcada. For a brief summary, see Amelang, *Honored Citizens*, 195–210.

27. L. Daunis, *Noticia histórica . . . la Cofradía del Santísimo Sacramento* (1923), 8–9. This brotherhood (also known as the Archconfraternity of the Minerva) was, to be sure, the only interclass penitential congregation within Santa Maria. The largest and most popular devotional associations were located elsewhere in the city, attached not to the parishes, but rather to the traditional mendicant orders. For craft and devotional confraternities in Santa Maria, see Bassegoda, *Santa Maria del Mar*, 2:231–52.

28. For example, the *obrers*, or vestrymen, of Santa Maria del Mar in 1653 included a gentleman, honored citizen, merchant, apothecary, and brocade maker (AHMB/XXII, Albarans, vol. 51, 18v).

29. I am indebted here to Peter Sahlins, who has reconstructed the various ways in which the crafty peasants of the Cerdanya Valley converted "political constraints" into "meaningful boundaries of territorial and social identities" in his *Boundaries: The Making of France and Spain in the Pyrenees* (Berkeley, 1989), 270. I have taken the double liberty of transposing this insight from the rural to the urban sphere, and focusing it on the most local of public identities, that of the neighborhood.

30. Craig J. Calhoun also distinguishes between popular mobilization within "traditional communities" and more formal political organization in his "The Radicalism of Tradition: Community Strength or Venerable Disguise and Borrowed Language?" *American Journal of Sociology* 88 (1983): 886–914.

31. "Che andasse fuora la nomina che le Chiozzotte xe baruffante": Goldoni, *Baruffe,* III, final scene.

The Social Transformation of the French Parish Clergy, 1500–1800

Andrew Barnes

My goal in this essay is to sketch the impact on the institutional character of the French parish clergy of the decree of the Council of Trent, which required that all aspirants to the curé of souls receive some previous training in seminaries erected explicitly for that purpose. Seminary education, I maintain, was the key factor in the emergence by the eighteenth century of a parish clergy not only capable of recognizing and maintaining a distance between itself and the laity, but capable also of using this difference to effect the withdrawal of the church from the role it had played for centuries in communal social relations. It may be that the most important way seminary education changed the priesthood was through the shift it forced in the social milieu from which most potential priests were recruited. Even so, by the eighteenth century, the ways seminary training molded these individuals, the behaviors it promoted, and the behaviors it suppressed, helped create a priesthood much different from its pre-Tridentine predecessor.

> Priests are for the most part so ignorant that they do not understand Latin. Their clothing and speech are no different from those of the laity. They wander around in short outfits of diverse colors, their cassocks remaining in the church along with their albs and other vestments, as worthy only of the altar. They wear their hair long like laymen; and like laymen they amuse themselves with the hunt or with games. They normally can be found in the cabaret, some can even be found who pass their evenings dancing and sporting with women.... Worse than this, there are some who

maintain debauched and scandalous lives, doing things so infamous and scandalous that one knows not how to read without horror the complaints made against them. Their evil goes to such an extreme that no one thinks anything of placing in the baptismal registers, after the name of illegitimate children, the name of their father along with notation of his priestly vocation, as if it was required that they leave for posterity the marks of their incontinence.[1]

Except for its failure to mention alcoholism or the disinclination of many priests to reside in their parish, this characterization sums up the assessment by the contemporary ecclesiastical hierarchy of the pre-Tridentine parish clergy. All that historians have added to the picture have been explanations of how it came about. They have postulated that the local priest was at best recruited from among the village elite. He acquired his knowledge of reading and writing, as well as of the duties and functions of the priesthood, through apprenticeship to an older priest. Perhaps he learned these things well enough to pass an oral examination administered by the bishop or his vicar general, but in many dioceses this requirement was not maintained; in many, the *visa*, the certification that permitted the priest to search for a parish, could be bought. Not that most priests had to look very far. The parish of their birth, or perhaps that of their mentor, was probably available, and if it did not provide sufficient revenue to live, there was always the option of moonlighting in other parishes or of singing masses for the soul of the mother of the local seigneur. Given the material circumstances of his life, is it so surprising that the priest lacked a sense of the distance between himself and the laity, that he lacked any incentive to learn to read or to perform the sacraments properly? Given the facts of his recruitment and training, is it so surprising that many priests could not discipline their sexual appetite?[2]

The nice thing about this explanation is that it both accounts for the type of complaints against the priesthood noted in the available records of pastoral visits and dovetails neatly with the conclusions of the ecclesiastics who attended the Council of Trent, who saw the solution to these complaints in education. For them the incapacities of the village priesthood could be traced to lacunae in what René Taveneaux labeled its *formation sacerdotale*,[3] lacunae that training or instruction in an educational institution specifically created for priests could fill.

I would suggest that the assessment of the types of deficiencies suffered by the pre-Tridentine priesthood implicit in the above view can be balanced by another, one which attempts at least to take better cognizance of the laity's perspective. The literature on sacerdotal reforms supports an assessment of the laity as being concerned foremost with the clergy's lack of attention to what it, the laity, perceived as the clergy's most important duties. There is little evidence that the laity traced this lack of attention to the insufficient training that contemporary ecclesiastics and present-day historians identified as the culprit. I will make the case that in fact the strength of the pre-Tridentine parish clergy was its awareness of local religious culture. The literature likewise supports an evaluation of the training routines implemented in post-Tridentine seminaries as being aimed at inhibiting the priest's performance of just those duties about which the laity was most concerned. Historical treatments of Catholic reform in France take as a given the idea that the emergence of the seminary-trained priest was a progressive step in the correction of the abuses that gave rise to lay alienation from the institutional church. A review of the pertinent facts about the nature of rural devotional life before and after the emergence of the new type of priest, however, argues instead for the conclusion that changes in the institutional character of the priesthood mostly caused older forms of alienation to be replaced by newer forms. In the end, the reform of the parochial clergy pushed the rural laity further away from the church.

Six types of complaints were leveled against the pre-Tridentine priesthood: that priests tended to be alcoholics; that they kept concubines; that they refused to maintain a dress code; that they refused to conduct themselves as priests—that they engaged in secular activities such as hunting and games, and even secular vocations such as farming and merchandising; that they did not reside in their own parish; and that they did not perform the functions of their office or performed them at times inconvenient for their parishioners.[4] From the brief notations that remain from pastoral visits, it is difficult to ascertain exactly who made these complaints, who perceived these behaviors as problems. I would argue, however, that the first four types of complaints were causes for concern primarily for ecclesiastical officials, and that only the latter two stemmed from the laity.

Regarding the question of celibacy, as the bishop of Autun observed in 1652:

> Concubinage here is extremely common and priests have no fear of maintaining in their quarters immodest women and the children they have had with them. They nourish and raise these children, train them to serve at the altar, marry them, dower them all as if they were legitimate. Parishioners are so accustomed to these practices that when interrogated about the morals and deportment of the clerics who keep these immodest women, they respond that these clerics live justly; and when it is brought home to these parishioners that the aforesaid priests are living with concubines and their offspring, they respond that these concubines and their children live quietly without noise, and so they see no evil, being so used to seeing their priests live with women that they assume it is acceptable.[5]

This statement suggests that when considering priestly sexual activity, we can profitably follow Jacques Solé, who argues that a distinction should be made between concubinage and adultery, the former definitely being the lesser of two evils.[6] In late medieval Germany, of course, priestly concubinage was sufficiently widespread to merit its own tax. There also it was perceived as an honorable alternative to philandering.[7]

Contemporary thinking on this matter is easy to comprehend. Priests' servants came from among the most impoverished, socially marginal local women.[8] Village society was not threatened when the woman who kept a priest's lodgings came also to share his bed. Such would not be the case if the priest turned his attentions to the wife or daughter of a socially prominent parishioner, that is to say, to a woman whose sexual actions did count in local social life.

Not surprisingly, what little comment we can extract from pastoral visits suggests that a critical factor in the village response to clerical concubinage was the way the priest's concubine sought to exploit her status. The complaint made against the priest in Saint Hilaire sur Yerre was that his concubine "criticized and badly injured the feelings of the honest women of the parish."[9] The young mistress of the priest in Saint Lubin d'Isigny so aggravated the parishioners with her presumption, that when she appeared for Sunday mass the congregation forced her out of the church.[10]

While undoubtably always topics of gossip, concubinage and the sexual activity on the part of the priest it implied were not necessarily points of contention between a curé and his parishioners. Conflict developed when, as in the above instances, the concubine attempted to exploit the liaison to improve her social standing. Or, keeping in mind that reporting the fact of the relationship to the episcopal visitor was itself an act of local social and political consequence, tensions occurred when a parishioner attempted to use information about the relationship as a weapon against the priest.[11]

This is not to argue that the laity did not perceive celibacy as a holy state, just that it did not expect curés to be holy. Perhaps the late medieval laity had fully assimilated the anti-Donatist argument, proselytized since the time of the Cathars, that the state of sexual purity of the performer had nothing to do with the efficacy of the rite being performed. More probable, I would speculate, is that celibacy, to the extent that it was perceived as a virtue, was expected only of those who aspired to the category of "holy man"—those men who had publicly left the world, such as friars, hermits, and penitents.

To the extent that parishioners sought to influence clerical behavior, as Taveneaux seeks to illustrate, it was in the direction of economic self-sufficiency and social congeniality.[12] Thus, it is reasonable to conclude that only churchmen would be concerned with whether or not curés sought to realize the Gregorian ideal of the social distance between the clergy and the laity symbolized by the cassock, or whether or not curés augmented their meager portions with meat from the hunt or earnings from some part-time trade. A bit more difficult is the question of drunkenness. Here also the personal act, in this case drinking, must be understood in its social context. The tavern was usually the center of village life, and since it was essential that the curé know all the latest happenings in the community, his regular presence there was probably perceived as useful. However, an inebriated priest must have been a nuisance, particularly if his physical state inhibited the performance of his duties. In the diocese of Chartres, complaints about clerical drunkenness were often simultaneously complaints about violent and abusive behavior. Drinking companions also were often a topic of concern, clerics being reported for sharing their wine with Huguenots and other disreputable sorts.[13] When the content of the laity's complaints about drunkenness is examined, it points toward a concern with how clerics behaved while inebriated, not with the act of drinking itself.

Parishioners may have ignored clerical concubinage. They may also have looked on silently at a curé's participation in secular social pursuits. Yet if available research provides any guide, when it came to the rural priesthood's diligence in the performance of the sacraments, the parishioners' expectations probably exceeded those of the hierarchy. In 1339, parishioners of the Church of Sainte-Marie-Madelaine of Besançon signed an accord with their curé specifying his duties. The contract ran to twenty-five articles, each one detailing minimum expectations in the performance of some ritual.[14] In 1455, the parishioners of Grissey in Burgundy signed a similar contract consisting of twenty-nine articles.[15]

The complaints about clerical absenteeism and nonperformance of services listed separately above actually may have been one and the same. In his study of the diocese of Geneva in the late Middle Ages, Binz identified clerical absenteeism as the primary concern voiced to episcopal visitors by rural parishioners. Binz's investigations revealed, however, that the major reason for such absenteeism was the fact that many curés held multiple cures, and that these curés gave preference to those parishes that rewarded their services the most highly. In late medieval Geneva, from the lay perspective, the major problem with the parish clergy was that it was never around to perform the sacraments.[16] In sixteenth-century Fréjus, absenteeism was comparatively less a problem. Still, as Louis Pignoli, vicar general, laconically noted again and again in the register of his 1546 trip through the diocese: "The parishioners complain against their priest ... for an improvement in the divine service."[17] In seventeenth-century Chartres, late (or non-) performance of sacramental services remained number one among the *négligences* for which the laity reproached the parish clergy.[18]

To appreciate why complaints about the performance of the sacraments were at the heart of lay concern about the curé's performance, one should briefly consider the nature of village social life. Social relations in premodern Europe, as John Bossy has characterized them, were normally in a state of conflict, of disintegration, such that "one [was] assumed to be at enmity with those to whom one [was] not related." The church took it upon itself to create a state of harmony, of integration, where "the peace which equals friendship, the peace in the feud," obtained. Its vehicle of conflict resolution was ritual performance of the sacraments, during which the conflicting parties were permitted to symbolically transcend their differences and emerge as a harmonious entity. Thus while marriage was for Bossy "almost by definition, 'a contract between two hostile groups,'" this point was significant only as a prelude to the dissipation of that hostility through performance of the marriage rites.[19] Whatever harmony existed in the medieval world was a function of the rites sanctioned by the medieval (pre-Tridentine) church. Essential to the assumption of this function was the fluidity the rites maintained in performance: they were not and could not be performed the exact same way each time. In this sense they fit within Hobsbawn's definition of a "custom" as a belief or practice that cannot afford to be "invariant" because it gives to any "desired change . . . the sanction of precedent, social continuity and natural law as expressed in history."[20] In performance, rites had to be sufficiently fluid so that participants could manipulate them to provide symbolic resolution of their conflicts. The obvious next question is how the parameters of performance were set. How was it determined that a particular set of acts and gestures constituted the marriage rite or the rite of baptism? I would suggest that it was here that the priest realized his true value to his parishioners. It was the priest who served as both the authenticator of a rite's validity and the guarantor of its sanctity.

In 1180, Henri, bishop of Senlis, feeling that it was beneath the dignity of the office of canon "to bless marriage beds, to purify women arising from confinement, [or] to render account to bishops of brawls and popular discords," promulgated that in the future no canon would be required to accept the care of a parish.[21] Henri's rather disparaging picture of the services expected of priests beyond performance of the sacraments nevertheless suggests that without the certification of the priest, few aspects of village ritual life could proceed. And since these rites were what held the village together as a community, the curé's dereliction in his duties put at risk not only the salvation of the parishioners but social harmony in the village as well.

The priest's role as agent for the village in its negotiations with the heavens is well understood. What requires more study is the part he played as facilitator and finalizer of more mundane negotiations between conflicting groups within the village. This latter function appears to have required far more time and far more diligence from the priest, as he was expected not only to be aware of the stress points in communal harmony but also to have some idea of the extent to which church rites had to be "customized" to relieve this stress. Whether or not he was the initiator of whatever innovation occurred in ritual performance is hard to say. At the very least he functioned like the referee in a modern sports contest, signaling, presumably in a less grandiose manner, when play had gone beyond some understood boundaries.

Saint Vincent de Paul, reminiscing, once complained that:

> Oh, if you only knew the diverse ways I have seen the mass celebrated these past forty years. It seems to me that nothing in this world is as ugly as the different ways it has been performed: some begin with a *Pater Noster;* others take the chasuble in their hands, intone the *Introit,* then put on the chasuble. I was once in Saint-Germain-en-Laye where I noted seven or eight priests all reciting the mass differently.[22]

But if my reading of Bossy is correct, this diversity was the key to the mass's social value, for each variation in performance reflected local sensibilities far more than reflecting, as the saint implied, the priests' ignorance. Perhaps the entire question of the corruption of the pre-Tridentine priesthood needs to be reexamined. The rural laity needed above all a resident clergy knowledgeable about local conflicts and the "customary" ways they had been resolved in the past. This clergy did not need to be literate, since the type of information upon which it had to act was accessible only through word of mouth. It did not need to know the "correct" way to perform the sacraments, since such knowledge would only get in the way of local custom. It did not need to be celibate, since available evidence suggests that ordinary folk never did buy the idea that the sexual purity of the priest had anything to do with the efficacy of the rites he was performing. What has been perceived as corruption was actually a reflection of the accommodation of the priesthood, as an institution, to the needs of premodern European society.

As radical as it may sound, perhaps the pre-Tridentine clergy was not as lacking in "sacerdotal training" as historians have assumed.

What the laity wanted was priests who were aware of its problems and competent to invoke the holy as an aid to the resolution of those problems. The *bon prêtre* of the pre-Tridentine era tried to live up to this ideal. To be sure, there were excesses. While it was good that the curé was in the tavern every evening, picking up the gossip that would make the performance of his office more socially effective, it was not good that he drank himself into a stupor in the process. It was also not good if he used these occasions to arrange liaisons with the wives of his parishioners; like every other man he was expected to content himself with the woman he had at home. While it was good that the priest got involved with his neighbors and not only heard but shared their problems, it was not good if he got involved to the point of taking sides in arguments. It was even worse if he took to withholding the sacraments from those from whom he was estranged. To the extent that they revealed the concerns of the laity, reports of pastoral visits evidenced frustration with the clergy's lack of performance of the services expected of them, not with the general nature of the priesthood itself. I would further suggest that to the degree that they anticipated the results of church reform at all, the rural laity probably was looking for a clergy more assiduous in the performance of these services, not the new entity that the post-Tridentine church sprang on them.

The pre-Trent rural laity saw nothing wrong with what the parish clergy was doing; they just wanted them to do it more conscientiously. The post-Tridentine hierarchy, however, traced the lack of commitment of the parish clergy to its involvement in the secular world. From this basic flaw sprang all the other problems the parish clergy, as a group, evinced. This perception on the part of the hierarchy helps explain one of the more confusing points about the education to which future priests were exposed in the seminaries that began to appear in most French dioceses during the second half of the seventeenth century. As Vincent de Paul complained, most priests were ignorant of even the rudiments of Catholic faith. Yet the thrust of the educational experience provided at seminaries led away from any sort of intellectual competence regarding the Catholic devotional experience and toward an internalization by the priest of a perception of himself as separate and distinct from the world around him. His complaint about priestly ignorance notwithstanding, Vincent de Paul himself sought to banish note taking by students in the seminaries he founded. He wanted both teaching and learning to be completely oral, viewing this to be the best method to prepare men for the pastorate.[23] Fortunately, none of the religious orders that came to specialize in the training of priests—the Sulpiciens, Jesuits, and Oratorians—was as anti-intellectual. Still, as Quéniart has described it, in the seminary the future priest was supposed to "empty" himself of the spirit of the world, and "fill" himself with the spirit of Christ.[24] Curricula deemed effective in producing this spiritual state placed a heavy emphasis on psychological isolation, they regulated social behavior, and they encouraged extreme deference and obedience to authority. To the extent that intellectual preparation was emphasized, it was, as Taveneaux notes about the study of the Bible, motivated by a concern to keep the priest one step ahead of the laity.[25]

The goal of seminaries, Quéniart stressed, was not to create evangelists or reformers, but rather to shape men capable of living for decades in self-imposed isolation in an environment perceived to be hostile to both their function and their salvation. Risk taking was trained out of priests; moral rectitude trained in.[26] As he explained the end result of the seminary process:

Transformed by multiple exercises in which it was required that he be a malleable paste in the hands of those who would fashion him, the priest was thus introduced to the piety and the virtues of the ecclesiastical estate: modesty, solemnity, self-control, benevolence, and, of course, obedience to the hierarchy now signaled the ideal priest, molded during his years at seminary by his relations with his superiors and with his fellow seminarians with whom he was not allowed to become familiar and whom he was required to address as "Monsieur." Intellectually, but also pyschologically, when he left seminary, after having celebrated there his first mass in order to avoid any worldly festivity being attached to such a serious event, he was different from when he had entered. Whatever were the differences of career, of spirituality or of character which appeared later, the conditioning he experienced in the seminary kept him close, in style of life, in preoccupations, in *mentalité,* to his brothers in the priesthood. He was deeply conscious of belonging not only to a social group, but to a corps whose function in the church placed it "above the angels" themselves; he was truly an outsider.[27]

Accepting Quéniart's conclusions prompts the task of reconciling his image of the post-Tridentine parish clergy with another image favored by historians, that of the clergy as the "shock troops of Tridentine Catholicism,"[28] to use Ralph Gibson's expression, the "agents of the Counter-Reformation,"[29] to use that of Philip Hoffman. Hoffman himself provides evidence to reinforce the traditional interpretation—the one Quéniart is attacking—that it was seminary training, supported by pastoral visits, retreats, and conferences, that turned the post-Tridentine priesthood into "cultural intermediaries who helped impose the harsh ethic and the urban sense of order favored by the post-Tridentine Church."[30]

The work of A. Lynn Martin and Louis Châtellier would suggest another possibility, that the reformed parish clergy acquired its new sensibilities along with the rest of the Catholic devotional elite through the network of secondary schools put into place by the Jesuits.[31] Still a third possibility is that curés gained their relentlessness from their confessors' manuals. Robin Briggs makes a powerful case for the "revolution" in thinking about Christian moral values that occurred between 1300 and 1600 as the source for the determination on the part of the post-Tridentine priesthood to expunge thoughts of certain types of behavior from the minds of the laity.[32]

I am more taken, however, with the possibility that the reformed clergy's affinity with what Bossy has labeled "ink divinity"[33] was instilled neither at school nor at seminary, nor learned from manuals, but rather was acquired at home. Fixation on determining the social composition and geographic origins of the post-Tridentine priesthood has lured historians away from investigation of an important fact about the priesthood's cultural background: the vast majority of the men recruited into the parish clergy from the late seventeenth century onward came from families who already made their living from literate and/or numerate intellectual skills.[34] Consistently across the eighteenth century, 60 percent of the men ordained in the diocese of Strasbourg for whom Châtellier could determine the family background came from families in which literacy and/or numeracy can be presumed.[35] More than 90 percent of the 353 priests from Upper

Brittany studied by Berthelot du Chesnay for the same period were from similar backgrounds.[36] In the centuries leading up to Trent, but for a small elite, few of the boys entering the priesthood could claim any systematic introduction to either letters or numbers. In the centuries following Trent, the majority of the boys entering the priesthood came from families where mastery of letters and/or numbers provided part of their livelihood.

In "Strikes and Salvation at Lyons," Natalie Davis told of how the spread of printing gave cultural status to those who participated in the print industry, and of how, when the old cultural elite refused to acknowledge the group's new status, many within the print industry turned toward Protestantism. I think facility with the written word empowered more than just those involved with printing. The use of texts for purposes of instruction in seminaries, the post-Tridentine dependence on the catechism as the preferred mode of lay instruction, and the emergence of the parish priest as record keeper of the state were just three of the developments—all tied to the encroachment of literacy on aspects of European culture previously left to oral tradition—that opened up the lower echelons of the Catholic clergy to the sons of groups who even before the invention of the printing press knew the value of the written record.

Quéniart found in the cities he studied in the four provinces of western France (Normandy, Maine, Anjou, and Brittany) that the number of clerics leaving estates that included personal libraries of more than one hundred books increased from 5 percent of the total in 1700 to 45 percent in 1730, 60 percent in 1760, and 80 percent in 1790.[37] Hoffman's much smaller sampling for Lyons during the seventeenth and eighteenth centuries confirms Quéniart's findings.[38] While their authors are justified in using these indices as measures of the growing immersion of the priesthood in literate culture, I would suggest that what these studies may also reveal is the gradual appropriation of the rural priesthood by the literate classes. As Châtellier points out for Strasbourg, prior to local implementation of the decrees of Trent, the city's cultural elite—those with university training—competed for positions only within chapters of canons. After the implementation of Tridentine reforms, rural parishes also became part of their playing field.[39]

There is a danger here of reductionism, but we should not let this danger impede an appreciation of the transformation in the cultural makeup of the parish priesthood stimulated by Trent. Reserving careers in the parish priesthood for those who had completed seminary meant reserving for Catholic Europe's expanding intelligentsia a vast number of positions, which, while they had not been closed to educated men before, usually had been awarded according to other criteria. Teachings on morality did change. But it took the appearance in country parishes of men with what William Christian has called "translocal" sensibilities—that is to say, intellectuals who structured their mental universe according to the ideas in their heads as opposed to the values of the surrounding society—to force-feed these teachings to the laity.[40] Europe's literate classes had been eager to assert some sort of control over the attitudes and antics of the unlettered, the "rustics," for centuries.[41] The Tridentine decree mandating the creation of seminaries granted them the opportunity to send their sons to initiate the process, an opportunity they did not fail to grasp.

I have argued that it was through his regulation of ritual performance that the pre-Tridentine priest played a positive role in the social life of the village. How conscious the post-Tridentine hierarchy was of this point is hard to say. According to Bossy, once a rite was written down, it lost its fluidity, its ability to be reconstructed to fit specific needs. Thus he took the publishing of the Roman Ritual of 1612 as signaling an end to the period when the performance of the sacraments played a socially integrative role.[42] His point is well taken, but in order for the missal to have such clout there had to be a clergy both capable of using it and willing to use it in the face of local opposition.

Quéniart notes that every seminary had a "master of ceremonies" charged with educating prospective priests in the right way to perform the sacraments.[43] Taveneaux mentions that liturgy was one of the few topics upon which there was theoretical discussion in seminary.[44] One of many manuals on how to perform the rites of the church, that written by Tronson, explained that these rites were to be performed with "a certain air not of this world, but of God."[45]

It is clear that there was contemporary awareness that the sacraments had to be reclaimed from the laity. It also would appear that the clergy were specifically trained to effect this reclamation. Curés became outsiders to the communities they served on two scores. They were educated to claim and maintain a status distinct from that of the rest of the inhabitants. Based on this status, they also were trained to repudiate a previously honored obligation to allow the sacraments to assume a social function. The advent of seminary-trained priests signaled the end of the institutional connection that had evolved during the Middle Ages between the village and the church. No longer did the church play a direct role in the maintenance of peace. No longer did the curé referee the resolution of conflict.

Not surprisingly, the laity reacted negatively to this development. Here, however, we must be careful not to confuse the response to the activities of clerical reformers with the response to the distance the curé now insisted on maintaining between the rites of the church and the needs of the community. In the hands of historians like Bercé, the violent reactions to the abolition of various rites and festivals by reforming bishops and curés has made great reading.[46] But these reactions provide little insight into how life came together again on the other side of such confrontations. Few dioceses or parishes were ever blessed with more than two reformers in a row; remote dioceses and parishes rarely had more than one in the time between Trent and the Revolution. It was up to the curé to make sure that once a rite had been suppressed, it stayed suppressed. First and foremost, the curé had to be capable of "just saying no."

What we should look for as responses to the change in the nature of the priesthood, however, are not violent or dramatic confrontations, but rather a coldness or lack of sympathy that reciprocated that of the curé. Bossy has argued that a "high proportion" of the charges of clerical sexual incontinence in the pre-Reformation period should be dismissed as "malicious gossip."[47] There is really too much evidence to the contrary to accept this conclusion for the time period to which Bossy refers. But it may work for eighteenth-century France. Tackett observed that "there was probably no area in which the parishioners exercised a more critical scrutiny over their curé than in his relations with women. His sexual purity was considered to be part and parcel of his religious holiness."[48] James Farr recently reported that accusations of sexual irregularities were a weapon used by more than one group of parishioners in their efforts to force the resignation of the resident curé.[49] Importantly, neither of the cases described by Farr had to do with concubinage. Rather, one had to do with accusations of an unrepressed libido in regard to village girls;

the other with an aged priest's dalliances with the wife of a local peasant.

In her survey of the priesthood at the end of the Old Regime, Rosie Simon-Sandras identified clerical adultery and concubinage as "crimes" of the sixteenth and seventeenth centuries.[50] In the *lettres de cachet* he studied for Upper Brittany for the eighteenth century, Charles Berthelot du Chesnay found that complaints against clerical morality had dropped to third place behind accusations of drunkenness and "bad behavior."[51] There are plenty of reasons why clerical sexual activity decreased during the eighteenth century. In this context, however, I would stress the disappearance of a sympathetic environment for this activity. The "holier than thou attitudes" of reforming priests, coupled with their determination to suppress the very rites that had made them so important in village life, made discovery of priestly hypocrisy a popular sport. As Philippe Boutry explains for the pays d'Ars, while throughout the nineteenth century only sixteen out of two thousand clerics in the region were ever accused of sexual improprieties, and the accusations were proven in only six of these cases, still "local authorities, state authorities, and eventually the anticlerical press took it upon themselves to give these incidents the widest possible publicity."[52] Post-Tridentine rural parishes no longer had a reason to cover for their priests. They did have many reasons to expose them.

Needless to say, this point applies also to the escalating conflict that first Pierre de Vaissière and then Tackett identified as developing between priests and various secular entities such as the parish board of trustees and the local seigneur.[53] The priests had to deny the recognition of a community of interest that these men demanded, where through the manipulation of ritual the priest helped regulate social tension and thereby assisted local elites in maintaining social control. The change that Hoffman discovered in the nature of litigation between priests and laymen in the late eighteenth century, where for the first time laymen began to prosecute clerics, reflects the fact that once his social value had diminished, attacking the priest was no longer out of bounds.[54]

This discussion has described the priesthood from the perspective of what it ceased to do. It is difficult to describe any positive directions in which the lower clergy evolved because it is not clear that there were any that are generalizable for the totality of the parish priest-hood for the rest of the ancien régime. Much has been written about catechisms and the priest's role in their diffusion.[55] Few priests seem to have relished the role of catechist, however, and most put the task off on someone else as soon as the situation permitted. Likewise, some historians have emphasized the role of the post-Tridentine priest as confessor and pastor. To be sure, seminaries spent a significant amount of time instructing priests in how to hear confession.[56] But it is only after 1760, after the Jesuit-Jansenist battle had extinguished the last fires of the seventeenth-century reform movement, that parish priests as spiritual directors can be said to have been anything more than pale imitators of the Jesuits and Jansenists they replaced.

Starting during the second half of the seventeenth century, the administrative role of the clergy took off, and during the eighteenth, the church and the state competed for the services of the curé as a local agent. But we should not exaggerate the amount of time it took to note births and burials. If the state had been permitted to make greater use of the parish clergy for the dissemination of its initiatives, then perhaps the curé's role as a royal agent would have made up for his withdrawal from the management of human relations. The church jealously husbanded the curé's time, however. And in the nineteenth century the state decided to develop schoolmasters as its own agents.[57]

Seminary-trained priests had a significant amount of time on their hands but not much they could do with it. In the second half of the eighteenth century, the lower secular clergy became a political force in France. One cannot help wondering whether these priests would have become so politically active if they had had more to do.

NOTES

1. From Léonard Chastenet, *La vie de Mgr. A de Solminihac,* as quoted by Jean Quéniart, *Les hommes, l'église et Dieu dans la France du XVIIIe siècle* (Paris, 1978), 43.

2. In addition to Quéniart, *Les hommes, l'église,* 41–50; see Michel Aubrun, *La paroisse en France des origines au XVe siècle* (Paris, 1986), passim; Pierre Pierrard, *Le prêtre français du Concile de Trente à nos jours* (Paris, 1986), 7–9; René Taveneaux, *Le Catholicisme dans la France classique 1610–1715,* 2 vols.

(Paris, 1980), 1:131–44; H. Roure, "Le clergé du sud-est de la France au XVIIe siècle: Ses déficiences et leurs causes," *Revue d'histoire de l'Eglise de France* 37 (1951): 153–87; Philip Hoffman, *Church and Community in the Diocese of Lyon, 1500–1789* (New Haven, 1984), 48–56; Louis Pérouas, *Les Limousins, leurs saints, leurs prêtres, du XVe au XXe siècle* (Paris, 1988), 18–30; Alphonse Jarnoux, *Le diocèse de Nantes au XVIe siècle* (Nantes, 1976), 61–64.

3. Taveneaux, *Le Catholicisme dans la France classique*, 135.

4. This list has been compiled primarily from Taveneaux, *Le Catholicisme dans la France classique*, 134–44; Quéniart, *Les hommes, l'église*, 39–50; Pérouas, *Les Limousins*, 26–30; Robert Sauzet, *Les visites pastorales dans le diocèse de Chartres pendant la première moitié du XVIIe siècle* (Rome, 1975), 130–41; Jacques Solé, "La crise morale du clergé du diocèse de Grenoble au début de l'épiscopat de Le Camus," in *Le cardinal des montagnes: Etienne Le Camus, évêque de Grenoble 1671–1707*, ed. Jean Godel (Grenoble, 1974), 179–209.

5. Taken from Taveneaux, *Le Catholicisme dans la France classique*, 1:140.

6. Solé, "La crise morale du clergé," 187–88.

7. See Steven Ozment, *The Reformation in the Cities: The Appeal of Protestantism in Sixteenth-Century Germany and Switzerland* (New Haven, 1975), 59.

8. See Louis Châtellier, *Tradition chrétienne et renouveau catholique dans le cadre de l'ancien diocèse de Strasbourg, 1650-1770* (Paris, 1981), 177.

9. "Fort injurieuse blasmant et offensant les honnestes femmes de la paroisse." Sauzet, *Les visites pastorales*, 138.

10. Ibid.

11. It could also be the case, as Binz reminds us, that reports of sexual misconduct were manufactured by laypeople in order to discredit priests. See Louis Binz, *Vie religieuse et réforme ecclésiastique dans le diocèse de Genève pendant le grande schisme et la crise conciliaire (1378–1450)*, 360–61.

12. Taveneaux, *Le Catholicisme dans la France classique*, 131–35.

13. Sauzet, *Les visites pastorales*, 134–37; 146–47; 151–54.

14. Aubrun, *La paroisse en France*, 245–50.

15. Ibid., 240–44.

16. Binz, *Vie religieuse*, 298–337.

17. Maurice Oudot de Dainville, "Une enquête dans le diocèse de Fréjus en 1546," *Revue d'histoire de l'Eglise de France* 10 (1924), especially 76–85.

18. Sauzet, *Les visites pastorales*, 131.

19. "Blood and Baptism: Kinship in Western Europe from the Fourteenth to the Seventeenth Centuries," *Studies in Church History* 10 (1973): 132. Note that in his discussion of the social role of the Sacrament of Communion in rural German Lutheran communities, David Sabean comes to essentially the same conclusion about the nature of village social relations as Bossy. See his *Power in the Blood: Popular Culture and Village Discourse in Early Modern Germany* (Cambridge, 1984), especially pp. 46 and 52. I would like to thank Lloyd Moote for bringing Sabean's work to my attention.

20. Eric Hobsbawn and Terence Ranger, eds., *The Invention of Tradition* (Cambridge, 1983), 2.

21. "De bénir le lit conjugal, de purifier les épouses relevant de couches,

de rendre compte à l'évêque des bagarres et des discordes populaires,"
Aubrun, *La paroisse en France,* 230.

22. See Taveneaux, *Le Catholicisme dans la France classique,* 137.

23. Ibid., 150. On the spread of seminaries in France, the main works are
of course Pierre Broutin, *La réforme pastorale en France au XVIIe siècle* (Paris,
1956), and Antoine Degert, *Histoire des séminaires français jusqu'à la Révolution*
(Paris, 1912). In addition, see François Lebrun, ed., *Histoire des Catholiques en
France* (Paris, 1980), 114–17 and 148–58; André Schaer, *Le clergé paroissial
catholique en Haute Alsace sous l'Ancien Régime, 1648–1789* (Paris, 1966), 105–
33; Alain Lottin, *Lille, citadelle de la Contre-Réforme (1598–1668)* (Westhoek,
1980), 98–106; Hoffman, *Church and Community,* 74–81; Timothy Tackett,
Priest and Parish in Eighteenth Century France (Princeton, 1977), 41–95.

24. Quéniart, *Les hommes, l'église,* 63.

25. Taveneaux, *Le Catholicisme dans la France classique,* 151.

26. Quéniart, *Les hommes, l'église,* 85.

27. Ibid., 65.

28. Ralph Gibson, *A Social History of French Catholicism, 1789-1914* (London, 1989), 16.

29. Hoffman, *Church and Community,* 98–138.

30. Ibid., 128. For his argument on the influence of seminaries, see pp.
74–81.

31. See A. Lynn Martin, *The Jesuit Mind: The Mentality of an Elite in Early
Modern France* (Ithaca, 1988); Louis Châtellier, *L'Europe des Dévots* (Paris,
1987).

32. Robin Briggs, "The Sins of the People: Auricular Confession and the
Imposition of Social Norms," in his *Communities of Belief: Cultural and Social
Tension in Early Modern France* (Oxford, 1989), 277–338.

33. John Bossy, *Christianity in the West 1400–1700* (Oxford, 1985), 100.

34. For examples of earlier approaches, see Tackett, *Priest and Parish,*
55–71; Dominique Julia, "Le clergé paroissial dans le diocèse de Reims à la
fin du XVIIIe siècle," *Revue d'histoire moderne et contemporaine* 13 (1966): 195–
216; Jean-Pierre Gutton, "Notes sur le recrutement du clergé séculier dans
l'archidiocèse de Lyon," *Bulletin du centre d'histoire économique et sociale de la
région Lyonnaise* (1974): 1–19.

35. Châtellier, *Tradition chrétienne,* 377. Note that families for which literacy/numeracy were presumed include those designated as having to do with
some type of administration, those in the liberal professions, merchants, and
mayors and local officials.

36. Charles Berthelot du Chesnay, *Les prêtres-séculiers en Haute Bretagne au
XVIIIe siècle* (Rennes, 1974), 108.

37. Quéniart, *Les hommes, l'église,* 73–74.

38. Hoffman, *Church and Community,* 102.

39. Châtellier, *Tradition chrétienne,* 372–87.

40. William Christian, *Local Religion in Sixteenth-Century Spain* (Princeton,
1981), 179.

41. See Alexander Murray, *Reason and Society in the Middle Ages* (Oxford, 1985), 237–51.

42. Bossy, *Christianity in the West*, 103.

43. Quéniart, *Les hommes, l'église*, 55–57.

44. Taveneaux, *Le Catholicisme dans la France classique*, 150–51.

45. See Quéniart, *Les hommes, l'église*, 93.

46. Yves-Marie Bercé, *Fête et révolte: Des mentalités populaires du XVIe au XVIIIe siècle* (Paris, 1976), especially chaps. 4 and 5.

47. Bossy, *Christianity in the West*, 65. See also note 11 above.

48. Tackett, *Priest and Parish*, 192.

49. James R. Farr, "The Power of the Holy: Reformers, Priests, and Parishioners," paper presented before the Social Science History Association Meeting, 19 October 1990. See also Farr's forthcoming book, *The Wages of Sin: Law, Morality, and Religion in Burgundy during the Catholic Reformation* (Oxford Unversity Press).

50. Rosie Simon-Sandras, *Les curés à la fin de l'Ancien Régime* (Paris, 1988), 91.

51. Berthelot du Chesnay, *Les Prêtres-séculiers*, 455.

52. "L'autorité locale, l'autorité civile et bientôt la presse anticléricale se chargent de donner à de tels événements la plus large publicité." Philippe Boutry, *Prêtres et paroisses au pays du curé d'Ars* (Paris, 1986), 227–28.

53. Pierre de Vaissière, "L'état social des curés de campagne au XVIIIe siècle, d'après la Correspondance de l'Agence du clergé aux Archives nationales," *Revue d'histoire de l'Eglise de France* 19 (1933): 24–53; Tackett, *Priest and Parish*, 170–93.

54. Hoffman, *Church and Community*, 153–55.

55. See Quéniart, *Les hommes, l'église*, 94–106; Taveneaux, *Le Catholicisme dans la France classique*, 166–89.

56. Quéniart, *Les hommes, l'église*, 56.

57. Jean-Pierre Gutton, *La sociabilité villageoise dans l'ancienne France* (Paris, 1979), 198–203.

Deep Play in the Forest: The "War of the Demoiselles" in the Ariège, 1829–31

Peter Sahlins

In May 1829, strange reports began to surface from the royal forests of the Castillonais, in the mountains of the Ariège department, along the Spanish border. Young peasant men, "dressed as women," with their faces and hands blackened and sometimes wearing elaborate masks, gathered in the forests at night to noisily expel charcoal makers and state forest guards. The Demoiselles of the Ariège (as the rioters soon came to be called) were protesting the application of the 1827 Forest Code, which severely restricted their use-rights, especially their right to pasture sheep in the royal and communal forests. They were also opposing the wealthy rural bourgeois owners of forests and ironworks, who systematically tried to restrict their rights. Drawing on festive traditions of carnival and *charivari,* popular rites used to enforce communal norms of marriage, the peasants enacted a dramatic claim to their inherited rights over the forest.[1]

Why did the peasants of the Ariège resort to such elaborate measures in their struggles to preserve their traditional rights to the forest against the state and local bourgeoisie? What, in particular, did it mean for the peasant men to disguise themselves as women? To the political and judicial authorities, as to the military officials sent in to quell the disturbances, the disguise played a dual role. On the one hand, it masked individual identities, allowing peasants to commit with impunity crimes against property and the state. On the other hand, the mask served as an "insignia" or an "emblem" of a collective enterprise, an "association" that could be prosecuted according to criminal statutes.[2] Historians of peasant culture have frequently used similar terms to interpret the significance of masking within popular

159

rebellions.[3] Yet a focus on the functions of disguise in peasant revolts cannot specify its meanings: in the war of the Demoiselles of the Ariège, the significance of the peasants disguising themselves as women was grounded less in utilitarian calculations than it was structured by a deeper, symbolic play with the cultural significance of the forest in nineteenth-century peasant society. This is not to deny the functional role of the forest within the political economy of the Ariège peasantry, nor to neglect the tactical moves of the rioters themselves in defense of their rights. Rather, I hope to suggest in this article how meaning structured function—how the meaning of the forest within local peasant culture was the condition for the possibility of both ecologically adaptive practices of forest management, and for the strategies of protest used to defend them.

The 1827 Forest Code stood in a long line of state attempts at forest management in the interests of affirming political authority, acquiring revenue, and abolishing the "disorderly" practices of local modes of forest exploitation. But unlike Colbert's Forest Ordinance of 1669, the bourgeois deputies in 1827 were especially concerned to safeguard the interests of private property against both state intervention and that "most redoubtable of dangers and the most fertile source of injury and abuses," local use-rights.[4] In denouncing these rights alongside the peasantry's destruction of forest lands, the 1827 Forest Code drew heavily on the ideology and practices of the imperial forest legislation in 1807–8, which in the Pyrenees had gone far toward securing the state's "property" over forests usurped by local communities, and toward restricting the peasantry's inherited rights to cut firewood, collect building materials, and pasture their livestock in the forests.[5]

The 1827 Forest Code forbade outright the pasturing of livestock in the forests (article 78), and gave the local communities two years to prove, in a court of law, their other use-rights to royal forests (article 61). Further provisions installed a costly and burdensome tutelage on the local communities, requiring them to place bells on all their flocks and refusing them the right to take the smallest branches from the forests without the authorization of the local forest guards (article 79), a practice that included the obtaining of firewood (article 81) and construction materials (article 84).[6] The code represented a concerted attempt to eliminate local management of royal and communal forests, while it actively encouraged the practices of leasing state forest lands to wealthy owners of ironworks who needed vast quantities of wood to make charcoal.

The code and accompanying ordinance strengthened the authority of state forest guards to execute its provisions. In the first half of the nineteenth century, these local guards—outsiders of the village communities where they were stationed—had terrorized the communities with their arbitrary and venal enforcement of state laws, practices that only increased with the new provisions of the code.[7] Collective resistance to these guards, as well as to charcoal makers in the employ of ironworks owners, often punctuated the first three decades of the nineteenth century. Most confrontations erupted in direct response to forest guards' seizures of illegally pastured herds in the forests. Men and women from the neighboring hamlets and villages rallied to the site and, armed with hatchets, sticks, or scythes, chased the guards off with threats of murder and mutilation.[8] But in May 1829, only men participated actively in the uprising, and they appeared in the forests at night "disguised as women."

Disguising as women was the focal element in a highly ritualized and dramatized encounter between the peasants and their enemies.[9] Their enemies were the forest guards, charcoal makers, and anyone who supported those groups (from innkeepers who housed them to the clergy who preached submission from the pulpit). The aim of the peasants was to expel the guards and charcoal makers from the forests. In loosely organized groups, ranging from a half-dozen to several hundred rioters, the male peasants appeared at night at the houses of the guards or the cabins of the charcoal makers. With great fanfare, the peasants menaced their enemies with threats of certain death, chasing them out of the forests, and frequently pillaging their belongings. The peasant rioters, for the most part younger men, drew specifically on the gestural and verbal codes associated with *charivari* or "rough music"—the discordant noise, invective, and derision used traditionally to punish marital transgressions. Solidly backed by members of the village communities, including women, the rioters enacted a popular judgment of their enemies.

Throughout the protest, the peasants were said to don feminine disguises. Yet technically speaking, the peasants were not "dressed as women" at all. "The disguise consists only in blackening the face," reported the prefect, "wearing a white shirt outside the clothes instead of leaving it tucked in, tightening the waist with a colored band, which gives the shirt the impression of a skirt."[10] There was as much variation in the headpieces as there was consistency in the uniform: on their heads the peasants wore sheepskins, pig bristles, "a false face made of cardboard left over from the carnival festivities," handkerchiefs, woolen bonnets, an old sieve, a woman's headpiece, and other improvised masks. Frequently, the peasants joined the insignia and language of the masculine military world to their feminine self-representation. As the protest was extended in space and time, "captains," "lieutenants," and "generals," proliferated, as did the signs and symbols of military culture. In their anonymous writings, the Demoiselles identified their organization in military terms—"regiments" and "troops"—and decorated their "uniforms" with military insignia. The effect was to create a powerful disjunctive image of women at war— the "War of the Demoiselles."[11]

If the peasants were seeking merely to hide their individual identities, they might have done much better. For the masks too frequently failed to cover up the identities of their bearers: "They were so little disguised," testified a charcoal maker about the Demoiselles at Saint Lary, "that someone from around here would easily have recognized them," a comment frequently reiterated by those who came close to the rioters.[12] And if they had merely wanted to express a solidarity among themselves, uniting the otherwise parochial and contentious villages of the mountain in a common front,[13] the rioters might have chosen any number of available signs or emblems—such as sheepskins—rather than necessarily representing themselves as women.

Natalie Davis has pointed to the feminine disguise of the Demoiselles rioters as evidence of how sexual inversion, drawing on the image of the unruly and disorderly woman, could be used by men to "defend the community's interests and standards, and to tell the truth about unjust rule."[14] One of the central insights in her work is an appreciation of the subversive functions that the world upside down might play. With the help of the Russian literary critic Mikhail Bakhtin and the American anthropologist Victor Turner, Davis turned the Englishman Max Gluckman on his head, along with the structural-functionalist paradigms of the 1950s, by demonstrating how sexual license could be used to criticize and subvert the social order, instead of merely affirming its formal hierarchies. In "Women on Top," Davis explored the cultural traditions that attributed disorderly qualities to women in their positions of structural inferiority and exclusion. Men drew on the perceived sexual power and energy of women to legitimate their resistance to the social and political order.

Yet in the case of the Demoiselles, it is possible to turn this formulation on *its* head. In the Ariège, as throughout the central and western Pyrenees where the feminine disguise not infrequently made its appearance in forest riots,[15] women had traditionally been able to act in public positions of authority. The peasant communities of the ancien régime that came to form the Ariège department had practiced a strict form of primogeniture, which valued the integrity of the household (the *casa*) over the specific sex of the household head (*cap de casa*). The result was that households were not infrequently headed by women, who held that right not simply as widows but as legitimate heirs with public responsibilites and privileges as local citizens, or neighbors (*bezi*). Such rights were recognized in the customary law codes of certain Pyrenean regions—such as Barèges, Labourde, Soule, and the Basque country—written down in the sixteenth and seventeenth centuries.[16] More detailed research is needed to describe the actual roles of women household heads in village public life under the ancien régime, but it is clear that as a function of customary inheritance laws, women could be empowered in the public domain of village life to a much greater extent than elsewhere in European peasant society. Moreover, within the household itself, French peasant women may have been better off than suggested by aristocratic and clerical misogynistic beliefs and practices. Recent reevaluations of the power of French peasant women in the domestic sphere, relying on interpretations of proverbs and contemporary ethnographic research, have usefully corrected the ideology of male domination with a more balanced appraisal of the reciprocal power relations in the household between wives and husbands, if not the hidden domination of the former.[17] It could thus be argued that peasant women in the Pyrenees during the centuries before the "war of the Demoiselles" were, relatively speaking, already empowered.

That "traditional" condition began to change in the central Pyrenees well before the French Revolution, when the monarchy—imposing the primacy of masculinity over primogeniture—intervened systematically in marriage and family practices at the expense of customary law.[18] Yet it was the state's unifying and centralizing revision of inheritance laws during the Revolution and under Napoleon, culminating in the Civil Code of 1804, which subjected women to patrilineal authority, and severely devalued their public status.[19] While peasant families throughout the Pyrenees evolved a set of marriage and inheritance strategies to subvert the legal order of bourgeois society in the interests of preserving the integrity of the household,[20] they were ultimately forced to comply with a legal order in which women were subordinated in civic and political life.

Like many peasant uprisings of the early modern period, the revolt of the Demoiselles, in its opposition to the twin forces of state building and capitalism, posited a return to a mythic past, a golden age of autonomy and freedom.[21] The peasants sought to restore a world of liberties and practices "passed on to us from our ancestors which we could not change without altering our existence and making life impossible," as the inhabitants of Prade claimed in a petition of 1841.[22] Part of the male peasants' self-representation as women in 1829 may have involved an invocation of a golden age in which women had held greater power and authority than in the present; after all, the same agency that took away the authority of women (the state) also usurped the peasant community's inherited rights to the forest.[23] Male peasants used the image of women to sanction their disobedience less, perhaps, because it signified the disorderly and unruly present condition of women than because it evoked their past power.

Hypotheses about the *uses* of the image of women could thus be turned over endlessly: men disguised themselves as women because women represented weakness and disorder, or they adopted a feminine persona as part of a claim about the past strength and authority of women. Not only do such explanations of functions yield contradictory interpretations, but they fail to disclose the meaning of the disguise as constituted within a broader idiom of gender, one that included the object of the peasantry's claim—the forests. To escape the functionalist impasse, I would like to shift the terms of interpretation, and to suggest that the peasant rioters, in adopting a feminine "disguise" to defend their relation to the forests, made reference in multiple ways to the feminine qualities of the forest itself.

In some notes on the cultural categories in the West that preceded our modern notions of "matter," the anthropologist Marcel Mauss drew on a line of early anthropological thought that linked the forest to conceptions of female power.[24] The Latin *silva*, on which Mauss wrote, designated the totality of forest lands under exploitation, whether as brush, forest, or pasture; in nineteenth-century Languedoc, *silva* was the name given to the forest lands as a whole. For Mauss, "*Silva* is the germinative power conceived as feminine, it is the forest. In this idea of forest there is ... something undisciplined, savage, and dangerous, but also animative, and receptive."[25] The dangerous but germinative qualities of the feminine forest in peasant culture were stated calendrically within the rituals of planting the "May trees" (*arbres de mai* or *mais*), which linked feminine fertility to the vegetative cycle.[26] But the feminine character of the forest was also stated more prosaically in the gendered ordering of the peasant political economy—in the forest's place in relation to agriculture and stock raising.

The forest provided essential products for the peasant livelihood, including firewood and building materials. But it was inherently destructive, the enemy of both arable lands below and of pasture above. Periodically, in the interests of livestock raising and cultivation of lands (linked by the importance of manure as the unique fertilizer used in agriculture), the forest had to be burnt back. This was the practice of clearing (*défrichage*) by fire.[27] Mauss noted the homologous qualities of fire and forest: both were at once dangerous and destructive, but also germinative and fertilizing. To reproduce itself, the forest needed fire. In the Ariège Pyrenees, where low-altitude clouds and fog gave to the medium elevations a generally fertile character, around and in the forest grew a great quantity of underbrush. Burning the forests thinned the trees, and the ashes of burnt wood fertilized the forests themselves, returning nutrients to the soil. The forest was thus an "obstacle," but it was also a necessary condition of productive life itself.[28]

Preserving the forests' ambivalent status within the local political economy, peasants exploited the forest according to a logic of production that recognized the "disorderly" and feminine qualities of the forest—and found itself at odds with the ordered, masculine rationality of state forest management. This local practice was known as "gardening" (*jardinage*), a name derived from the exclusively feminine work in the household garden.[29] Gardening in the forest was an adaptive technique linked to a profound knowledge of the environment and the generative cycles of the forests' reproduction as well as to a specified system of needs, especially the need to keep livestock.[30] In the largely beech forests—a slow-maturing hardwood that reproduced by shoots—gardening was a technique of letting forest growths reach their productive maturity, a relatively long cycle (sixty years). When the beech matured, shoots of the largest diameter from each trunk would be "gardened" by (male) peasants for use as firewood, building materials, and agricultural tools. The eco-logic to the system lay in the fact that the shoots would be thinned, and the larger of the uncut shoots would protect the newest growths from the deadening weight of the mountain snows and the teeth of pasturing animals.

In addition to allowing the forest to reproduce, the techniques of "gardening" provided the necessary condition for the fertility of arable land. In the largely infertile lands on the mountainside, with grain yields of less than 3 to 1, dung was an essential fertilizer. By gardening in the forests, peasants were able to maintain a large number of livestock, which they pastured in the forest in spring, before the summer pastures were clear, and for which the forests provided essential protection and sanctuary during summer storms. Hence the importance of local pasturing rights in the forest, rights which the forest administration consistently opposed.

Starting from the earliest attempts at state forest management in the fifteenth century, and continuing through to the time when the modern forest administration was created in 1827, the state considered *jardinage* to be a chaotic, disorderly, and intrinsically destructive way of exploiting the forest, and it was universally condemned. Etienne Dralet, the dominant legislator and ideologue of the modern French forest administration, decried in the early nineteenth century "this disastrous *jardinage*," and vehemently sought its prohibition.[31] In place of this "disorder," Dralet proposed—as had his predecessors—the regularized and rationalized "management" (*aménagement*) of forest lands. Without such "management," according to a printed instruction of 1828, "there is only disorder and confusion."[32] In place of gardening, the state called for the clear-cutting of areas, called *tire-aire* (with its sixteenth-century meaning of "arranged areas"). Certain growths were restricted from all usage, while others were divided into multiple areas of exploitation (*coupes*), which were either turned over to the local inhabitants for firewood and building material (but not pasturing) or leased to ironworks owners for making charcoal. "Forest lands must be exploited by *tire-aire*," wrote Dralet, "so that the growth is regular and easy to guard."

Despite the state's condemnation of forest "gardening" in the early nineteenth century, many sympathetic observers, including some forest administration personnel, recognized that in areas of abundant snowfall and steep slopes, gardening made more sense than exploitation by *tire-aire*. Not only would the forest reproduce itself more productively, but the local communities would thereby retain their necessary pasturing rights in the forest.[33] In his later writings, Dralet came to recognize the value and efficacy of *jardinage*, and within a century, French forest management sanctioned a modified version of the peasant technique.[34] But in 1829, the peasants had to fight to preserve their mode of production and their conception of a feminine forest with its "disorderly," dangerous, but germinative attributes.

In the late eighteenth century and throughout the nineteenth century, the practice of *jardinage* had been abused, and the delicate ecological balance of pasture, forest, and arable land had been put into question.[35] It was threatened from above, as the forest administration came to insist on the abolition of gardening, seeing this technique only as one of "devastation." It was threatened from below, as the system fell apart under extraordinary demographic pressure and due to a decreasing ability of village councils to enforce their authority over communal management of the forests.[36] Finally, the system broke down from an exhaustion of ecological resources: as Dralet himself estimated, one forge required 1,620 hectares of wood per year, and the "avarice" and "greed" with which the bourgeois owners of the more than forty-five ironworks in the Ariège destroyed both private and state forests had left the peasant communities with little for their own needs by the time of the 1827 Forest Code.[37] But if the system lost its effectiveness, it did not lose its cultural logic. The forest was a living feminine being, and the (male) peasants had to "master" (the word is from that time) the forest in ways that harnessed its disorderly and productive qualities.

The feminine attributes of the forest thus found expression within the practices and techniques of production in the forest, and the place of the forest, at once symbolic and practical, within the cyclical reproduction of the peasantry's agro-pastoral way of life. But the feminine qualities of the forest had a more obvious expression in the world of legend and myth, the supernatural world of the forest's numinous inhabitants.

The Demoiselles—by virtue of their disguise, the time and location of their appearances, their volatile relations with the guards, and their unflinching defense of conceptions of justice—parallel accounts of a class of supernatural, anthropomorphized beings of the forest: the fairies. Fairy beliefs have a long and complex history in western European culture. Since the medieval period, these rustic beliefs have been variously identified with the "fates," with the spirits of the ancestral dead, and with non-Christian or pagan ancestors,[38] even as literary cultures of medieval and early modern Europe consistently appropriated, while redefining, the significance of fairies.[39] Fairy beliefs were still strong in rural Europe in the late nineteenth and twentieth centuries, when folklorists were able to inscribe them with greater specificity. For the villages of the Ariège, where the Demoiselles had made their appearances, detailed ethnographic accounts of stories and legends were collected in the 1940s and 1950s.[40]

In these nineteenth- and twentieth-century accounts, fairies were called, throughout southern France, *demoiselles* or *dames blanches,* and in the Ariège, *hadas* or *encantadas.* These supernatural feminine beings lived in grottoes and caves and, more generally, in the forests— they were the permanent inhabitants of the sites where the peasant rioters played out their struggles. They invariably wore white cloth, sometimes specified as linen—the same material used in the shirts of the peasant men in Ariège. The variation in their headdresses was as great as that of the masks of the Demoiselles themselves, although the fairies generally wore only flora. And like most of the rioters, the fairies appeared only at night, frequently around midnight.

Much of their purported power was linked to fertility and reproduction, both natural and human. In many accounts, the fairies were identified with a mythical period of the forests' greatest extension and fertility, and, associated with running water, were seen from a distance around the streams, rivers, and water sources of the mountain communities. The Demoiselles had also gathered "at the bridge of Hioulat, where several rivers form a junction" in May 1829, and in July 1829, the Demoiselles of Fougaron warned the mayor that "he will meet his end at the fountain of Sallen" in the Saleich forest if he continued to accept the complaints that the forest guards lodged against the rioters.[41] Where the Demoiselles concerned themselves with the social "fertility" of the village communities, the fairies were literally identified with rain, given certain powers over the natural growth of vegetation, and could claim responsibility for human fertility as well. In the Pyrenees, their grottoes and sources were sometimes linked to fertility rites, practiced as recently as the 1950s, while elsewhere in rural France, the fairies were identified with a class of women who held social and ritual functions centering around the birth of children and the preparation of the dead for burial.[42] In both their mythic and their social representations, the fairies were closely linked to the process of washing: in the legends, they were invariably seen washing (with golden washboards) their (white) clothes, while ritually, the "women who help" (*femmes-qui-aide*) were responsible for washing the newborn and the recently deceased as well as for the annual "Great Wash" in the village, "as much a grand material-scouring as a generalized and symbolic whitening of spirits, of souls, of seasons, the timing of which within the calendar was not arbitrary."[43] It is perhaps not insignificant that the Demoiselles of Massat claimed that they intended "to wash" (*laver*) the forest guards who entered the forest.

With male peasants, the fairies entertained ambivalent relations. For one they were rarely seen up close: "here at one point, there at another, such that one can never get near to recognize any of them," wrote the subprefect in 1829 about the Demoiselles, anticipating later descriptions by peasants of the fairies' appearance. Men could make an appeal to their beneficent powers, but more often the fairies acted vindictively, punishing human offenses, with a developed sense of justice. Attacks on their persons and especially their properties—their golden washboard—brought swift and retributive justice. This sense of justice was shared by the peasant rioters, who claimed only to be restoring the peasant communities to their own, inherited possessions and source of livelihood, the forests.

In many of the tales recorded by Joisten, the peasant men attempted with high levels of success to possess the fairies in marriage, attracted by their gold fortunes or great beauty. The marriage was consummated and remained fertile (the household lands, productive) as long as the husband did not mention that his wife was a fairy. As soon as the words were spoken, generally in anger, the fairy disappeared from sight—a dimension of the tales that recalls the "secret" or "incomprehensible" language that the guards and charcoal makers reported was used by the rioters. In the tales, the fairies nonetheless remained around the household, leaving their marks in the linen cabinets—like the Demoiselles who sometimes ransacked these cabinets as part of their nocturnal visits to the cabins of forest guards.

Everything happened as if, to invoke the structuralist incantation, the peasant rioters in 1829 modeled their actions on the notions of retributive justice and supernatural power of the fairies of the forest. More generally, the peasant men of the Ariège identified with the forest *herself*, representing themselves and acting in accordance with the unruly and disorderly character of the feminine forest. As fairies of the forest, the Demoiselles protected their habitat against the thefts and assaults by the forest guards and charcoal makers. As representations of the disorderly forest, the rioters took on a feminine identity in their struggles against the usurpers.

But if the rioters represented themselves in female disguise, they also retained their identity as young men, as evidenced in the elaborate military symbolism that formed part of their "disguise." As young men, the rioters undertook an extensive *charivari* against the mismatched marriage of forest guards and the forest. The forest belonged to the peasants; they were married to it. But by the time of the 1827 Forest Code, the forest had been forced to marry another. The Demoiselles themselves did not use the marital metaphor, although they did argue that the forest had been "usurped by the guards," and they did claim to take over the role of the guards themselves.[44] In the structuring idiom of their relation to the forest, the male peasants sought to restore their proper role as husbands, and they thereby treated the guards and charcoal burners as cuckolds. The guards were publicly shamed and humiliated, obstructed in the fulfillment of their duties, and unable to take possession of their legally constituted spouse, the forest. When the elaborate *charivari* failed, in a frustrated "act of impossible love," the peasants burned the forests rather than see them possessed by another.[45]

The ambivalence of the disguise in the "War of the Demoiselles," containing both masculine and feminine symbolism, is thus rendered intelligible as part of the male peasantry's simultaneous identification with the forest and its marriage to it. The male peasants who undertook to defend their inherited rights to the forest were only partially "disguised as women": they remained at the same time young peasant men. The disguise was purposely ambivalent—and only with ambivalence were the identities of the peasants actually masked. The peasant community's dramatization of its project to exclude the forest guards and charcoal makers from the forest was done with several audiences in mind—the peasants themselves, the peasants' enemies, and the political and military authorities—and its form was conceived not from a logic of utilitarian calculation but as part of a deeper play with the image of the forest in local peasant culture.

Clifford Geertz borrowed Jeremy Bentham's concept of *deep play* to suggest the symbolic pursuits that underlay the apparently irrational (from a utilitarian standpoint) betting patterns at a Balinese cockfight.[46] I invoke the notion here to bring out the cultural framework of the Ariège peasantry's relation to the forest and the peasants' strategic defense of their inherited rights. The idea of the Demoiselles' revolt as a dramatic game in which the stakes and strategies were defined in terms of cultural values (possession of a feminine forest), which themselves structured issues of marginal utility (defense of pasturing rights), can add to an appreciation of the trees "from the natives' point of view" while not losing sight of the forest from the perspective of bourgeois political economy.

Yet I do not wish to suggest that the Ariège peasants were so completely enclosed in their own cultural logic and interpretations that they ignored both other possible strategies to oppose the state, or the wider political context of the revolt itself. For if the revolt of the Demoiselles was deep play in the forests of the Ariège, it also took place within a wider political upheaval in France surrounding the July Revolution of 1830, a Parisian affair that nonetheless transformed the language of revolt in the forests of the Ariège.[47]

The initial appearance of the disguise as women in the "War of the Demoiselles" was linked to the metaphoric expression of an identity between the peasant rioters and the forests. This deep play in the forests was loosely tied to the festive calendar: from May 1829 through the spring of 1830 the disguise had received its greatest elaboration as part of the festive season, which traditionally ran from Carnival through May and the summer patron saint festivals. Following a logic of seasonal festivity, the disguise, like the rioting itself, was relatively absent from August to December of 1829. But August 1830 proved different.

For the peasants of the Ariège, the news of the July Revolution led to a transformation in the language and goals of the uprising. "The Demoiselles are now unmasked and show themselves entirely uncovered," wrote General Lafitte to the war minister on 22 August 1830.[48] The language of "liberty" came to legitimate the actions of the rioting peasants, as they stepped up their attacks on the properties of iron-works and forest owners in the department. As stated in a letter to M. Ferreras, proprietor of the Esqueranne ironworks at Saurat, dated 20 October 1830, "The head of the regiment of Demoiselles has the honor to inform you that the ironworks which are close to the forest should be entirely destroyed and yours is one of them. *Vive la liberté.*"[49]

"The latest events," wrote the interior minister to the war minister, "have made them believe easily that liberty is liberation from the laws." Other officials were to comment on this "confusion" over the meaning of liberty in 1830, noting how the peasants thought that it meant "license" to do as they pleased.[50] But in fact, the July Revolution brought a different language of protest to the fore—a language and tradition of revolutionary self-determination. To the peasants of the Ariège, "liberty" meant "liberties," the recovery of their ancient rights and privileges to the forests, which was what 1789 had meant to them. The temporary absence of constituted authorities led them to "make themselves masters" of the public forests, and—following the examples of 1792—attack the *châteaux* of rich private forest own-ers.[51] The 1830 Revolution created for the Ariège peasantry the po-litical space in which the disguise as women was no longer the deter-mining idiom of protest—in which the mask was no longer useful. But in January 1831, as the revolutionary moment receded and the cycle of carnival festivities began, the Demoiselles reappeared in the forests of the Ariège. That spring, the state conceded: In February, March, and April 1831, the peasants secured a series of royal ordi-nances that permitted the pasturing of sheep in the forests, urged "leniency" in the application of the forest code, and gave amnesty for all past "crimes and transgressions." In the Ariège, deep play in the forests not only expressed the cultural values at the core of a political economy, it was also an effective strategy of protest.

NOTES

Thanks to Susanna Barrows, Marjorie Beale, Robin Einhorn, Tom Laqueur, Leslie Kauffman, and Irv Scheiner for their helpful criticisms of an earlier draft.

1. Useful general accounts of the "War of the *Demoiselles*" include J. Merriman, "The *Demoiselles* of the Ariège," in *1830 in France,* ed. J. Merriman (New York, 1975), 87–118; R. Dupont, *La guerre des Demoiselles dans les forêts de l'Ariège (1829–1831)* (Toulouse, 1933); and L. Clarenc, "Le code de 1827 et les troubles forestiers dans les Pyrénées centrales au milieu du XIXe siècle," *Annales du Midi* 77 (1965): 293–317.

2. The official records of the rioting spelled out these functions in this language; see, for example, the prefect's decree of 28 February 1830 in Archives Départementales de l'Ariège (hereafter, ADA) 7P 10.

3. For example, Y. M. Bercé, *Fête et révolte* (Paris, 1976), 82–86; E. P. Thompson, *Whigs and Hunters: The Origin of the Black Act* (London, 1975), 57–58 and 64; and Merriman, "The *Demoiselles* of the Ariège," 96. A continued insistence on the functional role of masking persists, I shall argue, even within interpretations that, following Natalie Davis, focus on the feminine symbolism of the disguise.

4. Archives Nationales (hereafter, AN) C*1 232 (Chamber of Deputies report, 26 December 1826); see P. Chevalier, "Le vote du Code forestier de 1827 et ses implications politiques," in *Actes du colloque de Lyon de l'association française des historiens des idées politiques* (Lyons, 1985), 73–84. On Colbert's 1669 ordinance, see *Les eaux et forêts du 12e au 20e siècle* (Paris, 1987), especially 131–64. Detailed descriptions of the conditions of the forests that were to make up the department of the Ariège, and the extremely limited and tolerant application of the ordinance by Louis de Froidour, can be found in ADA 2B 31, fols. 739–65 (*maîtrise* of Pamiers, 6 May 1670); and M. Durant-Barthez, "La maîtrise des eaux et forêts de Comminges avant 1789," (Thèse, Ecole Nationale de Chartes, 1937).

5. For the efforts of Etienne Dralet, administrator and theoretician of the imperial reformation, and his description of the forests in the Ariège, see Archive Départementale de l'Haute-Garonne (hereafter, ADHG) P 334 (Saint-Gaudens, 1807) and P 335 (Saint-Girons, 1808). Much of this material was incorporated into Dralet's *Description des Pyrénées,* 2 vols. (Paris, 1813). For a good discussion of the vexed problem of measuring the ownership, acreage, and condition of the mid-nineteenth-century Ariège forests, see M. Chevalier, *La vie humaine dans les Pyrénées ariègeoises* (Paris, 1956), 496–518.

6. M. Brousse, *Le Code forestier (1827) avec l'exposé des motifs, la discussion des deux chambres . . .* (Paris, 1827).

7. ADA 7P 11, Report of the Commission of Inquiry, 23–27 October 1830.

8. Examples include the *émeutes* in Oust during May 1806 (ADA 4U 16), in Boussenac in August 1820 (ADA 3U 40), and in la Barguillere during August of 1828 (ADA 3U 56). On forest riots and forms of peasant resistance during the early nineteenth century, see J. F. Soulet, *Les Pyrénées au XIXe siècle,* 2 vols. (Toulouse, 1987), 2:471–641.

9. The ritual and symbolic ("folkloric") dimensions of the protest have been well documented by F. Baby, *La guerre des Demoiselles en Ariège, 1829–1872* (Ariège, Montbel, 1972); see also P. Sahlins, "Rites of Revolt: The War

of the *Demoiselles* in Ariège, France (1829–1867)" (Honors Thesis, Harvard College, 1979).

10. ADA 7P 9, prefect to interior minister, 30 May 1829.

11. The extant letters and warnings of the Demoiselles are reproduced in Baby, *La guerre des Demoiselles*, 199–206, who also discusses the elaboration of military symbolism: 100 and passim.

12. ADA 3U 6, "Affair Saint-Lary," Interrogation, 6 April 1830, witness no. 5.

13. The village communities of the mountain districts were differentiated linguistically and culturally (Baby, *La guerre des Demoiselles*, 93–94); in the 1820s, they were largely endogamous, as approximately 90 percent of all marriage partners were drawn from the village itself (ADA, Etat Civil); and the antagonism among communities over disputed pastures and forests have been documented (see, for example, Chevalier, *La vie humaine*, 363–85). The unity among villages across the department was an explicit element of the Demoiselles' claims in April 1830: see, for example, ADA 7P 11, mayor of Rivernet to Sr. Trinqué, 5 April 1830.

14. Natalie Davis, "Women on Top," in *Society and Culture in Early Modern France*, 149–50.

15. Soulet (*Les Pyrénées au XIXe siècle*, 2:585–615) notes several cases in which the disguise as women formed an element within forest riots—in Castelloubon (Hautes-Pyrénées) in 1818; the Ossau valley in 1743; and Sainte-Marie d'Oloron (Pyrénées-Atlantiques) in 1767. He argues convincingly that in other respects as well, the revolt of the Demoiselles was a representative, if the most elaborate and dramatic, example of a forest revolt in the Pyrenees.

16. J. Poumarède, *Les successions dans le Sud-Ouest de la France au moyen âge* (Paris, 1972), especially part 2, where he argues that "coming up from the plain, the principle of masculinity penetrated only slowly in the mountainous zones made more conservative from their isolation"; J. F. Soulet, *La vie quotidienne dans les Pyrénées sous l'Ancien Régime du XVIe au XVIIIe siècle* (Paris, 1974), 219–29, offers some general descriptions of women in Pyrenean peasant society. For recent popularizations of the exceptional status of women in the Pyrenees, see Ph. de Latour, "D'un ancien féminisme du côté des Pyrénées et d'un anti-féminisme venu d'ailleurs," *Revue de Comminges, Pyrénées Centrales* 12 (1979); and I. Gratacos, *Fées et gestes. Femmes pyrénéennes: Un status social exceptionnel en Europe* (Toulouse, 1987).

17. M. Segalen, *Love and Power in the Peasant Family: Rural France in the Nineteenth Century*, trans. S. Matthews (Chicago, 1983); and S. Rogers, "Female Forms of Power and the Myth of Male Dominance: A Model of Female/Male Interaction in Peasant Society," *American Ethnologist* 2 (1975): 727–56.

18. Soulet, *La vie quotidienne*, 226–29; J. F. Traer, *Marriage and the Family in Eighteenth-Century France* (Cornell, 1980), 22–47.

19. Traer, *Marriage and the Family*, especially 166–91.

20. See, for example, R. Bonnain, "Droit écrit, coutume pyrénéenne, et pratiques successorales dans les Baronnies, 1769–1836," in *Les Baronnies des*

Pyrénées, vol. 2: *Maisons, espace, famille* (Paris, 1986), 157–77; and P. Bourdieu, "Les stratégies matrimoniales," *Annales* 27 (1972): 1025–1127.

21. Y. M. Bercé, *Revolt and Revolution in Early Modern Europe. An Essay on the History of Political Violence*, trans. J. Bergin (New York, 1987), 24–28.

22. Quoted in Chevalier, *La vie humaine*, 381. This attachment of peasant society to its past was widely decried by political officials in the nineteenth century: see, for example, AN F 20 164 ("Statistique du département de l'Ariège" by Prefect Brun, 1806).

23. Soulet, *La vie quotidienne*, 226–27, cites a folksong from the late eighteenth century that records the resentment in the Lavedanese valleys following the reform of customary inheritance laws in 1769: "All is suffering / in all the houses / especially of the heiresses / The King be damned / who has made the law / Against the heiresses" (my translation).

24. Marcel Mauss, "Conceptions qui ont précéde la notion de matière" (1939), in *Oeuvres*, ed. V. Karady, 2 vols. (Paris, 1968): 2:161–68. More recently, see C. Merchant, *The Death of Nature: Women, Ecology, and the Scientific Revolution* (New York, 1989), especially 1–41, for a discussion of the feminine attributes of the natural world in pre-seventeenth-century European intellectual traditions; and K. Thomas, *Man and the Natural World: Changing Attitudes in England, 1500–1800* (London, 1983), especially 192–223, referring to the "disorderly" and "savage" attributes of forests in early modern England. For similar attributes of the *silva* in Picard folk culture, see also M. Crampon, "Le culte de l'arbre et de la forêt: essai sur le folklore picard," *Mémoires de la société des antiquaires de Picardie* 46 (1936): 414 et seq.

25. Mauss, "Conceptions," 163.

26. On the *mais*, see for example Arnold Van Gennep, *Manuel de folklore français contemporain*, 4 vols. (Paris, 1943–46), vol. 1, pt. 4:1519 et seq.; and Fabre and Lacroix, *La vie quotidienne*, 222–27.

27. Chevalier, *La vie humaine*, 135–42; H. Cavailles, *La vie pastorale et agricole dans les Pyrénées des Gaves, de l'Adour, et des Nestes* (Paris, 1931), 49–51; and H. Gaussen, "La question forestière aux Pyrénées," *Revue géographique des Pyrénées et du Sud-Ouest* 8 (1937): 206.

28. Mauss, "Conceptions," 163.

29. On household gardening and the garden as a privileged site for women, see Fabre and Lacroix, *La vie quotidienne*, 172–73; Segalen, *Love and Power in the Peasant Family*, 43, 93; and F. Zonabend, *La mémoire longue: Temps et histoire au village* (Paris, 1980), 47–66.

30. The technique of *jardinage* is described in A. Campagne, *Les forêts pyrénéennes* (Luchon, 1912), 104–10; E. Dralet, *Traité du hêtre* (Toulouse, 1824), 110–16; Latour de Saint-Ybars, *De la question forestière en Ariège* (Toulouse, 1849), 12–13, and an unpublished response to this pamphlet by a forest guard in 1849 (ADA 7P 11).

31. Dralet, *Description des Pyrénées*, passim.

32. ADA 7P 1, no. 6: "Instruction sur les aménagements," 1828.

33. ADA 7P 11 (mayor of Cabannes to Forest Commission, 1830); ADA

12M 97 (1819) (memoir of a forest guard); ADHG P 381 (memoir of the justice of the peace of Aix to the forest administration, 27 April 1820).

34. Dralet, *Traité du hêtre*, 113–16; Campagne, *Les forêts pyrénéennes*, 108; J. Salvador, "L'aménagement et l'exploitation des forêts pyrénéennes," *Revue géographique des Pyrénées et du Sud-Ouest* 1 (1930): 58–71.

35. On the local administration of the forest and pastoral economy, "a reservoir of rules organized with a profound knowledge, acquired at the cost of historical essays of the possibilities of the environment," see Chevalier, *La vie humaine*, 375–84; and the descriptions sent to Dralet in 1815 (ADHG P 382/1, 30 June 1815).

36. For example, ADA 1J 378 (Village council of Alzen on its inability to enforce restrictions on forest usage against abuses both of its own inhabitants and neighboring villages, November 1786).

37. ADHG P 334: "Notice sur les mines et forges," by Dralet (1807); see also Archives de l'armée de la terre (hereafter, AAT) Mémoires et reconnaissances 1224, nos. 42–43 (22 February 1828); and the comments in ADA 12M 97, subprefect Saint Girons to Prefect, 1 September 1819; see J. Bonhote, "La destruction des forêts par les forges à la catalane en Ariège: problèmes de méthodes et sources," in *Lettre d'information, Institut d'histoire moderne et contemporaine*, no. 11 (1987): 31–35.

38. On the medieval period, see A. Maury, *Croyances et légendes du moyen âge* (Paris, 1896), who saw the fairies as the last vestige of paganism; and more recently, L. Harf-Lancner, *Les fées au moyen âge: Morgane et Mélusine: La naissance des fées* (Paris, 1984), especially 11–78. On the links of the fairy world to the powers of the ancestral dead, see A. Varagnac, *Civilization traditionelle et genres de vie* (Paris, 1948), passim.

39. L. Harf-Lancner, *Les fées au moyen âge*, passim; J. Le Goff and E. Le Roy Ladurie, "Mélusine maternelle et défricheuse," *Annales: économies, sociétés, civilisations* 26 (1971): 587–622; for the English case, see the work of K. M. Briggs, especially *The Fairies in Tradition and Literature* (London, 1967), and K. Thomas, *Religion and the Decline of Magic* (London, 1971), 606–14.

40. Classical folkloric sources include P. Sébillot, *Folklore de France*, 7 vols. (Paris, 1904–7), 3:253 et seq.; and "Légendes des forêts de France," *Revue des traditions populaires* 13 (1898): 656–61 et seq.; Laisnel de la Salle, *Croyances et legendes du centre de la France* (Paris, 1875), 99–125; see also H. Dontenville, *Histoire et géographie mythique de la France* (Paris, 1948), 165–200. For the Ariège, see C. Joisten, "Les Etres fantastiques dans le folklore de l'Ariège," *Via Domitia IX* (1962); and Gratacos, *Fées et gestes*, especially 25–75.

41. ADA 7P 9, district attorney (Saint-Gaudens) to minister of justice, 26 July 1829.

42. Y. Verdier, *Façons de dire, façons de faire. La laveuse, la couturière, la cuisinière* (Paris, 1979), 83–155.

43. Ibid., 122–35.

44. ADA 7P 11, letter of "Madame Laporte, Capitaine des Demoiselles," 1 April 1830.

45. Baby, *La guerre des Demoiselles*, 137.

46. C. Geertz, "Notes on the Balinese Cockfight," in *The Interpretation of Cultures* (New York, 1973), 412–53.

47. The best general account of the July Revolution remains D. Pinckney, *The French Revolution of 1830* (Princeton, 1972); see also R. Price, "Popular Disturbances in the French Provinces after the July Revolution," in *European Studies Review* 1 (1971): 323–50; and, for the Ariège, Merriman, "The *Demoiselles* of the Ariège," passim.

48. AAT E(5) 1.

49. ADA 7P 11: mayor of Aurat to the provisional administration, 21 August 1830.

50. AAT E(5) 2; "The liberty that His Majesty Philip I has just given to the French Nation has been badly interpreted by our mountain peasants, since they see themselves authorized to violate laws while throwing themselves without brakes into all the disorders which could be committed against the forest administration," ADA 7P 11: mayor of Parjole to Prefect, 13 September 1830.

51. ADA 1J 439, "Mémoire sur le département de l'Ariège," 4 October 1834, by the prefect. On the revolutionary attacks on *châteaux* in September 1792, see ADA 8L 32, and more generally, G. Arnaud, *Histoire de la Révolution française dans le département de l'Ariège* (Toulouse, 1904); for discussions of the forest question during the 1789 Revolution in France, see *Révolution et espaces forestiers*, ed. D. Woronoff (Paris, 1989).

Part 3
Cultural Identities

Between Oral and Written Culture: The Social Meaning of an Illustrated Love Letter

Elizabeth S. Cohen

Gradually, between the central Middle Ages and the nineteenth century, literacy transformed European culture. Recent historical discussion of this development has emphasized the complexity of the process by which writing, and later printing, little by little overwhelmed earlier oral practices.[1] Scholars have attributed to this evolution several different kinds of major social and cultural changes. Most often, literacy has been seen as a source of power, which, in politics, business, religion, and even family affairs, reorganized the relations between the dominant and the dependent, between elites and ordinary folk.[2] More abstractly, cultural commentators have posited a cognitive revolution, a new character for the very way people thought, which followed from the appropriation of reading and writing.[3] In one dimension of this psychological change, the expansion of literacy has been linked to the privatization of early modern life. According to this view, the possibility of silent, solitary reading offered the occasion for the elaboration of an autonomous mental life and a sense of bounded self.[4] Yet these broad, suggestive hypotheses beg for more thorough testing against the experience of real people. And, especially, there is need to explore how literacy's several consequences interacted. This essay examines one of many such conjunctions in an episode in which literacy and its lack shaped social power relations and notions of privacy. In particular, I will look at one obscure, odd, even comical text—an adolescent's love letter written in Rome in 1602, at its writer, its readers, and the court case to which it led. The document and—equally important—the acts of writing and reading

181

that gave it social meaning are rife with contradictions and conundrums. This tangle reflects in many ways the problematic conjunction of orality and literacy in early modern Rome and, more generally, in Europe.

Most early modern Europeans inhabited a culture suspended between orality and literacy. To the many people who could read and write only a little, if at all, written texts were a familiar but problematic medium for the pursuit of life's goals. Yet unlettered men and women were not mere unfortunate victims, trapped in an antiquated culture of orality. Since documents could work great good as well as great ill, everybody had a strong incentive to find ways to understand and respond to them. Semiliterate folk adapted and invented; often they sought help from others with skills greater than their own. One such custom was widespread reliance on reading aloud.[5] It is important to distinguish, however, between the collective reading of public texts—like government proclamations or religious books—and the transmission of written messages bearing personal or secret information and intended for an audience of one. In the second situation the need for intermediaries exposed the illiterate to quite different social and psychological challenges. The written document demanded the intervention of third parties, including, potentially, a surrogate writer, a surrogate reader, and even others who got ahold of something they were not supposed to see. Thus, writing facilitated communication in situations where speech was impossible or indiscreet. At the same time, writing reshaped the boundaries of privacy, but not in the fashion suggested for the educated. For the unlettered, the written word promoted not inner self-cultivation, but a complex of social transactions in an intermediate zone, neither communal nor intimate. For the majority of early modern Europeans, writing and privacy were not at first natural partners.

To pursue the problematic meanings of literacy for seventeenth-century Romans, I propose to undertake what the anthropologist Keith Basso calls the "ethnography of writing."[6] Basso asserts that, like colloquial speech, forms of nonliterary, nonacademic writing conform to rules and habits that reflect their cultural and social milieu. Thus, even routine, informal, or personal texts, studied in the context of the specific people who made and used them, can illuminate the larger world they occupied. This approach validates the close study of texts generated by people who were not experts in words, who were neither intellectuals nor public officials. One historian who has experimented boldy with such documents is Kristen Neuschel in her study of the correspondence of French noblemen.[7] Seeking to locate these texts in a culture both oral and literate, she analyzes both the social transactions and the language that characterized these documents. While her contention that letter writing reflected patterns of oral expression is not wholly convincing, she does demonstrate the value of such personal records for understanding not just individuals but the cultural practice of entire social groups. The study of Giovanantonio's love letter will, I hope, likewise prove fruitful.

I begin at the center with the letter itself, which I offer in its entirety, for the details of its form and content are the heart of this inquiry. Later, I will move outward into the larger circles of the letter's social, legal, and cultural contexts. The autograph document survives bound with the trials of the governor of Rome, the pope's chief municipal magistrate. It reads:[8]

Dearest sister, I have to tell you that last Sunday something happened to me. In the evening when I came home, that wretched spy Bertolino [a servant] had told my mother and Bartolaccio [her live-in lover] that I had had a key made and that I had come in through the window that night, and many other lies. And so when I got home, I had a big fight with my mother and she took away my door key. And Bartolaccio came up to my room and said that I had been going there in the evening to see you, and I said, "No, none of it was true." And he said he knew very well that I came there, because he had come there too. I'm not joking. If it's not all true what I'm saying, may Santa Lucia blind me. And so I got angry, and it's been two nights that I didn't sleep at home. And that way I got that scoundrel sent packing. My mother doesn't like me to be in that room any more, because she says I talk to you and doesn't want me going in there any more. But be patient; this hurts nobody as much as it hurts me. Believe me, if it weren't for love of you, my heart, I wouldn't want to come any more. Only God knows when we will see each other again, because I can no longer stay out past Ave Maria. Alas, I am losing my heart, my life, and everything good. I will be sleeping in that room under the loggia. But don't forget the one who loves you. And please plug up that hole; do me this favor. And please show yourself sometimes at the window. I don't know if I can come to your house any more while we are in this fix, because my mother goes and locks the door every night. But I have given you my heart and I will live always happy, if you love me. And really believe me that I'm in torment for you. So, love me and commend me to Caterina [Margarita's sister], because, indeed, I love her too. So, if you can send me a reply that both of you are well, that will please me. And keep me in your grace and tear up this letter, so no one sees it. Addio, I commend myself to both of you, and to you especially.

Wedged between this last word and the right edge of the paper is a sketch of a phallus, pointing right at a vulva, inscribed immediately below with the words "This is for you." Underneath is a second sketch, similar though slightly larger and pointing the opposite direction, labeled "And this is for Caterina." To the left of this drawing are two groups of words, added evidently as postscripts, penned in smaller letters, but the same hand, and squeezed to fit around the sketches and above the center foldline of the sheet of paper. The first message says, "Hot pot, juicy fig,[9] and prick up the ass to you both, and be it really big to give you more pleasure." The second adds, "I forgot one thing. In the evening I can't open my window, because my mother makes me keep my door open and comes up often to see what I'm doing. So, may your ladyship pardon me."

These words and drawings completely fill one and a half sides of the sheet of paper. Evidently, it had been folded first in the middle and then again in rough thirds, so that the blank half-side served as a covering and bore the address. Thus, even without an envelope the contents of the letter were protected from casual eyes.[10] The letter writer did not, however, feel inclined to hide his sentiments. The middle third of the empty side displays the words, "To my most worthy lady, Signora Margarita, heart of my life." Below, an elegant calligraphic ornament spirals down to a third rendering of the genital image, similar in its naturalistic details to the ones inside the letter, but here larger and inscribed with lettering. The testicles bear the initials *J* and *A*,[11] which correspond to the name of the presumed author, Giovan Antonio. The shaft of the penis proclaims, "ROMA," in what is presumably an echo of the classical anagram that puns on the name of the city and the Italian word for *love*.

There are several ways to approach the puzzle that this love letter presents. A literary critic would readily identify elements of both genre and rhetoric but also would find many quirks and inconsistencies. The letter's tone lurches from epistolary formality to adolescent whine, from romantic pleading to salacious doggerel. It combines words with graphic images. A postmodernist study would expect to account for these vagaries with reference to other literary texts. However, as a historian I am interested as well in investigating contexts, particularly social and circumstantial, as a source of explanation. I would like to assess the claims of intertextuality by asking not only what other writings offered parallels but also whether the letter's author was likely to have encountered them. I also want to trace not only how the letter came to be but also what it did. This question takes me into the realm where literate and oral culture intersected, for some of the people most strongly touched by the missive could not themselves read it. A microhistorical study of the events that the letter precipitated reveals the complexities of life in a partially literate world. The base for this reconstruction of the larger social and cultural context of the letter is another set of texts, the records of the interrogations conducted by the criminal magistrates during a lawsuit for libel against the letter writer. Following a historical analysis of these trial documents, I will return to addressing the letter as a literary text.

Literary texts are, of course, not the only ones that present problems of interpretation; the criminal court records pose their own difficulties. For my purposes here the biggest question is whether testimony fairly represented what people said and did.[12] The stories told by witnesses were inevitably incomplete. People lied to judges all the time and tailored their words to fit the demands of the law and of private interest. Yet with several versions of the same tale and information on the speakers' statuses, it is possible to make comparisons and take account of biases. Although ambiguities never disappear altogether, with a background knowledge of the culture the historian can often reconstruct a plausible rendering of events.

Let us begin with Giovanantonio, the son of Pietro di Seravalle of Piedmont. Despite his own testimony, which consisted largely of denials, and despite the absence of a record of the outcome of the trial, I will accept as true that this "beardless youth" was the author of the love letter.[13] His father, apparently dead, left no mark, of his social station or otherwise, on the trial. The rest of Giovanantonio's household, however, figured in his letter. Giovanna, his mother, had earlier set herself up to keep a boardinghouse but had soon given it up; at the time of the incident she lived with her son and a Signor Bartolomeo, probably her lover.[14] They employed a servant, confusingly also named Bartolomeo. With the help of these men, the mother succeeded in corralling her boy's romantic ambitions. There is no indication of whether Giovanantonio attended school or worked. The letter's neat chancery hand and courtly phrases suggest more than rudimentary education, but where the youth had mastered these is obscure.[15] Certainly, epistolary writing was a distinct skill, taught in special courses to those who aspired to posts as secretaries in courts and government bureaucracies.[16] It was also possible, however, to learn the forms and rhetoric from the proliferating manuals and books of models.[17] From these fragments of evidence, Giovanantonio appears as a young man with pretensions to social advancement through literacy, but who was not yet independent or launched in a career.

In the case before us, however, the youth put his education to work in service not of his career but of his love life. In the letter, Giovanantonio described in detail the occasion that prompted his resort to the pen. The servant, Bartolomeo, having lost his job over the incident, had little reason to accommodate in court the interests of his nemesis; nevertheless, the menial's testimony largely corroborated the boy's tale of frustration.[18] Giovanantonio had a girlfriend, Margarita, who lived in an adjacent building, where he had been visiting her at night. He had even acquired a copy of the house key in order to ease his nocturnal comings and goings. His mother, having gotten wind of his illicit outings, clamped down firmly, pocketing the key, forcing him to sleep in a different room, from which communication with the next house was less convenient, and keeping a close eye on his movements. Unable therefore to contact his girlfriend in person, he had to bemoan his plight to her in a letter. To someone with his epistolary training such a step may have come quite naturally. Writing offered a ready medium through which to pass information and feelings that were best kept private. Thus, Giovanantonio complained of his mother's severity, gloated over his revenge on the tattling servant, and trumpeted his sexual gusto, for not only the girlfriend but also her sister. Yet as he was anxious for secrecy, he urged Margarita to destroy the letter so no one could see it.

Taking advantage of writing's gift of privacy, however, depended on the girl's literate skills. If these matters were to remain between just the two of them, Margarita had to know how to read. The young man's request that she protect their intimacy by destroying the letter suggests that he assumed that only she need see it. But such presumption perhaps was foolish. On the one hand, Giovanantonio knew that Margarita was the daughter of a notary; women of such station often numbered among the small minority of literate females.[19] On the other hand, most women, including probably many urban wives of educated professionals, had little, if any, skill with letters. Furthermore, Margarita told the judges that she had warned her lover not to send a letter because she could not read.[20] Even if this claim was a bit of embroidery, inserted by the girl to lessen her own culpability, Giovanantonio had little grounds to assume her literacy.[21] What then did the beardless swain intend as he folded up his sheet of paper, covered with compromising words and pictures, tied it with a lute string, and flung it through the grating into the lower room of Margarita's home?[22]

Margarita's responses to interrogation by the magistrates, supported by those of Christofera, an older woman living in the household, supply further evidence about the episode of the letter.[23] At sixteen years of age, Margarita was the oldest child of the Fleming Pietro de Beques, a notary at the papal court of the Rota.[24] According to the girl, she had become acquainted with Giovanantonio when he moved into Piazza San Salvatore in Lauro over a year before. He had accosted her in the street several times, but conversation there was risky. So she decided to excavate a hole in the wall of her room, which, conveniently, lay opposite to Giovanantonio's window.[25] The testimonies disagree on the date of this ploy, but it must have occurred in January or February, when Margarita's mother, having quarreled with her husband, had gone off to stay with her cousin.[26] During this absence, Christofera probably had taken over some of the mother's role in the house, but she apparently exerted only lax discipline over Margarita and her younger sister. Indeed, the woman seems to have abetted the lovers' stratagems. Through the chink, like the classical lovers Pyramis and Thisbe, Margarita and Giovanantonio conversed at leisure, at times overheard by Christofera. It is she who reported that the boy spoke of marriage and, later, when he came to visit, brought gifts of silk—a scarlet belt with gold ornaments and a dozen multicolored laces. These promises and presents betokened a serious courtship.[27] Eventually, after many pleadings, Margarita consented to a clandestine visit, notably in the season of sexual license, which was the last evening of Carnival. That evening, while her father slept upstairs, Margarita gave up her virginity in the lower room of the house.[28] On this night, as on several others in the succeeding weeks, the lovers dallied for an hour or two.[29] The idyll ended when, as related in the letter, Giovanantonio's mother stepped in. No longer could the pair chat comfortably from their bedrooms; no longer could they meet. The suitor was forced to put his plight into writing.

The letter, then, marked a new phase in a consummated, clandestine love affair. Its rhetoric corresponded to real experience. The explicitly sexual words and pictures reflected more than adolescent wishful fantasy. The phrases about painful separation resonated with plausible emotion. But little of this communication could achieve its end if Margarita could not read.

When Margarita retrieved the letter from where it had landed, she adopted the resort common to nonreaders in a semiliterate world. She sought out someone to read it for her. Professional scribes offered such services, as did, more informally, many others who enjoyed the powers of literacy.[30] Modern sensibilities, which take for granted the skills and technologies necessary for private communication, may be surprised when early modern folk placed highly personal and even compromising material in the hands of a stranger, especially one who might well ply his trade in the publicity of the street. The cultivation of privacy, which scholars have highlighted as an increasingly salient feature of early modern culture, depended on the possession of both wealth and human capital, which remained very unequally distributed. Thus, private communication was a luxury many could not afford. In particular, reading and writing were activities that for many people were public rather than personal, shared rather than individual.

Even something so intimate and possibly compromising as a love letter often was a part of this social practice of public reading and writing. For example, another trial before the governor's court showed striking parallels with Margarita's experience. That case involved the illiterate wife of another notary of the Rota, seduced by a gentleman next door who threw *billets doux* (love letters), weighted with coins, into her yard.[31] Egged on by her scheming woman servant, the young lady had the letters carried to a convent, where her sister lived, to be read. While nuns might seem an unlikely choice as collaborators in a morally reprehensible intrigue, they contributed willingly, even to the point of invoking the magic of the holy altar to help the wife's cause. But there was always a risk that readers might betray those they served. Yet another case illustrates the hazards of dependence on the literacy of others. A young groom in the entourage of a cardinal plotted to run off with another man's wife. In order to determine when he should come for his beloved, he wrote to her neighbor, a midwife. That woman needed a reader for the letter, and, via the reader, the information found its way back to the jilted husband.[32] Thus, the choice of a reader could have serious consequences.[33]

Despite the need for privacy, in seeking a reader for her letter, Margarita was forced to opt for convenience over trustworthiness. Ignorant of the contents of the letter, the girl could not have responded to Giovanantonio's worry that there might be trouble if someone unsympathetic saw what it contained. The phallic image on the outside should, however, have warned her of the virtue of discretion.[34] Nevertheless, when Margarita made her choice, her principal reason was likely to have been propinquity. While she sometimes moved about in the street—as in her early encounters with her admirer—during the whole episode of the letter she seems to have remained inside and to have interacted with outsiders exclusively through openings in the walls.[35] Such restricted movement may have caused her to forgo the use of a public scribe, who might have exercised some professional tact. Instead she chose a neighbor named Ambrosio, a brass-smith, because he was one of the few literate people she could reach from within her house. Thus, she could catch his attention from her window, throw the letter into their joint courtyard, and listen as he read the contents aloud. In this way Margarita learned what Giovanantonio had to say, but without benefiting from the privacy of even a quiet conversation with her reader. Any passerby was a potential audience for her lover's endearments and protestations. As an additional threat to her privacy, the girl appears not to have known Ambrosio well; she had no special grounds to believe that he would protect her confidences.[36]

Ambrosio's attitudes about his role as literate surrogate were complex. He did Margarita a service as reader, possibly more than once.[37]

It is less clear whether he helped her to write a reply. From the first, the brass-smith obviously worried that his part in this affair would get him into trouble; he had been arrested once before amidst charges of sexual misconduct, although the case had been dropped.[38] In general, therefore, Ambrosio's testimony aimed at downplaying his role. Thus, he acknowledged reading the letter to Margarita and admitted that she had thrown him a sheet of paper on which to write a reply. But he denied her claim that he had cooperated in composing one. The girl's story of dispatching a mock reproach declaring her boyfriend a *monchione* may have conjured a rejoinder that was wishful rather than real.[39] Most telling, perhaps, in Ambrosio's response to Margarita's enlistment of his literate help was his refusal to return the letter to her.[40] His actions reflected mixed motives. Evidently, he wanted to protect himself, although why he felt safer in possession of the incriminating document is a puzzle. He may also have felt a responsibility to break up the immoral carryings-on, which had thus come to his attention. He did not rush to volunteer what he had learned. Yet several weeks later, when Margarita's mother complained to her neighbor of a youth hanging around in front of her house at night, Ambrosio said that he knew who it must have been. The conversation then led to the letter, which he handed over at the mother's request, as he had not at the daughter's.[41] Thus, the surrogate reader, perhaps justifying his action in the name of prudence or higher morality, betrayed the confidences of his supplicant.

Illiterate folk like Margarita, thus, readily sacrificed privacy in order to participate in the imposing, if sometimes dangerous, domain of written culture. In part, we may attribute the girl's somewhat imprudent enlistment of her neighbor to naïveté, even to brazenness. Also, unaccustomed to the practices of private written communication, she well may not have recognized that it was possible and desirable to keep things secret, as clearly Giovanantonio knew. On the other hand, Margarita's strategy was probably quite normal; she followed the steps of the many others similarly obliged to deal in a potent realm of signs they could not decipher. Ideally, unlettered people breaching privacy in order to communicate in writing kept the circle of interlopers as small as possible. Presumably, they preferred helpers who would respect their trust. Yet it is hard to tell what customs, if any, governed the informal relationship between the illiterate person in need and the literate person who could fill that need.

No one seemed to expect particular discretion from a surrogate reader or writer. This predicament sharply demonstrated the vulnerability of those who depended on such casual alliances. Nonetheless, when required, people did not hesitate to seek out literate helpers. To them, exclusion from the world of writing posed the greater risk.

The concerns that the brass-smith highlighted in his testimony, his preoccupation with the letter as a physical document and with his position before the law, led to questions about the resonance of this episode in the community beyond the lovers themselves. Margarita's illiteracy caused a private communication to enter the public arena and ultimately to come before the municipal judges. This phase of the letter's story also reflects on the social and cultural meaning of written words in the life of early modern Rome.

At first glance, it appears that Giovanantonio should have faced charges of defloration; nevertheless, the records classified the offense as libel, that is, as defamation in writing. Several legal technicalities justified this approach.[42] More importantly, the decision to highlight the alleged libel shows the serious concern over the power of writing in affairs of honor. Thus, in their lines of investigation, the magistrates expressed as much interest in handwriting as in sexual conduct. Expert witnesses included, besides two midwives, three scribes who compared the penmanship of the letter with Giovanantonio's signature on his deposition.[43] Nevertheless, in several ways the letter did not fit the standard notions of prosecutable defamation. The more typical targets of libel actions were public denunciations, such as scurrilous broadsides tacked on walls and doors.[44] Furthermore, to qualify as a criminal act, there had to be malicious intent. In contrast, the youth's missive was a private exchange and bore no evidence of a wish to blacken his sweetheart's name. On the other hand, by virtue of being a physical object that could be read again and again, the letter could pose a more enduring threat to reputation than the cascades of insulting words that regularly rang through the streets of the city. These spoken slanders frequently provoked legal complaints, but in general the judges declined to pursue them unless they accompanied some more serious offense.[45] Thus, the written word loomed more menacingly than the oral.

How then did Giovanantonio's problematic letter find its way into court? While not written to defame, it was nonetheless written, and it linked Margarita's name with explicit and unsanctioned sexuality.

As such it resonated with cultural and social meaning, whether or not intended by its author. As it moved into the public sphere of the larger community, it cast a shadow over the reputation of a respectable girl. The responsibility for protecting that social asset belonged to her parents, principally her father. Curiously, in Margarita's case, her father chose to absent himself from the whole judicial exercise. Instead, her mother initiated the proceedings and asked the court "to punish the one who deflowered and stole the honor of my daughter."[46] Perhaps the quarreling parents took this contest as an opportunity to act out their mutual anger. Perhaps the father, himself embarrassed by the fact that the defloration occurred while the mother was away and he was in sole charge of his children, would have preferred to negotiate a solution informally and to avoid the greater publicity of the court. Nevertheless, even the mother might have chosen a less visible recourse if the affair had not, unsolicitedly, already come to the attention of authorities. For, as Margarita's parents had been arguing over what to do about the letter, the chief of police, chancing to pass through the piazza, had heard the raised voices and gone to see what was happening. Inside, he obliged the notary to explain the problem and to relinquish the letter clutched in his hand.[47] Thus, the letter slipped, more by accident than by design, into an even larger circle of public significance. The police's intervention, the mother's formal complaint, and the magistrates' investigation all gave meaning to the document as something more than an adolescent's imprudent, but private, tribute to his girlfriend. The sheet of paper with its writing and drawings, in its social context, publicly challenged the canons of honor and sexual discipline.

Bearing in mind these multiple layers of the letter's social meaning, let us turn back to the text itself. I noted earlier its many contradictions of form and tone. Should those not lead me to dismiss the letter as the immature, culturally incoherent scribbling of a frustrated adolescent? Obviously, I have other ambitions. Letter writing, perhaps especially in the wake of the Renaissance, was a highly conventionalized undertaking. Even emotionally volatile teenagers, when they took up a pen, necessarily were directed by and made use of the ideas, forms, and words that their culture provided. In this realm of literary practice, we can explore one more dimension of the act of writing as an intersection of public and private, of cultural norms and individual impulse.

As several critics have remarked, the letter was, by its nature, the genre in which the tension between the strictures of form and the concerns of the individual was most acute.[48] There were many types of letters, to which convention assigned varying degrees of informality, more and less space for the diversity of personality. Nevertheless, even personal or, in Renaissance labeling, "familiar," letters were expected to conform to rules.

In the standard Latin curriculum, Cicero's *Familiar Letters* was a basic text for training young Italians in form, rhetoric, and appropriate content.[49] These studies classified words as high, middling, and low, and assigned them accordingly to different sorts of letters. Familiar letters might use the full range of vocabulary, but there was always the risk of discordance. Letter writing in the vernacular patterned itself on the Latin tradition, but also underwent its own rapid development from the midsixteenth and into the early seventeenth century. At first, published collections of letters set models; later in the century these were homogenized and standardized into manuals of types and phrases.[50] These offered culturally approved patterns in which to express quite personal concerns to an audience of only one. While the more informal "familiar" letters could tolerate a range of diction and other individual vagaries, such writing still took its shape from the prescriptions of teacher and handbook.[51]

The love letter, though a distinct type, resembled the familiar letter in its interest in private needs and experiences. Yet it, too, was subject to powerful stylization.[52] Looking back to Ovid, several Renaissance writers, including Petrarch and Pietro Bembo, revived the love letter as a form. Addressing their beloveds in lofty tones, these authors spun out lengthy plaints on the exquisite agonies of love. Both the rhetoric and the sentiments set the models for such correspondence. By the time of Giovanantonio's trial, this subgenre, like other epistolary forms, had been reduced to compendia of stock situations and phrases.

Between schools and books there was ample material in circulation to set the pattern for the several parts of Giovanantonio's letter. By what route he acquired his familiarity with these conventions, it is hard to say. Paul Grendler suggests that in sixteenth-century Italian cities, schools were fairly accessible.[53] But were they likely to have provided the models for the kind of letter this youth chose to write? Of course, he may have improvised on forms of more orthodox letters he had been taught in class. The physical appearance of the document—the folds, the arrangement of the address, the handwriting—make it look like a normal early modern letter, created by someone who had been instructed in epistolary proprieties. But the impact of cultural patterning did not end there. The phrases in which he writes of and to Margarita also were highly conventional. The high-sounding *colendissima* (most worthy) echoed traditional Latin rhetoric, and the use of superlatives typified the epistolary address of suppliants.[54] Similar in effect was his use of the more respectful second-person plural as in such courtly phrases as *tenetemi in gratia vostra* (keep me in your grace) and the concluding, *me perdoni vosignoria* (may your ladyship pardon me). Also, from the language of love literature came the several invocations of his beloved as his "heart." He inscribed *cor di mia vita* (heart of my life) on the outside of the letter and then inside recorded the classic lover's plaint, *hoime che perdero il mio core, la vita, and tutto il mio bene* (alas, I am losing my heart, my life, and everything good).[55] Yet all of these borrowings were just phrases, fragments of meaning, of the sort the young man might easily have extracted from guides to polite or amorous vocabulary or even heard in conversation.[56] While the letter did describe a situation standard to the lovers, where they face obstacles and the threat of loss, Giovanantonio developed this theme neither fully nor with the conventional sentimental rhetoric. Rather he interspersed his fancy words and romantic turns of phrase with many others belonging in vocabulary and sentiment to a lower, more popular style.

Rapid changes in rhetorical mode characterized the whole letter, even before Giovanantonio inserted the startlingly raunchy doggerel of the postscript and the illustrations. Blended with the fancy wordings were more popular utterances, for example, *se non e vero che Santa Lucia mi accechi* ("if it is not true, may Saint Lucy blind me"). But even such language probably fell within the tolerant boundaries for discourse appropriate in a familiar letter. Colloquial phrases accompanied preoccupation with details of daily life worthy of comic farce rather than romantic tragedy—for example, spying servants, blocked chinks, and changing bedrooms. The admixture of low and high, of common and proper, climaxed at the end of the letter. There both words and feelings became crude, even shocking. The love for not only Margarita but also her sister, which sounded courteous in the body of the letter, took on an explicitly promiscuous sexuality. The matched drawings of phalluses reinforced the indelicacy.

Nevertheless, this imagery also had its cultural roots. The youth perhaps had encountered books of salacious satire, which, among other jokes, played at juxtaposing the lofty and the scabrous. This genre subverted the high rhetoric of classicizing lovers with the earthy language of sex and sweat.[57] More specifically, the postscript's bits of dirty chant sounded remarkably like the sonnets that Aretino concocted for the engravings of *I Modi*.[58] This famous pornographic excursion was rapidly suppressed and probably was not available to stimulate adolescent hormones. But Aretino's poetry may well have drawn on an oral tradition of popular versifying that no doubt proved hardier than a printed artifact. Whatever the source, Giovanantonio probably did not invent his lines. A similar root in popular culture must account for the sketches, but the discretion of scholars has made it even more difficult to trace the history of sexual graphics than that of words. One Counter-Reformation theoretician of art censorship referred with dismay to the "immoral drawings" that were wont to decorate the walls of inns and public baths.[59] Presumably these resembled the *quattro cazzi* emblazoned on a defamatory placard that led to a trial before the governor's court in 1598.[60] Thus, there are hints of the existence of such images that offered a likely model for Giovanantonio's pen. But without more examples of the figures themselves, detailed analysis is impossible. Although the specific sources of these more popular elements of the letter are hard to pin down, it seems likely that they came out of the "oral" or, better, unlettered culture of the city. If so, this example should remind us that in the evolution of early modern life, literate practices responded to their oral environment as well as vice versa.

The final problem concerns the meaning of the love letter as a whole. Here I have traced various components of genre and language, of high and low culture that the missive used. Nevertheless, had the youth merely assembled a jumble of incongruent elements and packaged them into the form of a letter? Did the pieces all add up? Literary analysis rooted in the work of Bakhtin offers the concept of transgression, a notion that implies the acknowledgment of proper forms for conduct and their deliberate, though controlled, violation.[61] Unlike the satirists Rabelais and Aretino, Giovanantonio does not seem to me to have undertaken such an act of conscious crossing of the literary boundaries. While the youth may have taken pleasure from his surprising juxtaposition of the lofty and the scabrous, it appears an impromptu excursion, not a calculated cultural critique. Most probably, the crazy mixture of tones aptly represents a young man's culturally mediated ride on an emotional roller coaster.

Giovanantonio's letter took its character and its social meaning from the partially literate culture in which he and Margarita lived. While not a purely conventional artifact, the letter in its form and content drew in many different ways on the cultural habits of early modern Italy. It was a token of the advancing literacy of that culture that the young man wrote a letter at all and that he knew how to make a piece of writing look like a letter. Nevertheless, while he made use of public conventions, he intended to make a private communication. That it could not enjoy such a reading was also a product of that mixed oral and literate milieu.

As a written *and* illustrated document, the letter had a destiny of social significance beyond that anticipated by its author. For its readers meaning derived not only from the text, but also from the social relationships that linked the several members of its audience. Oddly, Margarita's reaction is least accessible. Because she could not read, because she could not move freely, her actions spoke more of her limitations than of her understanding. But clearly, Ambrosio (the surrogate reader), Margarita's mother, the chief of police, and the judges thought the letter mattered. It mattered in a complex way that resulted from the bringing together of its various disparate parts. I suspect that without the illustrations the letter would not have attracted so much attention. Yet the images had meaning not just because some people could not read, for the sketches bore only part of the message of the text. The full significance, and the puzzle it presented, arose from the conjunction of the pictures with the written words and with the culturally recognizable format of the letter. It was neither a normal love letter, nor a typical defamatory placard. Its creation was part accident, as was its fate. But the episode as a whole casts lights on many features of a shared cultural domain and demonstrates the social complexity of the "literacy process." In particular, the boundaries between public and private could not be the same as in a world where everybody was expected to read and to write. For the unlettered, the advance of written culture did not bring enhanced autonomy or occasion for introspection. Those were luxuries as yet beyond their means. Rather, for them, participation in the powerful new culture of writing demanded a sacrifice of privacy.

NOTES

1. François Furet and Jacques Ozouf, "Three Centuries of Cultural Cross-Fertilization: France," in *Literacy and Social Development in the West: A Reader*, ed. H. J. Graff (Cambridge, 1981), 214–31; Michael T. Clanchy, "Literate and Illiterate; Hearing and Seeing, 1066–1307," also in Graff, *Literacy and Social Development*, 14–45; B. V. Street, *Literacy in Theory and Practice* (Cambridge, 1984).

2. Furet and Ozouf, "Three Centuries," 215–16; Peter Burke, "The Uses of Literacy in Early Modern Italy," in *The Historical Anthropology of Early Modern Italy* (Cambridge, 1987), 110–31; Laura Antonucci, "L'alfabetizzazione a Roma fra XVI e XVII secolo," in *Roma e lo Studium Urbis*, ed. Paolo Cherubini (Rome, 1989), 65–68.

3. Walter J. Ong, *Orality and Literacy: The Technology of the Word* (London, 1982); Jack Goody, *The Interface Between the Written and the Oral* (Cambridge, 1987).

4. Roger Chartier, "The Practical Impact of Writing," in *History of Private Life*, vol. 3, *Passions of the Renaissance*, ed. R. Chartier (Cambridge, MA, 1989), 111.

5. Roger Chartier, "Publishing Strategies and What the People Read, 1530–1660," in *The Cultural Uses of Print in Early Modern France* (Princeton, 1987), 145–82.

6. Keith H. Basso, "The Ethnography of Writing," in *Explorations in the Ethnography of Speaking*, ed. R. Bauman and J. Sherzer (Cambridge, 1974), 425–32.

7. Kristen B. Neuschel, *Word of Honor: Interpreting Noble Culture in Sixteenth-Century France* (Ithaca, 1989), especially chap. 4. As evidence of oral culture, any written document is suspect. For any period before the present century, however, we have no other vehicle for even an attempt at understanding that very central aspect of so many past societies. Verbatim transcription of spoken testimony, such as we have in the archives of the Roman courts, come perhaps as close to artifacts of oral culture as we can expect to recover. The "orality" of these judicial records is not, however, our principal focus here. On the complex mixing of oral and written in the history of legal proceedings, see Clanchy, "Literate and Illiterate."

8. Archivio di Stato di Roma. Tribunale criminale del governatore. Processi, 1600–19, Busta 18, fols. 715–40. Below, references to this document will cite Busta 18 and appropriate folios. Other materials from this court will be cited as Processi or Investigazioni, with busta and folios.

9. The Italian is *fica fegna*.

10. The same pattern of folding is evident in the facsimile reproduction of the letters of Petrarch; see Armando Petrucci, ed., *Francesco Petrarca. Epistole autografe* (Padua, 1968), fig. iv, viii, xii.

11. The shaping of especially the *A* is somewhat ambiguous, but it is hard to say what else it could be. In the trial the letter was treated as unsigned, perhaps because that qualified it as a legally defined category of libel; see below. On the other hand, the court, while much concerned to prove the authorship of the letter, never mentioned the initials.

12. Elizabeth S. Cohen, "Court Testimony from the Past: Self and Culture in the Making of Text," in *Essays in Life Writing*, ed. Marlene Kadar (Toronto, 1992). Historians are mostly confident that, under the inquisitorial system, which the Roman governor's court shared with the church, the transcription of testimony accurately reported what was said; see Brian Pullan, *The Jews of Europe and the Inquisition of Venice, 1550–1670* (Oxford, 1983), 117–23. There is less consensus about how much what was said in court corresponded to what had happened in the world; see Thomas Kuehn, "Reading Microhistory: The Example of *Giovanni and Lusanna*," *Journal of Modern History* 61 (1989): 532–33.

13. The servant offers this description of the young man: Busta 18, fol. 729r. Giovanantonio's own testimony: fols. 722v–24v, 728r–v, 730r–31r, 733r–35r, 738r–40v. He persisted, even under torture, in denying any involvement with the girl. Of course, simply being prosecuted does not mean someone is guilty; my conclusion that he wrote the letter follows from an assessment of context and plausibility drawn from all the testimony in the trial.

14. In the letter Giovanantonio appends the negative suffix, *-accio*, to the name of his mother's lover. He refers to the servant by another nickname, "Bertolino."

15. During his interrogation, the boy tries to minimize his competence—*io so leggere et scrivere ancora un poco*—and persistently denies ever writing any letters: Busta 18, fol. 724r.

16. Paul F. Grendler, *Schooling in Renaissance Italy: Literacy and Learning, 1300–1600* (Baltimore, 1989), 229–31; Armando Petrucci, "Scrittura, alfabetismo ed educazione grafica nella Roma del primo Cinquecento: Da un libretto di conti di Maddalena 'pizzicarola' in Trastevere," *Scrittura e Civiltà* (1978), 185–93. The skills manifested in Giovanantonio's letter exceed those taught in at least the primary levels of Roman schools; see Guerrino Pelliccia, *La scuola primaria a Roma dal secolo XVI al XIX* (Rome, 1985), and Laura Antonucci, "L'insegnamento elementare a Roma nel XVI secolo," in *Roma e lo Studium Urbis* (Rome, 1989), 69–73.

17. Amedeo Quondam, ed., *Le 'Carte messaggiere.' Retorica e modelli di comunicazione epistolare: Per un indice dei libri di lettere del Cinquecento* (Rome, 1981).

18. Busta 18, fols. 729r–31r.

19. Busta 18, fol. 723r–v. The profession and household of his neighbor was one of the few topics on which Giovanantonio was willing to answer questions, and those evasively. On female literacy, Grendler, *Schooling*,

46–47; Guerrino Pelliccia, "Scuole di catechismo e scuole rionali per fanciulle nella Roma del Seicento," *Ricerche per la storia religiosa di Roma* 4 (1980), 237–68; Petrucci, "Scrittura, alfabetismo ed educazione grafica," 193–94, n. 38.

20. Busta 18, fol. 721v.

21. Margarita's mother, though hardly disinterested, testified that the girl was given to fantasies (*cricchi*). Busta 18, fol. 719r.

22. Busta 18, fol. 721v. Another example of lovers communicating through letters thrown from house to house: Processi, 16th century, Busta 48, fols. 645r, 661r–v.

23. Busta 18, fols. 720r–22v, 731r–32r.

24. Busta 18, fols. 716r, 719r. Among ordinary Romans, notaries were men of some prestige; Margarita may have been of somewhat higher station than her suitor.

25. Busta 18, fols. 720v, 731v. For holes in the wall in the service of courtship, see also Processi, 16th century, Busta 48, fol. 662r, and Busta 38, case 15, fol. 303v.

26. Busta 18, fol. 719r.

27. Busta 18, fol. 731r–32r. Christofera had a stake in legitimating the affair in order to justify her encouragement of it.

28. Busta 18, fols. 721r, 731v–32r. While in some ways this account follows a conventional scenario, it lacks several elements that typically appeared in prosecutions against abusers of virgins; here there is no talk of force or pain, for the girl clearly consented. Christofera testified that after the defloration, Margarita returned to the room she shared with her sister upstairs, told Caterina what had happened, but was ashamed by the blood on her clothing. See Elizabeth S. Cohen, "No Longer Virgins: Self-Presentation by Young Women in Late Renaissance Rome," in *Refiguring Woman: Perspectives on Gender and the Italian Renaissance*, ed. Marilyn Migiel and Juliana Schiesari (Ithaca, 1991), 169–91.

29. Busta 18, fols. 721r, 732r.

30. Professional scribes need further study; for a beginning, see Armando Petrucci, "Scrivere per altri," *Scrittura e Civiltà* 13 (1989): 475–87. On scribes as expert witnesses, as in this trial, see Laura Antonucci, "Scrittura giudicata: Perizie grafiche in processi romani del primo Seicento," *Scrittura e Civiltà* 13 (1989): 489–534.

31. Elizabeth S. Cohen and Thomas V. Cohen, "Camilla the Go-Between: The Politics of Gender in a Roman Household (1559)," *Continuity and Change* 4 (1989): 53–77.

32. Investigazioni, Busta 398, fols. 4r–6r, 9r–v, 10v (1606).

33. The choice of a writer was also potentially compromising. A law case in Leiden in 1606 involved a woman who had a scribe write a love letter to another woman and sign it with a man's name; see Rudolph Dekker and Lotte van der Pol, *Tradition of Female Transvestism in Early Modern Europe* (New York, 1989), 59.

34. It has been suggested that a semicloistered and illiterate girl such as

Margarita might have found the medium of written communication so unfamiliar as not to recognize the import even of pictures on the outside of the letter. Her sexual experience occurred in circumstances in which she may not have had too clear a visual encounter with male genitals. On the other hand, there is some indirect evidence to indicate that Margarita might well have understood what she had seen. While Roman culture of the period understood sexuality as potentially a powerful source of shame, it was not, in general, secretive or euphemistic about the subject. The young women who testified to the court about their defloration were often close in age to Margarita, although typically lower on the social ladder; those girls usually spoke forthrightly about their experiences with sex; see Cohen, "No Longer Virgins." Also, phallic images, presumably similar to those on the letter and publicly displayed, appeared sometimes on defamatory posters or as graffiti; see, for example, Processi, 16th century, Busta 310, fols. 1–18; Processi, 1600–19, Busta 10, fols. 151–62.

35. For other examples of locking up young women, see Processi, 16th century, Busta 48, fols. 649r, 655r; Processi, 1600–19, Busta 37, fol. 1391v.

36. Christofera suggested Ambrosio to Margarita as a reader; Busta 18, fol. 721v. Ambrosio, in his testimony, was keen to minimize his involvement and so claimed to know little of Margarita; but he may well have been speaking truly; Busta 18, fol. 726r.

37. So Margarita asserted: Busta 18, fol. 722r.

38. Busta 18, fol. 725v.

39. Busta 18, fol. 722r. A *monchione* is someone missing a hand, or more generally defective.

40. Busta 18, fols. 722r, 726v.

41. Busta 18, fols. 719v, 726v. According to the brass-smith, when the mother complained of her daughter as "una sfacciata," Ambrosio concurred that the girl was "una trista."

42. Unsigned letters as a form of libel: Giambattista De Luca, *Il dottor volgare, overo il compendio di tutta la legge civile, canonica, feudale, et municipale . . .* (Cologne, 1755), 5:375. A conviction for defloration would have been more difficult to secure. Even where a girl consented, taking her virginity could legally be prosecuted as offense against the honor of her family. In this case, however, where the father chose not to involve himself, such claims would not have had much credibility.

43. Busta 18, fols. 725r–v, 732v–33r, 735r–38r.

44. Peter Burke, "Insult and Blasphemy in Early Modern Italy" in *The Historical Anthropology of Early Modern Italy*, 95–109. For some examples, Armando Petrucci, *Scrittura e popolo nella Roma barocca, 1585–1721* (Rome, 1982), 24–25.

45. The *Investigazioni*, the books of complaints kept by the governor's notaries, are rife with such accusations.

46. Busta 18, fol. 720r.

47. Busta 18, fols. 716r–17r.

48. For example, see Quondam, "Dal formulario al formulario," in *Le 'Carte Messaggiere'*, 80–81.

49. Grendler, *Schooling*, 217–29.

50. Quondam, "Dal formulario," and Nicola Longo, "De epistola condenda. L'arte di 'componer lettere' nel Cinquecento," in *Le 'Carte Messaggiere'*, 13–156, 177–201.

51. In a study of modern letter-writing, Basso, "Ethnography," 429, notes that drawings are considered appropriate embellishments in the most personal and informal of letters. For premodern examples of this phenomenon, see Maria Savorgnan and Pietro Bembo, *Carteggio d'amore (1500–1501)*, ed. C. Dionsotti (Florence, 1950), opposite p. 98, and Emily Anderson, ed., *The Letters of Mozart and his Family*, 2nd ed. (New York, 1966), vol. 2, 654, 961.

52. Quondam, "Dal formulario," 96–120.

53. Grendler, *Schooling*, 104–5, 336–37.

54. Compare, for example, Girolamo Parabosco, *Libro primo delle lettere amorose* (Venice, 1571), fols. 3r, 4v, 5v, and passim.

55. In this type of language the letter sounds more like the feminine Madonna Celia, *Lettere amorose* (Venice, 1565), e.g., fols. 11v, 14r, 50v.

56. Literary elements can circulate through the oral medium.

57. For example, in Rabelais, *Gargantua and Pantagruel* (Harmondsworth, 1955), 240, Panurge courts a Parisian lady. Another satirist in this mode was Pietro Aretino.

58. Lynne Lawner, *I Modi. The Sixteen Pleasures* (Evanston, 1988).

59. Gilio da Fabriano, cited in Carlo Ginzburg, "Tiziano, Ovidio, e i codici della figurazione erotica nel '500," in *Tiziano e Venezia* (Vicenza, 1980), 127. In this article Ginzburg makes an interesting argument about the role of pictures in a partially literate culture. Sixteenth-century authorities disagreed over the relative danger of words and pictures as stimulators of lust. An oral culture might give more weight to images, which even the unlettered could "read." On the other hand, before the diffusion of printing, confessors' manuals displayed little concern over erotic pictures. Did graphics of the sort that embellished the letter change in significance with the advance of literacy? Did the increasing emphasis on sight, compared to the other senses, as the gateway to desire follow from the enhanced power that eyes could wield in a world of written and printed artifacts?

60. Processi, 16th century, Busta 310, fols. 1–18.

61. Peter Stallybrass and Allon White, eds., *The Politics and Poetics of Transgression* (London, 1986).

Print's Role in the Politics of Women's Health Care in Early Modern France

Alison Klairmont Lingo

The 1536 French translation of Eucharias Rösslin's *Der Rösengarten* was the first printed vernacular text on women's health and childbirth to be published in France.[1] This single text contributed to the expansion of a whole genre of medical writing on women's health and related topics that had begun to appear prior to the advent of printing.[2] Over the next hundred years, some twenty-two printed texts (eight translations and fourteen originals) were made available in French to a wider audience than ever before, on subjects including fertility, sterility, and infant care.[3] These publications reflect the surge of interest in everyday problems characteristic of early modern France.[4] The stated goal of many authors and translators of the time was to share practical information with those who needed it most—in this case, midwives, barber-surgeons, and mothers—in a language they could understand.

This study examines the politics of women's health care and the profound impact vernacular print had in shaping the field.[5] Authors who published in French had the ability not only to extend their reach to new audiences but also to organize and direct information so as to preserve social, occupational, and gender hierarchies.[6] We will also look at those authors who dared to go against the grain, using print to break barriers they thought prevented women from receiving the best care. Finally, this study looks at how print facilitated discussion, not only about obstetrical techniques but also about the ethics of employing them.

As today, candid treatments of sexual matters in print scandalized segments of the medical community, sparking disputes and even litigation. We shall see how these disagreements reveal in microcosm some of the religious, professional, and social divisions of early modern France. Before examining print's role in the politics of women's health care, however, it is useful to map the medical landscape of the day.

The Medical Hierarchy and the Politics of Women's Health Care

During the early modern period, those who practiced medicine were separated and pitted against each other on the basis of training and sex. The three official corps were composed almost exclusively of men, although a few women, often widows, practiced as surgeons or barbers within the guilds. Enjoying the highest status were physicians, who knew Latin and had studied a large corpus of learned medical texts at universities.[7] Next in the hierarchy were craft-based and apprentice-trained apothecaries, and finally surgeons, and barber-surgeons.[8]

Each of these groups jockeyed with the others for prestige and patronage. In order to advance themselves in the hierarchy, for example, lower-status male practitioners tried to associate themselves with university learning. Between the fourteenth and sixteenth centuries, Parisian surgeons aped physicians by learning Latin. They formed their own College of Surgeons within the university, wore long robes, and relegated the tasks of shaving and bleeding to the barbers.[9]

Physicians, who had most to lose by the social and professional advances of other medical practitioners, used different strategies to deflect their rivals. Sometimes they tried to enforce municipal and university regulations that distinguished the work of the physician from those lower in the hierarchy, and sometimes they played the lower-status groups against each other. During the fifteenth century, for example, university physicians encouraged the internecine rivalries between surgeons and barbers by lecturing to the barbers in French, much to the chagrin of the Latin-trained surgeons.[10] Ambitious barber-surgeons also read recently translated surgical texts and otherwise "appropriated" knowledge that had previously been the provenance of physicians and surgeons.[11]

During the sixteenth century, some barber-surgeons in Paris and other university towns were successful in their endeavors to acquire an aristocratic clientele that allowed them to move up the social ladder. Fluid professional boundaries and a growing economy allowed skilled and educated barber-surgeons to expand their territory and increase their prestige.[12] As we shall see, the success of the barbers intensified rivalries between them and those higher in the medical hierarchy.

Completely outside the official hierarchy were the empirics and charlatans, who had no formal training. They experienced repression and persecution by medical authorities from the thirteenth century onward. Yet through skill and guile, some empirics acquired royal patronage or municipal employment—fueling already sharp rivalries between official and unofficial healers.[13]

Many physicians saw conflict with female practitioners as part and parcel of their struggle against empirics. Both were seen as the "other," invading the body politic without the training or intelligence to heal properly.[14] But women's "otherness" went further. It reflected deeply-held beliefs about female nature and capacities, which in turn contributed to the systematic exclusion of women from the universities.[15] As a result, women never had the chance to acquire the knowledge or formal status the physicians condemned them for lacking.[16]

While women had been permitted to become surgeons and members of surgeons' guilds, they were gradually driven out of practice due to economic competition and jealousies of their male counterparts. In 1484, the Crown enacted legislation that made it illegal for all women except widows of surgeons to practice surgery.[17] In the late seventeenth century, surgeons' widows were prohibited from practicing as well.[18]

For a long time, midwives escaped regulation and conflict with men over territory and status. During the late medieval and early modern period, however, they came under official scrutiny for the first time. The fact that they practiced informally and without male supervision increasingly disconcerted religious and secular authorities concerned about the spiritual and physical health of mothers and children. And, as surgeons gained expertise in midwifery, midwives gradually lost the informal monopoly over childbirth that they had heretofore enjoyed.

The church was the first to set limits on the midwives' practice. Ecclesiastical legislation between 1404 and 1584 dealt with the spiritual role of the midwife. It set forth her duty to baptize a dying infant when no males were present and instructed her on how to baptize a child whose mother died before it had been completely born. Later legislation further specified that a midwife should never perform an abortion or aid a mother in committing infanticide. The church also attempted to limit the practice of midwifery to village matrons who had been chosen by their peers, had been given final approval by a local bishop, and had impeccable morals.[19]

The first secular regulation of midwives occurred in Paris in 1560.[20] While still concerned about religious and moral orthodoxy, the legislation also set forth new rules for instruction, examination, licensing, registration, and professional conduct of midwives.[21] Limiting the scope of the midwives' authority, the new laws forbade midwives to make reports concerning the chastity, pregnancy, or virginity of women unless in the presence of a doctor and two "sworn surgeons" of the king.[22] Indeed, the main thrust of the statutes was to put midwives under the aegis of the surgeons' guild.[23] Reflecting a growing conviction that surgeons were more skilled than midwives, the regulations further circumscribed the midwives' role by requiring that they call a surgeon, or one of the very few licensed "expert" midwives, when obstetrical complications arose during a delivery.[24]

The statutes of 1560 also required certified surgeons to instruct midwives in female anatomy, but it seems that few, if any, did so. Thus, midwives were excluded from the field of anatomy just as it gained preeminence in medicine and utility in midwifery.[25] Indeed, no formal instruction for midwives existed in France until 1630, when the Hôtel-Dieu in Paris began to provide training, though only for a handful of students at a time.[26]

It is against this backdrop of professional and gender rivalries that we shall review the hostility and discord between rival factions of physicians and surgeons over the appearance of sexually explicit material that appeared in vernacular works on women's health.

The Vernacular Debate: Boundaries and Border Control

In the 1530s and 1540s, there had been an earlier debate about the translation of medical texts for the benefit of "unlatined" barbers and surgeons, but this first round had not dealt with the sexual content of these works.[27] With the publication of the complete works of the barber-surgeon Ambroise Paré in 1575 and a "best-selling" work by the physician Laurent Joubert in 1578, however, came a second round of debates that took on a force of its own.

As in the earlier debate, a group of physicians associated with the medical faculty at the Sorbonne regarded vernacular translations as a threat to their monopoly on medical knowledge and as a challenge to their authority.[28] They felt that the French language did not have a technical vocabulary rich or precise enough to match that of Latin or Greek, and they questioned whether French was an "appropriate" vehicle for the presentation of ancient medical texts.[29] But it was the sexual content of the works that was the real source of furor this time.

The controversy began with the Paris Faculty of Medicine's censure of Paré in 1575. Self-taught, Paré had risen to become first-surgeon to four French kings. Between 1545 and 1590, he wrote manuals specifically for "unlatined" surgeons and barbers on a variety of topics, including obstetrics and gynecology.[30] When his collected works were about to appear in 1575, the Faculty of Medicine and some learned surgeons under the leadership of Dean Etienne Gourmelen attempted to prevent its sale on the grounds that it included subjects that were "immoral," "reckless," and capable of "incit[ing] youth to lust."[31]

Other concerns, personal and professional, also motivated Gourmelen's attack. As dean of the Faculty of Paris, and professor of surgery at the Collège royal, Gourmelen felt eclipsed by a "mere barber-surgeon." The dean argued that Paré's work trespassed into "sacred" medical domains. Gourmelen, who four years earlier had published two lackluster volumes on surgery, felt personally offended by the publication of Paré's complete works.[32] Upon Gourmelen's insistence, the faculty petitioned the Parlement of Paris to invoke a decree that assured the faculty's right to review all medical and surgical books before they went on sale.[33] The Parlement acceded to the demand and ordered both parties to supply evidence and briefs concerning the accusations.

In a memorandum to the Parlement, Paré responded that the source of the physicians' and surgeons' anxiety was that his book was written in a language anyone could understand and that he was giving away "medical secrets" to less trained, lower-status barbers, who would infringe on the learned surgeons' and physicians' professional territory.[34] He also charged that the "immodest" phrases his critics denounced had purposefully been taken out of context for effect and that his work in no way crossed the boundary into what was morally unacceptable.[35]

In a subsequent statement, Paré responded at greater length to every passage the faculty found morally reprehensible. In defending one such section, in which he discussed girls who "debauched" one another if they did not marry soon enough, Paré argued that he was not only providing information but, in fact, discouraging sinful behavior. "It seems to me that in this I have performed a service for parents as well as girls: counseling that they hurry to marry rather than falling into such inconveniences [i.e., debauching one another]."[36] Paré also pointed out that the material under discussion, as well as every other passage the faculty questioned, was already in the public domain. Others had translated and published the texts on which Paré based the offending passages long before his book appeared.[37]

Paré's lengthy self-defense suggests that he took his opponents' attacks seriously. The combination of his explicit descriptions of sexual activity and reproduction and his general popularity despite his low ranking in the medical hierarchy had touched a raw nerve among more elite medical practitioners.

Three years after this controversy, Dr. Laurent Joubert's *Popular Errors* (1578) again sent shock waves through the medical and literary communities. Its author, like Paré before him, dared to write frankly about sexual issues.[38] Even his status as physician and chancellor of the Faculty of Medicine in Montpellier did not protect him from his colleagues' wrath.

Joubert's motives were in keeping with strains of Renaissance humanism that emphasized practical matters and the unmasking of superstition. Hoping to correct the "popular errors" of lay persons as well as medical practitioners, Joubert examined the efficacy and validity of a variety of popular and learned medical beliefs and practices from cradle to grave.[39] The effusive, frank, and sometimes bawdy style in which Joubert explained reproduction and sexuality—including how to conceive, determine virginity, and deliver babies—scandalized some of his readers. Equally, if not more upsetting to some was the fact that Joubert *intended* his book to be read by women as well as men. His critics expressed particular dismay with the fact that he dedicated his work to Queen Marguerite de Valois (1553–1615).[40] His inclusion of midwives' slang for the hymen and other parts of the female genitalia in his discussion of virginity and use of the colloquial term *vit* for penis in another section further rankled his critics.[41] The popularity of Joubert's book (which was reprinted *ten times* in the *first six months* after publication) made it even more objectionable to those worried about dissemination of sexual knowledge.[42]

In his preface to a second edition of the book, Joubert noted how natural it was for wives to want to know about "conception, pregnancy, birth, and lying-in" and added that he had, he thought, "written rather modestly, considering the subject." He believed, moreover, that literal terms were "decent in any language, provided they are used decently and to the point."[43] Deferring to those alarmed by his chapter on virginity, Joubert suggested that maidens "abstain from reading" it. At the same time, he claimed that "girls can learn nothing from this . . . if they have not been instructed in these matters elsewhere."[44]

Contributing to this debate over the forthright discussion of sexual matters were the religious values that characterized Catholic dogma since Jerome and Augustine.[45] Although the church accepted the inevitability of sex in a post-lapsarian world, it ordained that such activities were permissible for reproductive purposes only. All other forms of sexuality were seen as sinful.[46] Catholic attitudes toward sex became further entrenched during the Tridentine debates and the Counter-Reformation. By contrast, many Protestant writers "treated sex as a normal part of conjugal relations, a sign of love between husband and wife, rather than a failing that required a procreative purpose to excuse it."[47] It is not surprising that Joubert was Protestant and Paré was rumored to be as well.

The works of these two medical authors thus raised questions as well as eyebrows. Was it appropriate for knowledge about the body and human reproduction to appear in vernacular texts available to any literate person capable of buying them? Projecting total chaos, critics worried about the social and moral disorder open discussion encouraged, particularly if such materials fell into the hands of pubescent boys and girls.

Intended Audiences

Some authors who opened new avenues of thought and knowledge to a wider audience by means of the printed word also used print to maintain and reinforce professional, social, and sexual boundaries. By the late sixteenth and early seventeenth centuries, male medical writers were gearing their works to both men and women, but with an important distinction. Path-breaking obstetrical manuals were directed to male practitioners, while less innovative works on childbirth were directed to midwives and/or literate laywomen. And while some innovative materials on childrearing, sterility, and female maladies were addressed to laywomen, they were directed to use them only under the guidance of their physicians.[48]

Paré set the trend with his *Brief Collection* (Paris, 1549). He addressed the book to young surgeons, assuming that only they would need to know the lifesaving technique of podalic version (manually turning a malpresenting fetus so it could be delivered feet first). Guillemeau, a student of Paré's, likewise wrote *The Happy Delivery of Women* (1609) "for the utility of the young surgeon."[49] Guillemeau stressed that only the most adept barber-surgeons (whom he presumed would be male) would be able to perform podalic version and wield surgical instruments. Utilized only sporadically before its popularization by Guillemeau, podalic version had the potential to save many lives by avoiding mutilation of mother and child in complicated deliveries. Barber-surgeons tended to be the only practitioners who were taught this method. Their expertise in this area of obstetrics contributed to their gradual takeover of wealthy, aristocratic clients.[50]

Following Guillemeau, the surgeon Jacques Bury and the physicians Jacques Fontaine and François Rousset also addressed their innovative midwifery manuals to young barbers and surgeons, whom they sought to bring up to date on the latest obstetrical techniques being developed in Paris and other French university cities.[51] Midwives were not among those expected to learn these new techniques.[52]

Two important works were, however, directed to midwives during this time: the vernacular translations of *Der Rösengarten* (1536 and 1586) and the original writings of the midwife Louise Bourgeois. The anonymous translator of the 1536 edition of *Der Rösengarten* addressed "midwives and birthing nurses [*gardes d'accouchées*] as well as all women in general [so they] would be able to have hereafter the means to better provide for their affairs than they customarily have had."[53] In these texts, the midwife's demeanor, duties, and skills were all carefully delineated. *Der Rösengarten* was a helpful, illustrated compilation of folklore and traditional practices from Hippocrates to the

Pseudo-Albertus Magnus. When it first appeared in German in 1513 and French in 1536, it broke new ground by assembling in print a variety of medical sources on women's health and childbirth in a format that could reach a relatively wide audience quickly and easily. This work was soon outdated by subsequent texts, such as Paré's work on podalic version, directed only to men. Although Rösslin mentioned podalic version for breech birth, he only advocated its use after the employment of other, less efficacious methods. There was a good chance that both mother and child would die before podalic version was ever tried. Midwives who followed Rösslin's advice would not have been as successful as those who intervened earlier, as directed by Paré and his disciples.

The midwife Louise Bourgeois wrote the only innovative book directed specifically to midwives.[54] In *Diverse Observations*, she instructed them on the most up-to-date techniques of her day.[55] Bourgeois also advised mothers and would-be mothers on fertility, prenatal care, choice of birth attendants, and infant care.[56] Adding a female perspective to the literature on women's health care, she discussed a variety of topics, including a woman's ability to control her emotions in order to protect herself from illness and the midwife's importance during delivery.[57] Not only were her innovative writings and protocols the only ones addressed to a female-only audience, but they also challenged Joubert's claim that "women have never invented a single remedy" or, by extension, anything else of medical value.[58] Bourgeois was, for example, the first to develop a protocol for management of umbilical prolapse.[59]

Bourgeois sounded a female voice in an otherwise all-male chorus and challenged stereotypes that portrayed women as inferior and inept in medicine. She also projected a unique vision of an alliance between medicine and midwifery. She sought to combine the book-centered culture of the university with her own experience both as a woman and as a midwife who had delivered thousands of babies.[60] Describing her book as a sample of her practice, she referred to it as a "school where Medicine is married to the industry of the midwife, for each one to learn the admirable effects of their [respective] divinity."[61] Her vision of a cooperative alliance between medicine and midwifery, in which each would learn from the other, never came to pass.

Another sort of female audience was targeted by those physicians who wrote on childrearing, sterility, and related matters. These male authors cultivated educated, aristocratic women who were having trouble conceiving, or who would benefit from knowledge of infant care, breastfeeding, and female maladies.[62] Those works concentrating on pediatrics also dovetailed with humanist literature stressing the importance of the maternal role.[63]

Above all, these authors hoped to make their expertise indispensable to those able to pay for their services. Self-medication or self-diagnosis was never advised. In the preface to his *Treasury of Secret Remedies for the Illnesses of Women,* Dr. Jean Liebault admonished readers that unless they were well versed in the mysteries of medicine, or "guided in the usage of them by some learned, wise, and well advised physician," the remedies he listed would be of little use.[64]

The only resistance to this reliance on experts was voiced by Gervais De La Tousche, a "gentleman from Poitou" and the only layperson to write on childbirth. Addressing laywomen from a singular perspective, he discouraged the use of midwives altogether and never even mentioned the possibility of male assistance. Instead, De La Tousche advised women to take care of each other. In his highly polemical tract, *The Very High and Very Sovereign Science of the Art and Natural Industry of Giving Birth,* he warned of the evils of midwifery and what he believed was the mercenary nature of midwives.[65] De La Tousche thought mothers would be better off if they trusted their own "natural" understanding of birth rather than the "ignorance" of midwives.

Neither reprinted (except in a nineteenth-century history of midwifery), nor picked up in the writings of others, De La Tousche's work remains an oddity. Surrounded by authors who sought to maintain professional and gender boundaries, De La Tousche was a radical, and some might say "crank." He used vernacular print as a means of promoting self-help among women who were otherwise being counseled to rely upon male professionals and trained midwives. In a quirky way, he challenged the mechanisms of and rationale for medical experts, at least in the area of midwifery. De La Tousche can be considered typical of his times only insofar as he expressed concern for the mother and unborn child. While bordering on the hysterical, his invective reflects the degree to which men and women of early modern France had come to be concerned about problems of everyday life.

Medical Ethics as Revealed in Midwifery Manuals

With vernacular print also came a heightened awareness that ethical, religious, and professional concerns were closely intertwined with questions of medical technique, protocol, and efficacy. As medical advances gave birth attendants a modicum of control over situations in which both a mother's and child's life were in danger, authors became increasingly aware that they needed to take a stand on whom to save. While print was not the only factor at play in bringing these struggles to the fore, it certainly facilitated the debate and extended the reach of those it touched.

Religion also played a key role in this controversy over whom to save when both mother and child were endangered. Contradictions in Catholic doctrine, to which many automatically turned for answers, helped to shape this debate in a unique way. On the one hand, the Catholic church favored saving the mother, already a member of the religious community, when a choice had to be made. On the other, it emphasized the importance of delivering the newborn alive, if only briefly, so it could be rescued from purgatory by baptism.[66] This ambiguity gave medical authors leeway to back either position, and it sharply divided opinion.

In his discussion of obstetrical techniques for complicated deliveries, Dr. Jacques Fontaine, a royal professor of medicine at the University of Aix-en-Provence, for example, articulated greater concern for the unborn and unbaptized child than for the mother. In a pamphlet entitled *Discourse on the Way to Take a Child out of the Uterus of the Mother by Extraordinary Violence against the Vulgar Opinion of Several Authors* (Aix, 1607), Fontaine opposed cephalic version (pulling the child out headfirst) or use of iron instruments to extract a malpresenting fetus even when all else failed. Concerned that these techniques could harm, even kill, the child, he advocated pulling the baby out manually by the feet (podalic version).[67] Fontaine's insistence on such lifesaving techniques, even when the infant seemed sure to die soon after delivery, arose from his desire to have even a weak or dying newborn baptized. A live birth was of greater concern to him than the health of the mother, who he assumed was (after all) already baptized.

Publishing only two years after Fontaine, Guillemeau on the other hand believed that it was "more expedient to lose a child than the mother."[68] Contrary to Fontaine, he argued that instruments, although "cruel," were sometimes necessary. Noting that one must decide quickly on some course of action, no matter how difficult and unclear the circumstances, he emphasized that

> both will die if one waits too long. And to save the mother (who is dearer than the said child) one must take a chance on this operation [with hooks]. But in this act, there are those who perform such an operation only [if the child is scarcely alive]; this is a point of Theology which I will let those who are more versed in that science than I decide.[69]

Here we have a rare case of a medical author describing the ambiguities of the situation and revealing his own ethical standards while leaving the theological resolutions to others.

Publishing the same year as Guillemeau, Bourgeois also favored saving the mother and used print to move the reader to embrace new techniques that aided in this.[70] Though also concerned about baptizing the baby, Bourgeois's protocol suggests that she was prepared to lose the child in order to save the mother.[71] Like Guillemeau, she wanted to avoid unnecessary family tragedies.[72] Unlike Guillemeau, however, she never advocated the use of instruments to extract a malpositioned infant. Most midwives avoided using instruments because of the high-risk surgical intervention involved. In any event, they were forbidden to do so by law.

The debate about saving the mother or the child continued for decades, and religious issues continued to inform arguments on both sides. In 1623, surgeon Jacques Bury argued against the use of instruments in all but the most extreme situations—grudgingly allowing them if, for example, a child had two heads or bodies and could not be extracted by any other means. In all other instances, he counseled against the use of instruments so the child could receive "the holy and august Sacrament of baptism, then [be] nourished, and raised."[73]

In each of these cases, we see authors struggling with issues of responsibility and authority as they explain how and why one should save the mother or the child in extreme situations. Their personal commitment to efficacy and morality emerged forcefully in their printed statements concerning emergency protocols. Authors who felt it necessary to articulate a position reveal sharp differences concerning the use of instruments, the extremes to which one should go in order to save a child's life, and an awareness of the opinions of others on the same matter. Printed vernacular works carried forward this debate with greater speed and reach than was possible in the era of manuscripts.

Conclusion

The early modern period in France saw increasing interest in what we today call "women's health care." The advent of vernacular print allowed fuller and faster discussion of new knowledge and techniques. As medical writings shifted from a language understood only by the elite to one of everyday usage, and from single manuscripts to printed works that could reach significantly larger audiences, medical writers were given a chance to engage in dialogue with each other about the newest birthing techniques and to debate the moral, religious, and ethical dilemmas that accompanied each advance.

Print's ability to bring more information to more people also brought with it a concern about how to halt, or at least redirect, discussion of socially sensitive topics. Treatises on reproduction and other aspects of women's health and sexuality raised questions of propriety, control, and power. What women knew about their own bodies, what they did to their bodies, who cared for their bodies, and how well they did so have had far-reaching social and political consequences.

NOTES

Thanks to Barbara Diefendorf, Monica Green, Nancy Selk, and Randolph Starn for their critical comments and helpful suggestions. Special thanks to F. Coon-Teters.

1. Translated into French as *Des divers travaux et enfantements des femmes* (Paris, 1536 and 1586), the text is referred to here by its original German title, by which it is most widely known.

2. On the genre of medical writing, see Michael R. McVaugh and Nancy G. Siraisi, "Introduction" to "Renaissance Medical Learning: Evolution of a Tradition," *Osiris* 2d ser., 6 (1990): 12. The number and variety of vernacular manuscripts on women's health and childbirth has yet to be thoroughly researched, especially in France. According to Thomas Benedek, "Before the 16th century only a few rather brief manuscripts and small sections in more comprehensive treatises were devoted to 'diseases of women.' Scant attention

was paid in them to the mechanics of delivery." Benedek, "Midwives and Physicians During the Renaissance," *Bulletin of the History of Medicine* 51 (1977): 558. Muscio's sixth-century version of the second-century Greek physician Soranus's *Gynecology* is the only exception to Benedek's statement. See Monica Green, "The Transmission of Ancient Theories of Female Physiology and Diseases through the Early Middle Ages" (unpublished Ph.D. dissertation, Princeton University, 1985), 136–40. On the French manuscript tradition, see Paul Meyer, "Manuscrits médicaux en français," *Romania* 44 (1915–17): 161–214 and Meyer, "Les manuscrits français de Cambridge," *Romania* 32 (1903): 18–120. For Latin printed texts on obstetrics and gynecology, see references in Ian Maclean, *The Renaissance Notion of Woman* (Cambridge, 1980), 102, n. 7.

3. See Elizabeth Eisenstein, *The Printing Press as an Agent of Change* (Cambridge, 1979), 63, 123, 128, and 242, on the vernacular translation movement. My survey has been compiled from a variety of sources including: Howard Stone, "The French Language in Renaissance Medicine," *Bibliothèque d'humanisme et renaissance* 15 (1953): 315–46; Paule Odile, "Etude statistique des ouvrages médicaux imprimés en français au XVIe siècle" (Thèse, Faculté de la Médecine, Université de Rennes, 1969); M. B. Quemada, "Introduction à l'étude du vocabulaire médicale (1600–1710)," *Annales littéraires de l'Université de Besançon*, 2d ser., vol. 2, fasc. 5 (1955); as well as H. L. Baudrier, *Bibliographie lyonnaise* (Paris, 1950–52); J. C. Brunet, *Manuel du libraire et de l'amateur des livres* (Berlin, 1922); *A Catalogue of Printed Books in the Wellcome Historical Medical Library . . . Books Printed before 1641* (London, 1962); Richard Durling, ed., *A Catalogue of Sixteenth-Century Printed Books in the National Library of Medicine* (Bethesda, Md., 1967); Peter Krivatsky, ed., *A Catalogue of Seventeenth-Century Printed Books in the National Library of Medicine*, (Bethesda, Md., 1989).

4. See Georges Barraud, *L'humanisme et la médecine au seizième siècle* (Paris, 1942); Natalie Zemon Davis, "Poor Relief, Humanism and Heresy," in *Society and Culture in Early Modern France* (Stanford, 1975), 17–64.

5. On vernacular print culture, see Davis, "Printing and the People," in *Society and Culture*, 189–226; Roger Chartier, "General Introduction," in *The Culture of Print: Power and the Uses of Print in Early Modern Europe*, ed. Roger Chartier, trans. Lydia G. Cochrane (Princeton, 1989), 1–10.

6. Davis, "Printing and the People," 190, 224–25.

7. Ernest Wickersheimer, *La médecine et les médecins en France à l'époque de la Renaissance* (Paris, 1906), 128–77.

8. Matthew Ramsey, *Professional and Popular Medicine in France: 1770–1830. The Social World of Medical Practice* (Cambridge, 1988), 17–70; Alison Klairmont Lingo, "The Rise of Medical Practitioners" (unpublished Ph.D. dissertation, University of California, Berkeley, 1980), 113–245; Wickersheimer, *La médecine*, 128–77. In Paris, in particular, distinctions were made between those craftsmen who learned Latin and wore long robes (surgeon-barbers) and those who did not know Latin and wore short robes (barber-

surgeons). In addition, such distinctions reflect the rivalry between surgeons and barbers and those two groups with physicians.

9. Alfred Franklin, *Les corporations ouvrières de Paris: du XIIe au XVIIIe siècle* (Paris, 1884), 3.

10. Alfred Franklin, *La vie privée d'autrefois: Les chirurgiens* (Paris, 1893), 12:37–48.

11. On cultural appropriations and their implications, see Chartier, "General Introduction," 1–2, and Eisenstein, *The Printing Press*, 270 and 539, on how print allowed "cross-fertilization" between disciplines and "intensified wrangling between diverse [medical] groups almost everywhere."

12. Robert Mandrou, *Introduction à la France moderne: Essai de psychologie historique* (Paris, 1971), 141–43; Pierre Goubert, *The Course of French History*, trans. Maarten Ultee (London, 1988), 82–86.

13. Alison Klairmont Lingo, "Empirics and Charlatans in Early Modern France: The Genesis of the Concept of 'Other' in Medical Practice," *Journal of Social History* 19 (1986): 583–604. In Lyons in 1581, the city hired an empiric "to save the home of Sieur de Mandelot" during the plague. *Inventaire-sommaire des archives communales antérieures à 1790*, ed. Fortuné Rolle (Paris, 1865–75), I, BB 52 1531–1534. And in 1603 Jerome Martin, "charlatan from Bologna," received a certificate of satisfaction from the city of Lyons where he "displayed publicly for sale several oils, unguents, and remedies for diverse maladies and operated several times, publicly and privately." Archives Municipales de Lyon, BB 107, fol. 168.

14. Lingo, "Empirics and Charlatans," 593–97.

15. Ian Maclean, *The Renaissance Notion of Woman* (Cambridge, 1980), and Londa Schiebinger, *The Mind Has No Sex* (Cambridge, Mass., 1989).

16. John F. Benton, "Trotula, Women's Problems, and the Professionalization of Medicine in the Middle Ages," *Bulletin of the History of Medicine* 59 (1985): 30–31.

17. Lingo, "Empirics and Charlatans," 594 and 602, n. 99. The Faculty of Medicine in Paris also encouraged the exclusion of women from the surgeons' guild. See Dr. Mélanie Lipinska, *Les femmes et le progrès des sciences médicales* (Paris, 1930), 55–56.

18. Mélanie Lipinska, *Histoire des femmes médecins* (Paris, 1900), 182.

19. Lingo, "Midwifery," in *Women's Studies Encyclopedia: Views from the Sciences*, ed. Helen Tierney (New York, 1989), 1:237; *Recueil des actes, titres, et mémoires concernant les affaires du clergé de France*, vol. 5 (Paris, 1768–71), cols. 71–78.

20. Richard Petrelli, "The Regulation of French Midwifery During the Ancien Régime," *Bulletin of the History of Medicine* 26 (1971): 272–92.

21. Ibid.

22. Ibid., 279; Jacques Gélis, *La sage-femme ou le médecin: Une nouvelle conception de la vie* (Paris, 1988), 22–55.

23. On this and other aspects of the changing identity of the midwife see Alison Klairmont Lingo, "Men, Women, and Science: The Tradition of Mid-

wifery in Early Modern France" (unpublished paper presented at the Seventh Berkshire Conference of Women Historians, Wellesley, Mass., 21 June 1987).

24. Wickersheimer, *La médecine,* 190; Petrelli, "The Regulation of French Midwifery," 277–78. Males outnumbered females on the board that licensed midwives, effectively counterbalancing the midwives' authority. Municipal authorities in other cities implemented similar regulations that were standardized in 1692 by royal edict. See Gélis, *La sage-femme,* 44–45.

25. On the midwife's ignorance, see Laurent Joubert, *Popular Errors,* trans. and annot. Gregory David de Rocher (Tuscaloosa, Ala., 1989), 172–73.

26. On instruction for midwives, see Gélis, *La sage-femme,* 42–43, and Wickersheimer, *La médecine,* 188–90.

27. Ferdinand Brunot, *Histoire de la langue française des origines à 1900* (Paris, 1906), 2:35–55.

28. Marcel Fosseyeux, "L'humanisme médical au XVIe siècle," *Bulletin de la société française d'histoire de la médecine* 28 (1934): 77; Stone, "The French Language," 315–46.

29. Evelyne Berriot-Salvadore, "'L'irrévérence' des ouvrages médicaux en langue vulgaire," *La Catégorie de l'honneste dans la culture du XVIe siècle, Actes du Colloque International de Sommières,* 2 (Saint-Etienne, 1985): 65–77; Davis, "Printing and the People," 222–25; Stone, "The French Language," 315; Brunot, *Histoire de la langue,* 2:36–53 and 67–70.

30. See Eisenstein, *The Printing Press,* 541 and 541, n. 58.

31. *Les oeuvres de M. Ambroise Paré* (Paris, 1575); "Responce de M. Ambroise Paré, premier chirurgien du Roy, aux calomnies d'aucuns médecins et chirurgiens, touchant ses oeuvres," in *Ambroise Paré d'après de nouveaux documents . . . ,* ed. Stéphen Le Paulmier (Paris, 1887), 224.

32. Paule Dumaître, *Ambroise Paré: Chirurgien de quatre rois de France* (Paris, n.d.), 287–89.

33. See Janet Doe, *A Bibliography of the Works of Ambroise Paré* (Chicago, 1937), 105.

34. Paré, "Mémoire d'Ambroise Paré . . . ," in *Ambroise Paré d'après de nouveaux documents,* 222. The text was written in 1575. See also Doe, *A Bibliography,* 75–76.

35. Paré, "Mémoire," 223.

36. Ibid., 233. This is a loose translation of the text.

37. Ibid., 233, 236, 237.

38. Brunot, *Histoire,* 2:43 and 53; Davis, "Proverbial Wisdom and Popular Errors," in *Society and Culture,* 260–61. Although Joubert's *Popular Errors* did not specifically focus on women's health care, significant portions were devoted to the subject.

39. See Davis, "Printing and the People," 224, and Joubert, *Popular Errors,* 173, 176.

40. Also known as Marguerite de France, she was daughter of Henry II and Catherine de Medici and wife of Henry of Navarre, future Henry IV of France.

41. Joubert, *Popular Errors,* 209–25, particularly 212–13, and 283, n. 1. Joubert claimed that the word's inclusion was due to a typographical error.

42. On editions and reprintings, see de Rocher's "Introduction," in Joubert, *Popular Errors,* xx–xxi.

43. Joubert, *Popular Errors,* 6–7.

44. In its second printing, Joubert used asterisks to identify offending passages. Ironically, this may have served to make the materials more visible to the eye instead of less. Ibid., 6–10.

45. James A. Brundage, *Law, Sex, and Christian Society in Medieval Europe* (Chicago, 1987), 80–93.

46. Decretists and later canonists debated the relative sinfulness of what was called the "marriage debt," i.e., a husband or wife's obligation to submit to the sexual needs of his/her spouse. Ibid., 236, 241–42, 281–84, 358–60, 505–7.

47. Ibid., 574–75.

48. While there was a fairly high degree of literacy among males, particularly in the medical community, it is unlikely that there were many educated midwives. The few midwives who could read, however, might have shared their knowledge with their colleagues by reading texts aloud or passing the information on informally. See Davis, "Printing and the People," 210; Davis, "City Women and Religious Change," in *Society and Culture,* 72–74; David Harley, "Historians as Demonologists: The Myth of the Midwife-Witch," *Social History of Medicine* 3 (1990): 1–26; Roger Chartier, "Publishing Strategies and What People Read, 1530–1660," in Roger Chartier, *The Cultural Uses of Print in Early Modern France,* trans. Lydia Cochrane (Princeton, 1987), 152–54; Eisenstein, *The Printing Press,* 60–61.

49. Guillemeau, *De l'heureux accouchement des femmes, où il est traicté du gouvernement de leur grossesse* (Paris, 1609), fol. e iii.

50. Male authors also attempted to exalt the role of the male midwife by linking it with antique, learned traditions. In his obstetrical manual, Guillemeau glorified the male tradition of learned obstetrics and gynecology by tracing its roots to such venerated thinkers as Hippocrates, Soranus, and Galen.

51. Jacques Bury, *Le propagatif de l'homme et secours des femmes en travail d'enfant* (Paris, 1623). Jacques Fontaine, *Deux Paradoxes appartenant à la chirurgie, le premier contient la façon de tirer les enfans du ventre de leur mère par la violence extraordinaire . . .* (Paris, 1611), and *Livre Second de la particulière façon de tirer les enfans par la violence* (n.p., n.d.). François Rousset, *Traitte nouveau de l'hysterotomotokie ou enfantement caesarean* (Paris, 1581).

52. Rousset, *Traitte nouveau;* Jacques Bury, *La propagateur de l'homme et secours des femmes en travail d'enfant* (Paris, 1623). Jacques Du Val addressed midwives and surgeons in his *Traité des hermaphrodits parties genitales, accouchemens des femmes* (Rouen, 1612) but assumed that women would not use instruments. While he included instructions for midwives on how to perform podalic version, he followed Rösslin in not advising its use until all other

methods had failed. Du Val, *Traité des hermaphrodits,* 194–95. Also see Yvonne Knibielher and Catherine Fouquet, *Histoire des mères du Moyen Age à nos jours* (n.p., 1977), 70.

53. *Des divers travaux et enfantements des femmes* (Paris, 1536), fol. lxxxvii.

54. Also directed to laywomen, the first edition of Bourgeois's *Observations diverses sur la sterilité, perte de fruict, foecondité, accouchements, et maladies des femmes et enfans nouveaux-naiz* (Paris, 1609), includes vol. 1. The editions of Paris, 1617, and Rouen, 1626, include vols. 1 and 2. The edition of Paris, 1626, includes vol. 3. Page references for vols. 1 and 2 are to the 1626 Rouen edition, and for vol. 3, to the 1626 Paris edition.

55. Ibid., 1:75–91, on podalic version for various fetal malpresentations.

56. She probably hoped men would read her text as well. She criticized her male colleagues throughout the text. See ibid., 1:113, 3:35.

57. Ibid., 1:35, especially 2:96 on control of anger.

58. Joubert, *Popular Errors,* 171.

59. She also offered a detailed description of face presentation and its management during a delivery and was the first to cut the cord between two ligatures when it was wrapped around the neck. See Philip A. Kalisch, Margaret Scobey, and Beatrice J. Kalisch, "Louyse Bourgeois and the Emergence of Modern Midwifery," *Journal of Nurse-Midwifery* 26, no. 4 (1981): 3.

60. Bourgeois, *Observations diverses,* 1:111.

61. Ibid., "Au lecteur," n.p.

62. The Parisian physician Guillaume Chrestien dedicated his translation of Hippocrates, *De la nature de l'enfant ou ventre de la mère* (Reims, 1553), to the Duchesse de Buillon, the daughter-in-law of Diane de Poitiers, and a translation of Galen, *De la formation des enfans au ventre de la mère* (Paris, 1556), to Queen Catherine de Medici. In the former, Chrestien recounted how the Duchess had called upon him during the previous winter to help a poor woman of Sedan who was having a difficult delivery. At the time, the Duchess asked him many questions about "conception, formation, nutrition, and childbirth." Chrestien, "Preface," *De la nature de l'enfant.* Simon De Vallambert wrote his *Cinq livres de la manière de nourrir et de gouverner les enfants des leur naissance* (Poitiers, 1565) for the Duchess of Savoy and Berry to help her raise her son, the Prince of Piedmont. Dr. Louis De Serres of Lyons dedicated his *Discours de la nature, causes, signes, et curation des empeschements de la conception et de la sterilité des femmes* (Lyons, 1625), to Dame Françoise De Bonne, maréschalle de Créqui and to other women to whom "God had not given any children in the first years of marriage."

63. Also see Ruth Kelso, *Doctrine for the Lady of the Renaissance* (Urbana, Ill., 1956), 117–20.

64. Giovanni Marinello, *Thresor des remedes secrets pour les maladies des femmes,* trans. Jean Liebault (Paris, 1585), "Au Lecteur."

65. De La Tousche, *La très-haute et très-souveraine science de l'art et industrie naturelle d'enfanter . . .* (Paris, 1587) in G.-J. Witkowski, *Accoucheurs et sages-femmes célèbres. Esquisses biographiques* (Paris, 1891), 296–302.

66. St. Thomas Aquinas, as quoted in Renate Blumenfeld-Kosinski, *Not of*

Woman Born: Representations of Caesarean Birth in Medieval and Renaissance Culture (Ithaca, 1990), 26–27, stated: "'Evil should not be done that good may come,' according to St. Paul [Rom. 3:8]. Therefore one should not kill the mother in order to baptize the child; if, however, the child be still alive in the womb after the mother has died, the mother should be opened in order to baptize the child." Thus, the church approved of Caesarean section if the mother had died in childbirth.

67. "In that way there will never be a need to use tools or hooks that kill children. . . . The invention of tools is born of . . . impatience and the difficulty created by pulling them by the head; . . . fearing the loss of the mother and the child, [the surgeons] elect to lose the child to save the mother." Fontaine, *Discours de la façon,* 13–14.

68. Guillemeau, *De l'heureux accouchement,* 252.

69. Ibid.

70. Bourgeois, *Observations diverses,* 1:69.

71. Ibid., 1:64.

72. Bourgeois and Guillemeau followed Paré's protocol for podalic version in cases of breech birth and other fetal malpresentations. Bourgeois, *Observations diverses,* 1:75–91; Guillemeau, *De l'heureux accouchement,* 272–300.

73. Bury, *Le propagatif,* 96–97.

Deadly Parents: Family and Aristocratic Culture in Early Modern France

Jonathan Dewald

I begin by juxtaposing two well-known plays. In Sophocles' *Antigone*, Creon—newly installed in power—condemns Antigone and is himself destroyed as a result.[1] His son Haemon commits suicide, his policies are revealed to be impure, and he can only exile himself from the city. His lineage extinct, he has no claim to political power, or any interest in it; the son's death destroys the father's life. Jean Racine's *Thébaïde*, of 1664, recounts the same events but reorders them. Racine condenses the action, so that the fatal battle between Antigone's brothers, Jocasta's death, and Antigone's death all occur on the same day. Following the model of Euripides' *Phoenician Women,* he gives Creon a second son, who kills himself in a vain effort to bring peace to the city; Haemon (the character does not appear in Euripides' version of the story) now dies in battle, also in a glorious effort to restore civic peace. But above all Racine changes Creon's response to these events. His Creon is less a patriarch ambitious for his dynasty than a *gallant* wildly in love with Antigone herself. His son's death, so he wrongly believes, removes the only obstacle to winning the girl's love. His son's death destroys Sophocles' Creon and shakes Euripides', but Racine's Creon exults:

No one's happiness matches mine; and you'll see, in the course of this fortunate day, my ambitions crowned and my love enthroned . . . I lose much less than I expect to gain. . . . In depriving me of a son, the heavens eliminate a rival. . . . It's all like a dream: I was a father and a subject; now I'm a lover, and king.[2]

His exultation is appropriate, for all along Racine's Creon has manipulated events toward this conclusion, slyly encouraging Oedipus's sons to fight each other and thus, indirectly, causing his own sons' deaths. Only news of Antigone's death ends Creon's joy and brings on his own death. In Racine's story, it is the object of sexual desire, not the son, whose disappearance destroys Creon's hopes and leaves him unwilling to continue living.

Such comparisons illuminate the degree to which seventeenth-century dramatists reworked the classical models on which they based their work, changing both details and essentials so as to reflect contemporary preoccupations; the changes must have been the more striking precisely because they entailed the deformation of well-known cultural models. In the *Thébaide,* this reworking produced a grim vision of the family, for the play inverts our expectations about Oedipal relations. Here it is a father who (in effect) sacrifices his sons to his sexual and political desires.

Racine's play tells us important things about familial tensions in seventeenth-century Parisian high society. Assumptions of conflict, I want to suggest, permeated seventeenth-century discussions of the family and undercut some of the most deeply held ideologies of the age. For belief that familial conflict was pervasive and murderous stood against belief in either patriarchal authority or dynastic tradition. Figures like Racine's Creon implied that patriarchy, whether familial or political, rested on a combination of paternal violence and filial sacrifice; here the father symbolized not an ordered and nurturing cosmos, but rather danger and loss. In turn, such a vision of patriarchy raised questions about the aristocratic lineage itself. Aristocratic ideology presented the lineage as a basic social reality, from which individuals derived their personal qualities and for whose advancement they directed their efforts. The lineage gave purpose and meaning to individual lives. Such plays as the *Thébaide* suggested instead that the lineage achieved its ends at great personal cost and that paternal aims had no necessary legitimacy. Whereas the ideology of the aristocratic lineage drew an easy convergence between personal and familial fulfillment, Racine suggested potentially violent conflict between them.

Figures like Creon were commonplace on the seventeenth-century Parisian stage and in other literary genres. Racine's *Mithridate* presents a father who has already killed two sons, and its plot centers on his efforts to kill two more; *Iphigénie* of course describes a father killing his daughter; *Bajazet,* an older brother killing a younger; the Hippolyte of *Phèdre* dies because of his father's curse. *Britannicus,* *Andromaque,* and *Bérénice* offer the same pattern in attenuated form. For though sons survive their parents in these plays, their parents have effectively destroyed their hopes of happiness and autonomy. Nero describes his inability to rule, even to speak, when his mother is present; neither Titus (*Bérénice*) nor Pyrrhus (*Andromaque*) can have the woman he loves because of the obligations that each has inherited from a dead father. Pyrrhus is urged to kill the boy he contemplates raising as a son, since he risks his life by allowing the boy to live, and die himself for attempting to violate his father's legacy. A comparable catalogue could be drawn from Corneille, and his play *Rodogune* summarizes the mixture of violence, guilt, and filial renunciation that the tragedians saw in the transfer of authority from one generation to the next: "Can you not allow us to reign in innocence?" asks a son of his mother in that play. The play concludes with her decisively negative answer: "Because of one crime and then another, there you are, finally king. For you I've killed your father, your brother, and now myself. May the heavens take you [my son and your bride] for victims, and rain down on you the punishments that I have earned."[3] Corneille's preface to *Rodogune* stressed the playwright's liberty to reformulate ancient stories for his own purposes,[4] and all of these plays showed a similar readiness; most built on only slight ancient authority.

In all of these plays, a further preoccupation accompanies discussions of inheritance, a preoccupation with illicit sexual desire. There are of course the Oedipus plays, of which Corneille, like Racine, wrote a version. Racine's version, as we have seen, presents a doubling of sexual competition between fathers and sons, adding the mortal competition between Creon and Haemon to that between Laius and Oedipus, and other plays use similar techniques, drawing attention to the problem of sexual desire through parallels and doubles and deforming classical models so as to serve new purposes. Thus Racine's *Mithridate* displays two brothers in love with their father's new bride, a girl who has long been in love with one of the brothers; the play thus matches paternal sexual rapacity against a doubled filial desire. Corneille's *Rodogune* employs a milder version of the same pattern, with two virtuous brothers in love with their dead father's bride. In *Phèdre* there is not only the heroine's incestuous love for her stepson, but also Hippolyte's love for a girl who his father has adopted and to whom he has forbidden marriage. *Bajazet* presents a royal wife in love with her brother-in-law, and *Andromaque* and *Bérénice* present still more muted versions of the theme; for in each a dead father's legacy prohibits the hero's love.[5] In all of these plays, images of incest place the denial of personal desire at the center of familial life and emphasize the ferocity of conflict within the family. Family members are driven by the most powerful urges, those of sexual desire, to want the same objects.

Finally, all of these plays explicitly attach problems within the family to problems within the political order. *Bérénice* presents a famous and reasoned exposition of relations between political and personal realms. If he is to reign justly, so the play concludes, the king must renounce his personal wants and accept the prohibitions that his paternal inheritance demands. In this play, the requirements of succession are rational, though painful. But other plays present harsher, more troubling accounts of the political aspect of patriarchy, stressing its potential violence and lawlessness. Thus Racine's infanticidal Mithridates is also a heroic political figure, struggling for national independence against Roman imperialism. The *Thébaide* stresses the violence that underlies political activity: all characters in the play agree that the frenzy to rule shown by Eteocles, Polynices, and Creon will overcome their sentiments of familial love. *Bajazet* makes the same point, by describing the place of systematic fratricide in the Turkish political world; the needs of successful rule destroy familial attachments. Again, it is Corneille who provides the fullest discussion of the collision between personal and political worlds. His *Horace* portrays a brother who kills his sister, with their father's vociferous approval, and a father arming to kill his son, in the mistaken belief that the son has dishonored the state. The same father defines his stance as an affirmation of public over private needs. "It is wrong to weep for private losses, when one sees them producing public victories," he proclaims, and the play concludes by confirming his view. Because of young Horace's usefulness to the state, the king overturns laws against murder and pardons his act.[6] Here again the needs of the public world destroy the private, in a sequence of violent acts; the play's conclusion notes the lawlessness of some of these acts, but argues that the state must sometimes discard law as a potential threat to its own functioning. In their different ways, all of these plays ascribe to the public realm a destructive violence. At best, the states that they describe constrict the realm of personal feeling; at worst, they violently assault it.

Seventeenth-century drama was an exceptionally public form of art, in which success with the public provided explicit justification for artistic choices. "Poets fit themselves to the tastes of their era," as Racine's son said of his father, and both Corneille and Racine repeatedly made the same point; audiences' enthusiasm justified their efforts, even when these violated critical doctrines.[7] Their vision of the family, in short, touched contemporaries, and was fashioned in order to do so. But one can see comparable images in other sixteenth- and seventeenth-century writing. Thus Montaigne's insistence on parents' bitterness at watching their children coming to enjoy adulthood;[8] thus Jean Bodin's enthusiastic endorsement of parents' right to kill their children. "In any rightly ordered commonwealth," wrote Bodin, "that power of life and death over their children which belongs to them under the law of God and of nature, should be restored to parents. . . . If this power is not restored, there is no hope of any restoration of good morals, honors, virtue, or the ancient splendor of commonwealths."[9]

And thus the two opening stories of the *Contes de Perrault,* one of the most popular books of the late seventeenth century and one explicitly directed to a refined and courtly group of readers. The opening tale, "Griselidis," claims to teach by the example of the heroine's patience—but it is also a story of symbolic infanticide and incest. Her husband the king tells Griselidis that their daughter has died and follows this imagined death by locking the girl in a convent. Neither parent sees her for the next fifteen years, when she emerges as a beautiful young lady; still testing his wife, the king (who alone knows that the young lady is his daughter, and who knows as well that she is in love with a young courtier) announces that he will divorce Griselidis and marry the girl—before finally revealing the truth, arranging the girl's marriage to her lover, and returning to his own wife. Like Racine, Perrault thus imagines the sexual rapacity of the old and their readiness to deny their children's happiness, or indeed to deny them existence. "Griselidis" presents such possibilities as play rather than reality, but in the next tale they take on greater seriousness. In "Peau d'Ane," the father so desperately desires his daughter that he kills his gold-producing donkey in order to have her. After a series of narrow escapes, the heroine's flight and marriage finally cure him of his "odious flame," but even then "the little [of his incestuous desire] that remained served only to strengthen his paternal love." Sexual feeling cannot be entirely banished from familial relations, however well they function.[10]

Both tales, furthermore, underline the political implications of the tensions that they describe. Both fathers are kings, and they are described in terms that would have reminded readers of Louis XIV's propaganda for his regime (some of it produced by the Perraults themselves). Griselidis's husband combines "all the gifts of body and soul." He is suited to war; "he ardently loved the arts"; he loves victory and "great undertakings," but above all he seeks "the solid glory of making his Peoples happy." Peau d'Ane's incestuous father is "the greatest king on earth, gentle in peace, terrible in war; . . . his states were calm, and under his protection both the virtues and the arts flourished."[11] For late seventeenth-century readers, these must have been troubling descriptions, suggesting as they did the potential lawlessness of great and constructive kings; in fact their royal powers allow these kings to pursue their destructive designs. In Perrault as in Racine, the image of the dangerous parent extends to the collective parent, the king, and it does so in a striking way. Medieval commentators had warned of the moral dangers of public life, but in these stories danger lies in the private realm of the family.

I have suggested that these images of the parent had more than private significance, emerging as they did in some of the seventeenth century's most public art forms.[12] It remains to ask how these images functioned in the private lives of real people. In the remainder of this essay, I want to suggest that images of familial murder and incest touched contemporary audiences because they gave mythical form to important aspects of contemporary reality. Drama expressed the seriousness of the conflicts that divided families and the painful emotions that these created; it allowed viewers to imagine, as in a thought-experiment, the extreme consequences of a commonplace experience, that of family members desiring the same objects, competing for them, and ultimately submitting to paternal domination.

Thus literary chronicles of the great nobility's lives drew attention to the anger and dislike that prevailed between generations. Early in the fifteenth century, Jean Froissart described the events that led Gaston de Foix, in many ways his ideal example of chivalric behavior, to murder his son. The murder itself was accidental, Froissart concluded, but it followed a long history of conflict within the family. Gaston's wife had already fled the household, and his father-in-law had attempted to poison him, manipulating the boy for the purpose.[13] Three centuries later, Saint-Simon gave familial conflict a similar centrality in his narratives of the great. There was the prince de Conti: "His son, young as he was, he could not abide." There was the prince de Condé: "For [his son], it was only politeness. They feared each other; the son, a difficult and capricious father; the father, a son-in-law of the king. But from time to time the son would trip up the father, and the father's attacks on the son were furious." And likewise the duc de La Rochefoucauld: "His feelings for his children were less than lukewarm; and though they served him well, he made their lives very difficult."[14]

Families' private papers include similar events and reflections. We can follow these with exceptional ease in the case of the La Trémoille family, leading Protestant nobles from the southwest. An exchange from 1642 illustrated tensions between the family's brothers. In that year, the comte de Laval, the duc de La Trémoille's younger brother, died in Venice; the family dispatched a dependant to the scene to unravel the comte's affairs and recover familial property. After extended negotiations with the comte's widow, this emissary reported back that "M. de Laval carried off to the other world, and wanted to leave behind here, marks of the hatred and aversion he had for Monseigneur [the duc] and Madame."[15] Twenty years later, the same duc de La Trémoille entered into a new conflict, believing himself insulted by his forty-two-year-old son, the prince de Tarente. "After God's service," he wrote his son, "serving myself and the family ought to be your principal object and employment. . . . Consider that having received from us life, honor, and property, you can give us nothing that is not infinitely beneath what you owe." Ten days later, after the son had attempted to justify his conduct, La Trémoille's anger rose to new heights. "Learn that except for my mercy, you ought to beg for nothing but leave to die," he told his son.[16]

All of these issues were replayed by the next generation of La

Trémoille. The prince de Tarente, so his daughter remembered, "distinguished sharply between my brother and me; for since he was always timid and serious, and I very bold and gay, [our father] had a preference for me, which followed the sentiments that he had felt from the start." Soon after, the prince abjured his Protestantism and encouraged his son to do the same. The son's resistance provoked furious rage: Tarente threatened "to place him between four walls, on bread and water, for the rest of his life."[17] Among the La Trémoille family, experiences like this had hardened into conventional wisdom. In the later seventeenth century a cousin wrote to the duchesse de La Trémoille that "it's so common to receive neither pleasure nor satisfaction from anyone that it no longer surprises one, . . . for those who are most obliged by birth and friendship take the greatest pleasure in upsetting us."[18]

Given the well-known diversity of familial unhappiness, such conflicts within specific families might perhaps be dismissed as isolated events. For this reason, it is helpful to turn to examples of relatively successful familial relations and to explore some of the language in which contemporaries described them. I offer two such examples. The first comes from 1649 and concerns the Nicolay family, one of the great Parisian robe families. In that year Nicolas de Nicolay succeeded his father as first president of the Chambre des Comptes of Paris, and he used his first speech to the court to reflect on his father's generosity in resigning the position to him. "When I consider," he began,

> that I could not be a part of this illustrious body without my father—who has had the happiness of being its leader—departing from it; that I could not have arisen to this place of honor without his lowering himself; that I could not climb to the glory of my ancestors save by the same steps that I see him descending; that my good fortune can only be built on the ruins of his; when I reflect that his fall is the price of my happiness . . . [19]

The Nicolay had successfully negotiated one of the difficult transitions that every aristocratic family encountered, the moment of inheritance, and Nicolas de Nicolay accurately appreciated his family's success in this task. Offices, honors, and wealth had passed from one generation to the next, without apparent conflict. But Nicolay also spoke of what the process cost. He spoke of his father's "fall," his descent (*il s'abaisse*), the "ruins of his situation." The father had sacrificed himself for the son's advancement. Underlying Nicolay's rhetoric was a hierarchical vision of familial roles, which accorded only one family member a leading position. The son could advance within this hierarchy only if the father fell; two generations could not coexist as full adults.

For this reason, not all families managed the transition as well as the Nicolay. Early in the seventeenth century, two members of the Busquet family, notable Rouennais magistrates, disputed the possession of an office before the assembled Parlement. The father accused his son of attempting "shamelessly to despoil him of his position"; the son responded by claiming that the father sought "to reduce him to indigence."[20] "Hurry up and die," says Molière's Dom Juan to *his* father; "it's the best thing you can do. Everyone must have his turn, and it enrages me to see fathers who live as long as their sons." The father responds in kind: "this son . . . is the bitterness and torment of my life."[21] Nicolas de Nicolay's speech praised his father and celebrated his family's continuity, yet his assumptions converged with the Busquets' and Dom Juan's. One generation did in fact despoil the next. There could be no resolution of the conflicts between them without loss on one side or the other.

My second group of examples concerns parental love for children. Seventeenth-century parents certainly felt love for small children, love that in some instances acquired surprising intensity. The military nobleman Henri de Campion described his first daughter, born in 1649, as "so beautiful and so delightful that from the moment of her birth I loved her with a tenderness that I cannot express." When the girl was two, Campion found himself forced to spend some months at his country home, and there he spent "part of my time reading, or in playing with my daughter, who despite her youth was so amusing that everyone who saw her felt enormous pleasure, and I more than all the rest together." But two years later the child died, and Campion felt his life blighted. Years later Campion wrote that "since then, I've felt no real joy. I had so firmly convinced myself that my daughter would be the consolation of my last years, and I had begun so to associate her with all my actions, that I feel it a form of theft to take any pleasure without her."[22] Campion's fascination with his daughter and delight in playing with her suggest modern ideals of familial life, but the language in which he expressed these emotions deserves close attention. For Campion interpreted his love in terms of the child's specific qualities. His love corresponded to her beauty and ability to amuse, to her worth. Thus the survival of another child afforded Campion no consolation for the loss of this one. Affection for children was closely related to discriminating judgments between them.

Other seventeenth-century parents used the same language. What this meant for children themselves can been seen in the autobiography of Charlotte Amélie de La Trémoille, from the later seventeenth century. Charlotte Amélie, it has been seen, knew that her father loved her and knew why he preferred her to her brother: her ease of manner contrasted with her brother's timidity. With their mother, the situation was reversed. Early on "my mother could not endure me," because of the liberal manner in which she had been raised. Yet a halting relationship developed between them, a by-product of the pressures that Protestant families like the La Trémoilles faced after the midseventeenth century. A Catholic uncle sought to have the thirteen-year-old Charlotte Amélie and her brother placed under his care; to prevent this enforced conversion, their mother suddenly appeared at the family's estate to carry the children off to Holland. "I awoke, I looked at her," recalled Charlotte Amélie, "and thinking that I was dreaming (which had happened to me several times) I rolled over and tried to get back to sleep." The poignancy of the moment lay both in the child's longing for her mother and in her conviction of her mother's indifference. "I knew that my mother had never loved me," she remembered in her autobiography, "but things improved somewhat; for seeing that she received my little efforts well gave me courage, and I gained ease with her much sooner than I would ever have hoped; and this truly won my mother's heart, so that she did sincerely what she had resolved to pretend—that is, to treat me well and to love me."[23]

Like Henri de Campion, then, Charlotte Amélie understood parental love to be conditional, a response to the child's merits. The child's capacity to display affection convincingly was especially important. As she became more at ease with her mother, she could begin to win her mother's love; her brother's reserve stood in the way of affection from their father. (The same process had occurred a few years earlier in the king's household: when Louis XIII found his son excessively reserved toward him, he threatened to remove the boy from his mother's care and bring in new tutors).[24] Charlotte Amélie's experiences convinced her that parents demanded such courtship throughout their lives. "Assuredly," she reflected as she thought about her childhood, "I believe that blessings or curses from fathers and mothers, and especially at the hour of their deaths, have great importance, and draw upon their children blessings or sufferings; that's why every child ought to seek religiously to observe the fifth commandment, as something of great importance."[25] Parents might well give love, in this view, but they remained dangerous, a source of blessings if placated, of efficacious curses if slighted. In either case, responsibility lay with the child, whose behavior and character called forth the parent's responses.

Images of the dangerous parent, this paper has suggested, pervaded seventeenth-century high culture, and expressed with surprising directness fears of violence and of incestuous sexuality. Seventeenth-century fascination with such stories, of course, recalls our own readiness to understand familial structures in terms of the Oedipal myth, but with differences. Whereas the twentieth century has focused on the rapacious, violently desirous child, the seventeenth century gave these qualities to parents, and notably to fathers; whereas the twentieth century has tended to see in the myth a narrative of the child's triumph, in an eventual adult autonomy, seventeenth-century Oedipal narratives describe the child's destruction. In these narratives, fathers rather than children threaten violence and pursue illicit sexual relations. In contrast, sons are dutiful, self-sacrificing, and often timid. *Phèdre* makes the point explicitly: young Hippolyte opens the play by contrasting his modest achievements and sexual restraint with his father's heroic deeds, violence, and endless record of seductions and rapes.[26] Such images, I have suggested, undercut two of the ideologies that the seventeenth century took most seriously. They contradicted the belief in the king as father of his people, and they made more difficult the belief in the aristocratic lineage as the appropriate basis for social organization. The image of the dangerous parent carried significant ideological costs.

Why then the seventeenth century's fascination with the image? Experience of daily life offered numerous instances of familial conflict, but these do not explain a readiness to interpret familial life in terms of conflict—that is, to see conflict as a norm of familial relations rather than an unhappy accident. In fact one might have expected ideas about parental violence to recede over the seventeenth century, as manners improved and the "civilizing process" did its work of reducing personal aggression among the aristocracy. Patriarchal ideas also became more powerful during the course of the seventeenth century. Louis XIV and his writers produced lavish celebrations of the king's importance to the society and of the need for obedience to him. During the same years, new genealogical requirements limited access to high positions at court, and sharper distinctions emerged within the nobility itself; under Colbert the Crown began inspecting nobles' credentials and publicly humiliated those who claimed high status without the proper background. Venality of office had similar effects. The price of both civil and military positions increased dramatically during the first three-fourths of the seventeenth century, making inheritance a more central moment in most nobles' careers and making the lineage a more prominent institution. In these and other ways, patriarchal ideas and realities were acquiring greater force as the seventeenth century advanced.[27]

All of these changes glorified paternal authority, teaching that society functioned on the basis of obedience to fathers and devotion to the interests of the lineage. Jean Racine and Charles Perrault themselves produced florid versions of such ideas in their work as historians and propagandists for Louis XIV.[28] That Racine and Perrault were at the same time among those writers most fascinated by antithetical images of paternal authority, as lawless and destructive of personal happiness, suggests the complexity of paternalism's apparent triumph in the seventeenth century. The murderous royal parents that they and their contemporaries created expressed what many felt to be implicit in patriarchal ideology, its sacrifice of personal wants to political ard familial ends. The problem of personal autonomy, in other words, lay embedded in patriarchal ideology itself. The ideology's successes over the seventeenth century only sharpened the problem, by making more oppressive the ideology's demands on individuals. Racine, Perrault, and the others expressed the painful nature of these demands; at the same time, their work demonstrated the inherent instability of patriarchal ideology and the personal resistances that it created even as it advanced.

NOTES

1. Some of the evidence and arguments presented in this article are developed at greater length in my book *Aristocratic Experience and the Origins of Modern Culture: France 1570–1715* (Berkeley, 1993), and are used here by permission of the University of California Press.

2. *Oeuvres complètes*, I: *Théatre-poésies*, ed. Raymond Picard (Paris, 1950), 166. The understanding of Racine offered here owes much to Roland Barthes, *On Racine*, trans. Richard Howard (New York, 1977).

3. Pierre Corneille, *Oeuvres complètes* (Paris, 1963), 437.

4. Ibid., 416.

5. For stress on the shocking nature of even muted forms of incest in early modern England, see Roland Mushat Frye, *The Renaissance Hamlet: Issues and Responses in 1600* (Princeton, 1984), 77–82.

6. Corneille, *Oeuvres complètes*, 262 and 267.

7. Racine, *Oeuvres complètes*, I, 39; for other instances, ibid., 242, and Corneille, *Oeuvres complètes*, 835.

8. Donald Frame, ed., *The Complete Essays of Montaigne* (Stanford, 1958), 280.

9. Eric Cochrane et al., eds., *Early Modern Europe: Crisis of Authority* (Chicago, 1987), 232.

10. Jean-Pierre Collinet, ed., *Perrault, Contes* (Paris: Folio, 1981), 114.

11. Ibid., 59 and 98.

12. For other examples of sixteenth- and seventeenth-century images of parents destroying their children, see Jean Delumeau and Daniel Roche, eds., *Histoire des pères et de la paternité* (Paris, 1990), 205–9.

13. Jean Froissart, *Chronicles*, trans. Geoffrey Brereton (London: Penguin, 1968), 266–74.

14. Louis de Rouvroy, duc de Saint-Simon, *Mémoires*, ed. Gonzague Truc (Paris, 1958–63), 3:55, 99, 142.

15. Archives Nationales, Paris (hereafter, AN) 1 AP 642, Allard to Monsieur, 6 September 1642.

16. AN 1 AP 396, fols. 308, 314–15.

17. AN 1 AP 444, 34 and 51.

18. AN 1 AP 435, marquise de La Moussaye, 7 December 1641.

19. AN 3 AP 256, "Harangues de mon grand-père," 73.

20. Jonathan Dewald, *The Formation of a Provincial Nobility: The Magistrates of the Parlement of Rouen, 1499–1610* (Princeton, 1980), 302.

21. Molière, *Oeuvres complètes*, 14 vols. (Paris, 1873–1900), 5:178 and 175.

22. Henri de Campion, *Mémoires*, ed. Marc Fumaroli (Paris, 1967), 199, 201, 212.

23. AN 1 AP 444, 28.

24. See for instance A. Lloyd Moote, *Louis XIII, the Just* (Berkeley, 1989), 282.

25. Ibid., 21.

26. Racine, *Oeuvres complètes*, 1:751–52.

27. My understanding of these issues owes much to the work of Ralph Giesey and Sarah Hanley on the legal organization of dynasticism in early modern France.

28. Orest Ranum, *Artisans of Glory: Writers and Historical Thought in Seventeenth-Century France* (Chapel Hill, 1980).

Revolutionary Histories: The Literary Politics of Louise de Kéralio (1758–1822)

Carla Hesse

> Quid foemina possit?
> (What couldn't a woman do?)
> Aeneid, book V

In June of 1787, one of France's most noted journalists, Jacques Mallet du Pan, announced in the *Mercure de France* that:

> There exist an overwhelming number of Histories and Historiographers, but very few Historians. Up until now we have not seen in France a *Historienne;* Mlle de Kéralio, I think, is the first. . . . And yet another singularity is joined to this one, the Author's choice to trace the lives of two Women . . .[1]

Mallet du Pan thus credited the author of the *Histoire d'Elisabeth* with more than the publication of an admirable history, he attributed to her the invention of a new authorial identity, the woman historian. Why did Mallet du Pan consider the achievements of Mlle de Kéralio to be so unprecedented as to require, if not the invention, then at least a neologistic usage of the term *historienne*?[2] The question deserves serious reflection because we know, from the work of Natalie Davis among others, that there had been histories of women written in France for several centuries before the publication of Kéralio's *Histoire d'Elisabeth, reine d'Angleterre* in 1787. And there had been many women writers of history as well.[3] Moreover, Mallet du Pan was a man of considerable learning and no doubt well aware of these facts. In what then did he perceive her innovation to consist? By what new light did she cast all those who came before her into shadow? How did Louise de Kéralio come to be recognized as France's first and only *historienne* on the eve of the French Revolution? And in her hands what fate awaited the history of women in the Revolution itself?

This essay will examine the discursive dilemmas and achievements of one writer, Louise de Kéralio (1752–1822), as she sought to constitute herself as a historian and women as subjects of historical knowledge in the period spanning the French Revolution, that is from 1780 to 1810. Her career makes it possible to recapture the French revolutionary project of remaking history from a woman's point of view. I will first consider Kéralio's coming into voice as a published writer and as a *historienne* and then turn to the dilemmas of Kéralio as a revolutionary historian attempting to overcome the past. And, finally, I will examine Kéralio's abandonment of historical writing in favor of the novel in the postrevolutionary world of the First Empire.

The Making of a *Historienne*

Louise Félicité Guynement de Kéralio was born in Paris in 1758, into an old noble Breton family who exemplified, through their anglophilia and reform-mindedness, the enlightened liberal aristocratic literati in the later half of the eighteenth century. The intellectual world of Louise de Kéralio's parents was a world sharply delineated along gender lines, lines that are now becoming familiar to literary and cultural historians of the eighteenth century.[4] Her father, Louis Félix Guynement de Kéralio, wrote erudite military histories and was a member of the Royal Academy of Inscriptions and Belles-Lettres.[5] Her mother, Marie Françoise Abeille, wrote and translated fiction. But like most women writers of her generation, she published her works anonymously, declining to sign or to publicly acknowledge her literary achievements.[6] Louise de Kéralio was an only child; her intellectual career can in many respects be seen as a struggle to come to terms with this dual inheritance of paternal historical erudition and her mother's passion for writing and translating fiction.

Indeed, Kéralio proved from the very start to be a virtuoso at bending the rules of both gender and genre as far as they could bend without breaking them. The issue of Louise de Kéralio's gender affiliation was raised from the very day of her christening when she received her father's names (Louis Félix), with the endings feminized: Louise Félicité. Further, by Kéralio's own testimony as well as that of others, it was her father, rather than her mother, who took charge of her education.[7] And though Kéralio's first published works appear to descend smoothly from her maternal side—a series of translations from Italian and English and a novel published anonymously in 1782—closer inspection reveals that Kéralio had elaborated a much more complex configuration of her gender identity and her choice of literary genre. Kéralio's first work, *Adélaïde ou les mémoires de la marquise de* *** may have been a novel, but it was a memoir-novel, and as Nancy K. Miller has recently observed, the decision to write a memoir-novel was an extremely unusual one for an eighteenth-century woman writer, and especially for a woman who was only twenty-four years old when she published this book in 1782. Miller notes that "the first-person feminine retrospective was left largely to the male imagination."[8] Thus by authoring an anonymous memoir-novel, even one written in the first-person feminine, Kéralio was in fact adopting an authorial persona that was publicly coded as masculine.

Moreover, *Adélaïde* proves upon reading to be a violently antimaternal novel. In the opening pages, the young heroine introduces her mother as a haughty and vain woman whose

> pride of birth—the kind that is inspired by rare beauty—and the sentiment of her superior enlightenment heightened her passions to an extreme vivaciousness; and my mother submitted to their empire, imagining not that either her equals or her inferiors should ever resist her. My father, who had experienced all the inconveniences of this kind of character, gave me an education which was completely opposed to it. Through wise precepts and useful examples he rendered me capable of thinking and feeling.[9]

The tragic story of Adélaïde begins when she falls madly in love with a young count, Rofaure. He loves her in return, and, moreover, her father delights in her choice. But her father dies before they are wed, and she soon discovers that her mother had secretly been seeking the affections of the young count for herself. Now the thwarted rival, her mother determines never to allow the lovers to marry. The plot of mother-daughter rivalry, jealousy, and persecution grinds relentlessly through a gruesome forced marriage and repeatedly thwarted attempts by the lovers to reunite. The book ends tragically, inevitably, with the triumph of the mother's will—the definitive separation of the two lovers.

This first novel reveals four themes that were to be reworked continuously throughout Kéralio's literary career: (1) her identification with her paternal inheritance; (2) the adoption of an authorial persona that was at once recognized as feminine, but publicly coded in the masculine; (3) the creation of an oeuvre populated almost entirely by powerful female figures; and (4) a central preoccupation with the problem of female rivalry.

In 1786, four years after the publication of *Adélaïde*, Mlle de Kéralio began publishing openly under her own name the first volumes of what were to be her two greatest intellectual projects: a five-volume *Histoire d'Elisabeth, reine d'Angleterre*, which she prefaced with an effusive dedication to her father, and twelve volumes of a *Collection des meilleurs ouvrages français composés par des femmes*, dedicated in turn to her mother. These two publications marked a change, indeed an inversion, of the configuration of gender identification and literary genre that Kéralio had established in her earlier work. She now publicly claimed authorship of her work as an unmarried young woman. But at the same time that she abandoned her anonymity, she also abandoned the novel for a decidedly masculine genre: history.

Of course, the term *histoire* was very slippery in the eighteenth century, and the boundaries between history and the novel were not as clearly fixed as they would become in the nineteenth century. The term *histoire* could mean either history or story, or both. Indeed, in the standard eighteenth-century dictionary, the editor, Furetière, gives two definitions of the term, one referring to an official record of public political events, and the other referring to *histoire particulière*, which recorded private lives and events that could be as equally invented as not.[10] Further, by the end of the seventeenth century, these two different notions of history were also clearly coded in gender terms. Public history was written almost exclusively by and about the political and military actions of men documented in official records. *Histoire particulière*, in contrast, was written most often by women to advance their own, often feminist interpretations of the social, moral, and even political order of the Old Regime.[11] Louise de Kéralio left no ambiguity as to where her own works stood within contemporary understandings of historical practice. Her histories, like those of her erudite father, she announced, were to be histories of public lives, based upon a verifiable record of historical fact. The aim of history, she asserted, is to reconstruct the truth found in public records.[12] They were, however, to be public histories of *women*.

Though both were historical works, the *Collection* and the *History of Elizabeth* nonetheless represented two distinctively different paths toward the construction of a public historical identity for women: one literary, one political; one separatist, one integrationist. The *Collection* was an explicitly feminist attempt to construct a literary tradition for women writers, from Heloise to the eighteenth century. But as extraordinary as this work is, it was also the less controversial project. Working strictly within the traditional conventions of historical writing about women established by Renaissance histories of *femmes fortes* (women worthies), the *Collection* presented a series of portraits of exceptional women, followed by a selection of each author's works.[13] Thus, although the work is organized chronologically, it retains the structure of a series of timeless exemplary portraits offered as models to the women writers of her own age.

The *History of Elizabeth* was by far the more innovative and more monumental project. Here Kéralio departed radically from the *femme forte* histories by situating Elizabeth's reign squarely within the history of male political sovereignty. For example, she writes: "Under Titus, Trajan, Marcus Aurelius, Gustavus Adolphus, Henry IV, and Elizabeth, virtue dared to reappear" (II:3). The *History of Elizabeth* was thus not merely a history of women. It was an attempt to write a woman into the history of men.

Moreover, following the historiographic path paved by Voltaire in his *Siècle de Louis XIV*, Kéralio intended her history to be the history of "a celebrated era" rather than an exceptional individual ruler (I:i). The achievements of Elizabeth's reign can only be understood, she insists, within the wider context of the European Reformation. Finally, citing Locke and Montesquieu as her authorities, she wrote that her ultimate aim was "to assess Elizabeth's contribution to the progress of the law" (I:vii).[14] And it was here that her historiographic goal became clear: to establish Elizabeth's reign as a linchpin in the history of English constitutional law that had issued from the pens of David Hume and William Blackstone after the English Revolution of 1688.[15] Thus she argued that the real founder of the modern—by which she meant secular—constitutional state was not Henry VII, as past histories had claimed (and one might add, as current histories now do), but rather Elizabeth. Why? Because she believed in religious tolerance and was the first ruler to successfully establish secular over religious rule. And though she acknowledges that the queen ruled too much by prerogative and too little through Parliament, she asserts that the reign of Elizabeth nonetheless marked the critical turning point in the path toward a secular constitutional monarchy, which would only be fully, or nearly (she hedged here), embodied by the principles of 1688.

Kéralio knew that she was working against received ideas, and in anticipation of her critics she deployed the entire arsenal of skills she had inherited from her father, the *érudit*, to make her case. "If I am daring to raise my voice against the opinion of the majority, who still attribute to Henry VII the present government of England," she wrote, "it is not without proof for what I am advancing" (I:4, note 1). Her history, she announced, was the result of ten years of research, extensive consultation of previously unexamined archival material, an exhaustive reading of all available histories, and scrupulously critical cross-examination of the documentary evidence (I:i). She copiously footnoted every point and published a fifth volume devoted entirely to *pièces justificatives*, along with a critical bibliography of existing sources. Even Mallet du Pan found this was excessive. But it was effective!

This magisterial synthesis of English constitutional history and the critical methods of historical erudition, issuing from the hands of a twenty-eight-year-old woman, became one of the literary sensations of the pre-Revolution. Mallet du Pan's fourteen-page review in the *Mercure de France* was not the only one to laud Mlle de Kéralio, if not as the first and only then at least as the "premier" woman historian of her age.[16] The royal censor charged with evaluating the book wrote in the official approbation that he was

> astounded that a refined woman would devote herself from the first years of her youth to such a demanding work; she has consulted all the original sources, and all the men of Queen Elizabeth's reign; and her discussions, her reflections, and her style merit praise.[17]

In 1787 she became one of only three women ever elected to the Academy of Arras.[18] The *History of Elizabeth* had succeeded in translating the history of female sovereignty from the Renaissance genre of the *femme forte* into the enlightenment idiom of a critical history of the law. Herein lay the innovation that Mallet du Pan recognized as singular and without precedent.

But Mallet du Pan did not find Kéralio's work without flaws. Most centrally, he was perplexed by her preoccupation with the relationship between Elizabeth and Mary Stuart. Indeed, he observed, it was really a "history of two women," as she devoted almost half of the four volumes to documenting their relationship. And he acutely observed that this extended narrative of female rivalry worked like a kind of riptide against the dominant movement of the work. While her overarching thesis celebrated the queen and lodged her firmly in the camp of the pro-Elizabethan historiography of Hume, when it came to Mary Stuart, Kéralio parted ways with her respected English predecessor. In Kéralio's estimation, Mary Stuart was the innocent victim of plotting male courtiers and of a queen who was blinded by her own narcissistic jealousy of Mary's greater beauty and feminine charm. But despite Kéralio's copious archival documentation of Scottish court intrigue, Mallet du Pan found this depiction of Elizabeth as Mary's jealous rival implausible. Hume's portrait of the queen, he judged, was more coherent and hence more convincing.

While Kéralio depicted Elizabeth as the nearest to a model of enlightened constitutional monarch that the sixteenth century could have possibly produced, as a model of womanhood she represented her in profoundly ambiguous terms. Indeed, at the very heart of Kéralio's history was a war between two differently, yet equally flawed and equally tragic, conceptions of womanhood, embodied on the one hand by Elizabeth and on the other by Mary Stuart. The book ends with the following double portrait of the two queens. Of Elizabeth, she wrote,

> When one sees such great achievements accomplished by the genius of a woman, all the defects, all the weaknesses of her sex, of her character, disappear even in face of the most severe judges.... One can almost pardon her exercise of absolute power.... If all of these male characteristics place her amongst the ranks of great kings, one cannot credit her with having united

them with the charms of a refined woman. But it should be observed that gentleness, weakness even, which are the real charms of a woman in private society, would have marred her virtues as a sovereign; and Mary Stuart, who possessed all the graces and the charms of her sex, would perhaps have been able successfully to resist her formidable rival, if she had been, like her, less amiable, and if she had had her strength, her power, and her greatness of character. The death of this princess is the only blemish that cannot be removed from the life of Elizabeth; it is inexcusable.[19]

Mary Stuart, a successful woman, by virtue of this success failed as a ruler and was destined to be dominated by her rival. Elizabeth, in contrast, abandoned womanhood to become a successful ruler. And in the one moment in her career when she permitted her desire to be loved as a woman to express itself (in her jealous rivalry with Mary), she failed as a ruler.

In these two painfully tragic portraits, Kéralio exposed the inherently paradoxical nature of the concept of female sovereignty in a political culture that coded public virtue as masculine and private virtue in the feminine.[20] In fact, a history, begun as a celebration of female rule, ended as a poignant testimony to its impossibility. It also ended with the repetition of the warning to women which she first sounded in her novel *Adélaïde:* women in positions of absolute power (for example, widowed mothers or sovereign queens) are dangerous not so much to the men whose equals they become, as to other women, whom they come to reign over.

It should be underscored, however, that Kéralio herself appeared in 1787 to have succeeded in the cultural sphere where Elizabeth had failed in the political. That is, she had managed to acquire masculine authority without losing her identity as a woman, by feminizing masculine identities: just as Louis Félix begot Louise Félicité, so too the academic historian was succeeded by the *historienne,* and then the *académicienne.*

From Historian to Antihistorian

The dilemma of taking on male characteristics in order to acquire public power was not merely an intellectual issue for Kéralio. By the time the Revolution erupted in 1789, Kéralio had proven herself to be extremely adept at forms of covert literary cross-dressing in order to acquire male cultural privileges and prerogatives. Despite the laws prohibiting women from becoming publishers, in 1785 she launched a publishing business behind a man's name.[21] And in 1789 she took a step further. She threw herself openly into a new career as a revolutionary journalist-printer, founding her *Journal de l'Etat et du Citoyen* two weeks before the National Assembly officially declared the freedom of the press in August 1789. The Revolution, she announced, not only offered, but also demanded, a new role for the author in French society:

> A new order has been established in the nation; the great work of French liberty has been accomplished in a week.... But it is a small thing to build ramparts, you must defend them... this is without doubt the most worthy employment of literary talent.[22]

Over the fall of 1789 Kéralio deployed her pen and her presses in the service of the political and cultural vanguard of the Revolution.[23]

But in moving from history to politics, Kéralio began to encounter firsthand the limits of the gender-genre system she had so painfully analyzed in her *History of Elizabeth*. By the end of October 1789 she found herself publicly characterized by radical journalists as a *phenomène politique*, and an *amazone*.[24] Moreover, by 1789 Kéralio was thirty-one years old and still single. She was thus becoming increasingly vulnerable to the threat of social marginalization as a *vieille fille*. Indeed, hostile pamphleteers were already beginning to attach the stereotypical attributes of the *vieille fille—laide, susceptible aux fureurs utérines*—to her name.[25] In December of 1789 Kéralio announced that her *Journal du Citoyen* was folding, and that a new journal, the *Mercure National*, would serve as its continuation. But the prospectus of the *Mercure* announced that the journal was to be edited by three soldiers of the National Guard—Louis Félix Guynement (formerly de Kéralio), Hugou de Basseville, and François Robert—and of "a citizeness, daughter and wife of two of them."[26] Denounced as a "political amazon," and an "old maid," Kéralio at last married at the age of thirty-two, and took refuge behind the names of her father and her new husband, Pierre François Robert. Madame Robert did continue to contribute articles to the *Mercure*. But she now had to contend with the emergence of women as a central element of popular counterrevolutionary political mobilization.[27] Initially she attempted to rescue the political reputation of women as radical political activists by publicly denouncing counterrevolutionary women in the *Mercure*. But within an increasingly antifeminist revolutionary environment, her public role as revolutionary writer became more and more untenable, even as a denouncer of other political women.[28] She steadily withdrew not only from politics but from writing and publishing as well—at least in her own name.

In 1791 a new work of women's history, entitled *Les Crimes des reines de la France depuis le commencement de la monarchie jusqu'à Marie Antoinette*, appeared *anonymously*, from the Parisian publisher Louis Prudhomme. It was immediately attributed to Kéralio.[29] This work is most frequently cited as part of the flurry of anti–Marie Antoinette polemics of the early revolutionary period. This is of course not entirely incorrect. But because of its length, and its content, it stands apart from the porno-polemical tracts used most commonly to attack the queen.[30] I would like to consider it here rather as a part of Kéralio's historical writings, as a work of history, rather than a polemical tract, if only because the *Crimes* raises equally interesting questions about the problem of writing history in a revolutionary moment, and in particular about the problems of women writing women's history in a political moment in which women were being driven out of public life.

The Crimes of the Queens of France was an attempt at a generic inversion of Kéralio's *History of Elizabeth*. And just as the *History of Elizabeth* had taken the genre of the *femme forte* and reworked it, transforming it from a series of portraits of exemplary queens into an institutional history of female sovereignty, so *The Crimes of the Queens of France* attempted to perform a similar revision of the evil twin of the *femme forte* histories, the histories of bad queens.

There were numerous models for this kind of generic inversion dating from earlier political crises. As work by Rachel Weil, and more recently Elizabeth Dudrow, has shown, in both the Wars of Religion and the Fronde, histories of bad queens were deployed by opponents of the monarchy who felt that Catherine de Medicis and Anne of Austria had overstepped the appropriate political roles prescribed for queen-regents.[31] Indeed on the eve of the Revolution there was a canon of bad French queens (most frequently, Clotilde, Frédégunde, Brunhaut, and Catherine de Medicis) readily available to any polemicist who needed historical illustrations of the sorry consequences of permitting women an equal role in public life. *The Crimes of the Queens of France* drew heavily upon these past models but broke with them in ways that merit further consideration.

First, earlier black histories had been written with the purpose of restoring the monarchy to what the authors envisaged as its proper course. The histories of bad examples held up against Catherine de Medicis and Anne of Austria in particular were intended as attempts to call bad queens who had overstepped their authority "back into order." They were reformist narratives. *The Crimes of the Queens,* in contrast, had a revolutionary purpose: to condemn the institution of queenship itself. This gives the narrative an overdetermined and vertiginous quality: in the end all queens, by the very fact of being queens, are bad. Like the *History of Elizabeth, The Crimes* was not a history of exemplars. Rather, it was a history of political institutions.

Robert advanced two different arguments against queenship. On the one hand she argued that the problem with queens was that they were women. And here she deployed traditional rhetoric about women's greater passions, and their lesser capacity for self-control:

> Drunkenness from wine produces greater vice in women than in men; so too, the inebriation of power, the lust for domination, is more hideous and deadly in the former than in the latter; ... a woman who can do anything is capable of anything.[32]

Then she went on quickly to advance a kind of corollary principle: as women deformed politics, so too politics deformed women. She writes, "a woman who becomes a queen changes sex, she thinks everything permitted to her, and defers to nothing." This line of argument, however, simply returned her to the problems of male monarchy itself, the absence of checks upon absolute power. To get back to the problem of queens in particular, she then took another turn, this time toward a Rousseauvian critique of the institution of queenship. She writes,

> The queens who have held the scepter in their own names are not those who have done the most evil; they were accountable, if not to the law, then at least to opinion, which sometimes condemns more quickly than the law: it is the wives of kings, who insist on

being called queens, who have had the most damaging influence on the destiny of empires and the happiness of peoples.... These queens have only escaped public resentment because they have known how to hide their intrigues behind the dignity of their marital status. (*Crimes*, vii)

Salic law, far from restraining French queens, rather made them worse than any others, precisely because it put their power outside of the law and beyond the reach of public opinion. French queens ruled through deception because they were not allowed to rule as men, that is in their own names. It is hard to read these lines without wondering if Robert also meant to sound a warning to republicans who sought to exclude women from public life, and who drove them to act through men. She momentarily strayed toward such musings, invoking an even earlier, premonarchic past under the Gauls, when she wrote, "several *gauloises* took seats in the senate and voted and deliberated the same as the men ... " (x–xi). One wonders where this text might have gone, in another moment, or in the hands of a less misogynist editor than Prudhomme. Perhaps Mme Robert might have found a historical model for women's political inclusion in the new regime. But she did not. This was a text written against the past. In fact it was not history, but antihistory. She pursued the course taken by the broader revolutionary movement toward women: to write them out of public life.

Thus, when it came to Marie Antoinette, she deviated from the tactics of the porno-polemicists. Instead of denouncing her private vices as public crimes, she insisted that the queen's personal vices should be of interest to the queen's conscience alone. Unlike the revolutionary prosecutor, Fouquier-Tinville, Kéralio insisted that the ex-queen should be tried only for her political crimes, her conspiracy, her waste of public funds. Kéralio's solution to the problem of Marie Antoinette was to remove the issue of her sexuality and her sex from public discussion; to recast her as a private woman. *The Crimes of the Queens of France* wrote an end to the history of women insofar as that history had been understood as a story of public political action. This negation of the history of women, for its author, was also an act of self-negation. The end of history represented the end of the historian. With the *Crimes*, Robert's career as a historian ended. In 1793

Louise Robert published an open letter announcing her retreat from public life. She published nothing further for fifteen years.[33]

Postrevolutionary Fiction, History by Other Means

If the Terror had attempted to purge the nation of a corrupted past, Thermidor precipitated a recovery of memory, and, on the part of male cultural elites, a return to the writing of history. The French nation needs a "new history," Henri Grégoire proclaimed upon the floor of the National Convention in 1795.[34] But for the former historian of women, Mme Robert, the problem of coming to terms with the past could entail no mere reprisal of past means. In 1808, a five-volume novel entitled *Amélia et Caroline, ou l'amour et l'amitié* appeared under the hyphenated signature, Mme Kéralio-Robert.[35] This third revision of her public signature itself expressed a desire to recover a sense of historical continuity across the rupture of the revolutionary period, which in her case was also a passage from the name of her father to that of her husband. Mme Kéralio-Robert acknowledged as much in the dedication of the novel to her husband:

> In former times I dedicated the first work that I published in my name to my father. For twenty years I have published nothing. For twenty years I have been yours, and it is to conjugal love that I dedicate this work.

But if the hyphen between Kéralio and Robert sought to create a continuity, it also betrayed a discontinuity and the impossibility of naming that brief revolutionary moment in the fall of 1789 when she had been neither daughter nor wife but rather an amazon, a *phenomène politique*. Indeed, in stating that she had published nothing for twenty years, that is since 1788, she denied authorship of her publications of the revolutionary period.

In the preface to her novel, Kéralio-Robert expanded more openly upon the problem of postrevolutionary lineage as a literary problem. She acknowledged that in former times she had written a history of Queen Elizabeth. The success of that work, she now wrote, had given her the courage to embark on publishing a collection of women writers, but the Revolution had forced her to abandon it (vii). And since the Revolution, she continued, French literary "taste has been deformed," and there would be no market for these women writers of the past: "The French imagination has gone off to distract and lose itself in catacombs and tombs..." (ix–x). Kéralio-Robert was not a great partisan of gothic novels. She found their lack of *vraisemblance* (plausibility) dissatisfying. Moreover, she found their representations of women undignified. It was difficult for her to believe that women wrote them (xiii). Of course it was true, she continued, that every historical moment had its own style, and its own mores, and it was the job of the novelist to capture this specificity of each era. Novels were in their own way a record of their era. Indeed, the novel, she wrote, "is the history of private life" (xvii).

Mme Kéralio-Robert thus reworked her own literary past, and created a new lineage for herself, descending this time from the maternal, rather than the paternal line, from the woman's novel rather than the male lineage of academic history; from her *Collection des meilleurs ouvrages*, rather than the *Histoire d'Elisabeth*. Yet, at the same time as she reidentified herself with the novel, Kéralio-Robert also assigned the novel the status of a historical genre, albeit a "history of private life." The novel, in her hands, thus became a pursuit of history by other means, a history written from within the feminine register of fiction.[36]

Amélia and Caroline engages with the problem of historical writing and historical identity at a number of different levels. It is a work of historical fiction in the sense that it is set in the past: it is set in the English Revolution of 1640–60. This choice was not a politically indifferent one. Contemporary readers would have immediately recognized this setting as an allegory for their own revolution, and at one moment in the text the author explicitly echoes the common contemporary analogy between Cromwell and Robespierre (I:197). But the choice of period had a more particular meaning within the oeuvre of Kéralio-Robert. It is difficult not to see this work both chronologically and thematically as a continuation of the *History of Elizabeth*. And it too is a "history of two women."

Further, *Amélia and Caroline* is not simply the story of private lives set into a historical landscape. Rather, it unfolds as a double narrative, tacking back and forth between two generic registers, one recounting the public history of the English Revolution and the other detailing the fictional story of the private lives of its two heroines,

Amélia and Caroline. The novel thus plays continuously with the *double entendre, histoire-histoire,* "history-story." Moreover, this double *récit* is clearly marked in gender terms. The public history is that of men in revolution. Here Kéralio-Robert meticulously reconstructs the events of the English Revolution, replete with direct quotations from primary sources and footnotes to key authorities. For example, she quotes from a letter Cromwell wrote to Parliament when detailing his religious views (II:6) and offers detailed descriptions of the battles of Naseby and Maarston Moor, based upon citations to the historians Clarendon, Gumble, and especially Hume (III:126, 140–41, 168–69).[37] This history is interwoven with the fictional narrative recounting a struggle between mothers and daughters.

The political narrative of the Revolution was no mere historical backdrop for a romance. Indeed the whole interest of the novel lies in showing how the histories of public and private life, and the histories of men and women, do not simply parallel one another, but rather, are profoundly and inextricably implicated in one another. Thus, as the novel closes, a minor character remarks philosophically, "The troubles of state traversed everyday life . . . and opened up different vistas in the affairs of private individuals who found themselves wounded in the wars between competing factions" (V:109). Kéralio-Robert's novel thus rebelled against the postrevolutionary ideology of separate spheres. Indeed, the whole point of the book was to reveal that the histories of public and private life are profoundly implicated in one another.

But it is at the level of plot that the book reveals itself most clearly as a history rather than a romance. Rather than beginning with the problem of desire and ending with that of marriage, the novel opens with the problem of origins and ends with that of inheritance. Charles, the émigré son of a cavalier, rescues a girl named Caroline from robbers who have killed her guardian. Caroline does not know who she is, though she has retained a jewel box which she has been told contains the secret of her identity. Charles and Caroline fall in love. His mother consents to their marriage, because, she reflects philosophically, in revolutionary times, all lineages are called into doubt. Suddenly the daughter of Oliver Cromwell, Adélina, and her own daughter, Amélia, arrive at the neighboring chateau. The shrewish and vain Adélina becomes the young Caroline's persecutor, first attempting to seduce her beloved Charles, and then when that fails, to have the two of them captured and put to death as counterrevolutionary traitors. But, Adélina's daughter, Amélia, becomes Caroline's best friend and protector. After volumes detailing the horrible persecutions of the two girls by the bad mother, who like a queen manipulates her father's men and thus turns the whole political world against Caroline and Amélia, we finally discover that Caroline is in fact the daughter of the wicked Adélina's husband by his first marriage. Caroline's mother was the source of the entire family fortune, and so Caroline is hence to be the true heiress to the family fortune. Caroline and Amélia thus are not only friends, but half-sisters. When these truths of their identities finally come to light, Adélina, the wicked mother, attempts first to kill Caroline and then Amélia, and finally, failing in both these attempts, she kills herself.

Were this novel a mere historical romance it would have ended in the marriage of Charles and Caroline. And although this marriage is of course implied, the book does not in fact end with it. The closing pages are concerned rather with the problem of settling the inheritance of the two half-sisters, Caroline and Amélia. Their father announces that by the terms of the maternal will Caroline, as her mother's natural daughter and the eldest of the two, is to receive the entire fortune. But Caroline rebels. No, she insists, she will not accept the inheritance, unless it is divided equally between herself and her sister Amélia:

> You have two daughters, Milord, and my mother's fortune is in your hands; let it be shared between both of them. At this price, I will accept the inheritance of my mother, when it has been dispensed as I desire it to be. (V:167)

And she continues, these two sisters "were united by unhappiness; wealth shall not have the deadly power to divide them." (V:168–69). This revolt by the daughters against the inequities of the maternal will at last put an end to the deadly inheritance of maternal tyranny, female rivalry, and domination.

Amélia and Caroline was in fact not a continuation of *Adélaïde*, nor of the *History of Elizabeth*, nor of *The Crimes of the Queens*, rather it was a postrevolutionary rewriting of their female plots. Through fiction, Mme Kéralio-Robert was able, at last, to write a truly revolutionary, indeed a utopian plot, in which the problem of female rivalry is resolved through the suicide of the queen mother, and the daughter's rebellion in the name of equality and sisterly love.

Recent work by Joan Landes, Dorinda Outram, and Lynn Hunt, among others, has demonstrated that the French Revolution marked a moment of assault upon the public figure of the *femme forte* and her evil twin, the bad queen. In this essay I have attempted to examine a dimension of this story that has not yet been fully confronted: the part played by women in this republican assault on the public women of the Old Regime. Some years ago Natalie Davis commented in a seminar that feminist historians had paid perhaps too much attention to the conflicts and tensions between men and women and devoted too little time to exploring the complicities between the sexes in the construction of gender systems. And I think she was right. Louise de Kéralio's role in killing off the queen needs to be explained, rather than explained away.

Feminist historiography of the closing years of the Old Regime has tended nostalgically to lament the prerevolutionary period as a period of greater public possibilities for women.[38] I would like to suggest that Kéralio's histories cast that world in a different and more anguished light. Her histories should give us pause before regretting the demise of that world of possibilities, for they expose the limits of the model of the *femme forte* as a model for female and feminist identity. Her histories record the cruelty of the political culture of absolutism toward women who sought, or who found themselves in, public roles. And further, she reveals the ways in which absolutist modes of power, as surely in the hands of women as in those of men, pitted mothers against daughters and sisters against one another. The exceptional woman, like the absolutist queen, was someone who lived beyond the law, as an exception to the rule, and thus accountable to nothing beyond her own desire.[39] However painful a truth it may be for feminists to accept, Kéralio's histories reveal why it was necessary not just for revolutionary men, but also for revolutionary women, to kill off the queen. In order for women to have a real revolution, to achieve the power of self-determination and the power to lay down more equitable laws in their own names, it was not only the absolutist fathers that had to go, but the tyranny of mothers as well.

Further, Kéralio-Robert's oeuvre helps to explain how female literary subjectivity was refashioned over the course of the French Revolution. We know that the Revolution imposed a more rigorous gender order upon the social world than had existed under the Old Regime. And it was an order which relegated women strictly to the private realm. The consequences of this for women's history are evident. Insofar as the writing of history continued to be conceived as a task of recording the events of public life, women ceased to be subjects of history. Kéralio-Robert turned to prose fiction instead. Her postrevolutionary novel, however, reveals that this turn toward fiction could in fact represent an opportunity to move beyond the constraints of past models for writing women's history and offer the freedom to write a truly revolutionary plot. Of course, it is needless to say that this fictional plot of equality and sisterly love, this daughter's rebellion, was not the kind of plot that the Napoleonic censors would have been on the lookout for.

NOTES

Epigraph cited by Louise de Kéralio in the "discours préliminaire" to her *Histoire d'Elisabeth, reine d'Angleterre*, 5 vols. (Paris: 1786–88), I:iv. Kéralio miscites the passage as appearing in book II of the *Aeneid*, and adds an interrogative (I am grateful to Shaun Marmon for this observation and to Ann Blair for her assistance with the Latin translation). All translations are my own unless otherwise noted.

1. Jacques Mallet du Pan, review of the *Histoire d'Elisabeth, reine d'Angleterre*, by Louise de Kéralio in the *Mercure de France*, 23 June 1787, 151–65.

2. For a discussion of the etymology of the term *historienne* see Michel Delon, "Les Historiennes de Silling," in *Actes du Colloque: L'Histoire au XVIIIe siècle*, Centre Aixois d'Etudes et de Recherches sur le XVIIIe siècle, 1–3 May 1975 (Aix, 1980), 102. According to Delon, "Trévoux et Furetière l'admettent en tant que féminin d'historien, mais remarquent que 'ce mot est peu d'usage, et ne se dit que dans le style familier.' Ils citent un exemple tiré de Marie-Jeanne L'Heritier de Villandon: 'Je suis historienne, dit Mlle L'Heritier, et une historienne, aussi bien qu'un historien ne doit pas prendre parti.' Becerelle, repris par Littré, ajoute un sens figuré, illustré d'une citation de Rivarol."

3. See Natalie Z. Davis, "'Women's History' in Transition: The European Case," *Feminist Studies* 3 (Spring-Summer 1976), 83–103; and Ian Maclean, *Women Triumphant: Feminism in French Literature, 1610–1652* (Oxford, 1977). For a discussion of the precedents for women writing history, see Faith Evelyn Beasley, *Revising Memory: Women's Fiction and Memoirs in Seventeenth-Century France* (New Brunswick, 1990).

4. The classic study of the association of writing and reading novels with

women in the eighteenth century, and with feminism in particular, is Georges May, *Le Dilemme du roman au XVIIIe siècle* (Paris, 1963). See especially chapter 8. The most path-breaking recent work on gender and literary culture in eighteenth-century France has been accomplished by Nancy K. Miller. See Nancy K. Miller, ed., *The Poetics of Gender* (New York, 1986); Nancy K. Miller and Joan DeJean, eds., *The Politics of Tradition: Placing Women in French Literature* (New Haven, 1988); and Nancy K. Miller, *Subject to Change: Reading Feminist Writing* (New York, 1988). For the most recent synthesis of the gender issues in eighteenth-century literary culture, see the relevant sections of Denis Hollier et al., eds., *A New History of French Literature* (Cambridge, Mass., 1989). For a sociocultural history of men of letters in the eighteenth century, see Daniel Roche, *Le Siècle des lumières en province: académies et académiciens provinciaux, 1680–1789*, 2 vols. (Paris, 1989; first published, 1978).

5. See Roger Chartier, "Historiography in the Age of Absolutism," in *A New History of French Literature*, ed. Denis Hollier et al., 345–50. For further discussion of official historical writing in the eighteenth century, see Blandine Barret-Kriegel, *Les Historiens et la monarchie*, 4 vols. (Paris, 1988), see especially vols. 2 and 3:261 and 284. For explorations of other uses of history and historical writing, see the *Actes du Colloque: L'Histoire au dix-huitième siècle*, and Michel de Certeau, *L'Ecriture de l'histoire* (Paris, 1975), especially 182–96.

6. On the complexities of female literary anonymity during the period under consideration see Roger Bellet, "Masculin et féminin dans les pseudonymes des femmes de lettres au XIXe siècle," *Femmes de lettres au XIXe siècle: Autour de Louise Colet*, ed. Roger Bellet (Lyons, 1982), especially 251; Nancy K. Miller, "A Feminist Critic and her Fictions," *Diacritics* 12, no. 2 (Summer 1982): 48–53; Joan DeJean, "Lafayette's Ellipses: the Privileges of Anonymity," *PMLA* 99, no. 5 (October 1984): 884–902; Carla Hesse, "Reading Signatures: Female Authorship and Revolutionary Law in France, 1750–1850," *Eighteenth-Century Studies* 22 (Spring 1989): 469–87; and Nancy K. Miller, "The Gender of the Memoir-Novel," in *A New History of French Literature*, ed. Denis Hollier et al., 437–38.

7. The essential biographical information on Louise de Kéralio has been compiled by L. Antheunis, *Le Conventionnel belge François Robert (1763–1826) et sa femme Louise de Kéralio (1758-1822)* (Wetteren, 1955), especially 11–13. According to contemporaries, Kéralio read Greek and reportedly spoke and read Latin, English, and Italian fluently. For evidence that her father was responsible for her education, see Antheunis, ibid. See also Louise de Kéralio, *Histoire d'Elisabeth, reine d'Angleterre*, 1:ii; and *Collection des meilleurs ouvrages français, composés par les femmes*, 12 vols. (Paris, 1786–88), I:vii; and Joseph François Michaud and Louis Gabriel Michaud, eds., *Biographie universelle, ancienne et moderne nouvelle édition*, 45 vols. (Paris, 1843–65), 21:535–36.

8. Nancy K. Miller, "The Gender of the Memoir-Novel," in *A New History of French Literature*, ed. Denis Hollier et al., 437–38. The following discussion is indebted to Miller's interpretation of the gender politics behind Mme de Tencin's *Mémoires du comte de Comminges* which was published anonymously in 1735.

9. [Louise de Kéralio], *Adélaïde, ou les mémoires de la marquise de ***. Ecrits par elle-même* (Neuchâtel, 1782), 2.

10. See Chartier, "Historiography in the Age of Absolutism," 345–50; Georges May, *Le Dilemme du roman*, especially chap. 5; Suzanne Gearhart, *The Open Boundary of History and Fiction: A Critical Approach to the Enlightenment* (Princeton, 1984); and Michel de Certeau, *Heterologies*, trans. Brian Massumi (Minneapolis, 1986), especially chap. 15, "History: Science and Fiction," 199–221.

11. See Beasley, *Revising Memory*.

12. See in particular, her preface to the *Histoire d'Elisabeth, reine d'Angleterre*, 1:i.

13. See Davis, "'Women's History' in Transition," 83–103; Beasley, *Revising Memory;* and Maclean, *Women Triumphant*.

14. She cites John Locke, *The Second Treatise on Government*, and Charles de Montesquieu, *The Spirit of the Laws*.

15. The two works she cites most frequently are David Hume, *The History of England*, and Sir William Blackstone, *Commentaries on the Laws of England*. The first volumes of Hume's *History* were published in Edinburgh in 1754. The completed six-volume edition appeared in 1762. A French translation of the completed work, by Mme Octavie Belot, was published in 1769. The first edition of Blackstone's *Commentaries on the Laws of England* was published by Clarendon Press, Oxford, between 1765 and 1769. It went through ten editions before 1785. There was no French translation until the nineteenth century.

16. Reviews of the work appeared in the *Journal encyclopédique*, no. 8 (1787), 267–78, 436–47; Jacques Mallet du Pan, *Mercure de France* (23 June 1787), 151–65; and Lans de Boissy, *Journal Littéraire*, Nancy, 34 (1787): 106–19.

17. See the "approbation du roi," signed by the royal censor Démeunier, 7 December 1786, and printed at the end of volume five of the *Histoire d'Elisabeth, reine d'Angleterre*.

18. None of the 116 regular members of the Academy of Arras in the eighteenth century were women. Of the 124 honorary members only three were women, and all of them single. Mlle de Kéralio and Mlle de Masson le Golft were both admitted as honorary members on 3 February 1787, and Mlle du Chastellier was admitted as an honorary member on 16 October 1789. See E. Van Drival, *Histoire de l'Académie d'Arras depuis sa fondation, en 1737, jusqu'à nos jours* (Arras, 1872), 223–55. It was typical for academicians to come from the older nobility, but Mlle de Kéralio was unusually young (29) at the time of her election. For a sociocultural profile of the Academy of Arras in the eighteenth century, see Daniel Roche, *Le Siècle des lumières en province*, 1:189–210, and 2:209 and 213. Roche also documents an increasing academic interest in historical subjects during the last two decades of the century. See ibid., 2:295. Unfortunately Roche does not offer any figures for the number of women admitted to the provincial academies in the eighteenth century.

19. Kéralio, *Histoire d'Elisabeth, reine d'Angleterre*, 4:666–67.

20. For further discussion of the gendering of public virtue as masculine, see Joan Landes, *Women and the Public Sphere in the Age of the French Revolution* (Ithaca, 1988); Dorinda Outram, "Le langage mâle de la vertu: Women and the Discourse of the French Revolution," in *The Social History of Language*, ed. Peter Burke and Roy Porter (Cambridge, 1987), 120–35; and Dorinda Outram, *The Body in the French Revolution: Sex, Class, and Political Culture* (New Haven, 1989), especially chap. 8.

21. On the complexities of the relationship between the legal and familial status of women in the eighteenth century, see Adrienne Rogers, "Women and the Law," in *French Women in the Age of Enlightenment*, ed. Samia Spencer (Bloomington, 1984), 35–37; Elisabeth Guibert-Sledziewski, "Naissance de la femme civile. La Révolution, la femme, le droit," *La Pensée*, no. 238 (March–April 1984), 34–48; Michèle Bordeaux, "Droit et femmes seules. Les pièges de la discrimination" in *Madame ou Mademoiselle? Itinéraires de la solitude féminine, 18e–20e siècle*, ed. Arlette Farge and Christiane Klapisch-Zuber (Paris, 1984), 19–57; and Hesse, "Reading Signatures," 469–87. By contemporary accounts, the business did spectacularly well, especially with her history of Elizabeth, and by 1789 the publishing house had gained notoriety in Parisian cultural circles as an important source of enlightenment philosophy and new novels. See Bibliothèque Nationale, MSS fr. 6687, "Mes loisirs," the journal of Siméon-Prosper Hardy, vol. VIII, entry for 21 January 1789; Archives Nationales (hereafter, AN), V 1 553, memorandum of the office of the book trade concerning Mlle de Kéralio, 12 November 1789; Michaud and Michaud, eds., *Biographie universelle*, 21:535–36; and Archives de Paris, fond "faillites," D4B6, cart. 105, doss. 7454, 30 March 1789.

22. See the *Prospectus du journal de l'état et du citoyen proposé par souscription, chez mademoiselle de Kéralio, rue de Grammont, no. 17*. The *Prospectus* is undated but appeared shortly after 6 August 1789. The first issue of the journal appeared on 13 August 1789. On the founding of her printing shop, see her memorandum to this effect of 12 November 1789, which she addressed to the royal administration of the book trade: AN, V 1 553.

23. For examples of the radicalism of her ideas, see her comments on Jean Joseph Mounier and Jean Paul Marat in the *Journal de l'Etat et du Citoyen*, no. 4, September 1789 and the supplement to no. 14, 22 October 1789, and her *Observations sur quelques articles du projet de constitution de M. Mounier* (signed Mlle de Kéralio) (Paris, n.d. [1789]).

24. *Journal de l'Etat et du Citoyen*, supplement to no. 14, 22 October 1789, 229. These accusations originally appeared in the *Révolutions de Paris*, no. 16, 32.

25. On the social realities and the stereotype of the *vieille fille* in eighteenth-century France, see Cécile Dauphin, "Histoire d'un stéréotype, la vieille fille," in *Madame ou Mademoiselle?*, ed. Farge and Klapisch-Zuber, 207–31; on the medical attribution of the particular susceptibility of single women to *fureurs utérines*, see Arlette Farge, "Les temps fragiles de la solitude des femmes à travers le discours médical du XVIIIe siècle," in ibid., 251–63. For the attri-

bution of *laideur* and *fureurs utérines* to Louise de Kéralio, see the anonymous pamphlet, *Les Crimes constitutionels de France, ou la désolation française, décrétée par l'assemblée dite Nationale Constituante, aux années 1789, 1790, et 1791. Accepté par l'esclave Louis XVI, le 14 septembre 1791* (Paris, 1792), cited by Lynn Hunt, "The Many Bodies of Marie Antoinette," in *Eroticism and the Body Politic*, ed. Lynn Hunt (Baltimore, 1991), 120 n. 42.

26. Prospectus for the *Mercure National* (n.p., n.d. [1790]).

27. For the counterrevolutionary mobilization of women, see in particular Olwen Hufton, "Women in Revolution 1789–1796," *Past and Present* 53 (1971): 90–108; and Suzanne Desan, "Redefining Revolutionary Liberty: the Rhetoric of Religious Revival during the French Revolution," *Journal of Modern History* 60 (1988): 1–27.

28. For Kéralio's efforts to distance herself from counterrevolutionary women, see her "Adresse aux femmes de Montauban" in *Mercure National* 6 (23 May 1790): 429; also published separately as the *Adresse aux femmes de Montauban . . . par Mme Robert* (n.p., 1790).

29. For the contemporary attribution of this work to Kéralio, see Hunt, "The Many Bodies of Marie Antoinette," 120–22, especially n. 42.

30. Ibid. For further discussion of the pamphlet literature attacking Marie Antoinette, see also Robert Darnton, "The High Enlightenment and the Low-life of Literature," reprinted in *The Literary Underground of the Old Regime* (Cambridge, 1982), 1–40; Chantal Thomas, *La Reine scélérate: Marie Antoinette dans les pamphlets* (Paris, 1989); Sarah Maza, "The Diamond Necklace Affair Revisited (1785–1786): The Case of the Missing Queen," *Eroticism and the Body Politic*, 63–89; and Elizabeth Colwill, "Just Another Citoyenne? Marie Antoinette on Trial, 1790–1793," *History Workshop* 28 (Autumn 1989): 63–87.

31. See Rachel Weil, "The Crown has Fallen to Distaff: Gender and Politics in the Age of Catherine de Medicis, 1560–1589," *Critical Matrix* 1, no. 4 (1985): 4, especially 17–19; and Elizabeth Dudrow, "Anne of Austria and Political Rebellion: Depictions of the Queen during the Fronde," (unpublished seminar paper, University of California, Berkeley, Spring 1990), especially 17–19, 22–23, 34, and 38–39. I would like to thank Beth Dudrow for her permission to cite this paper.

32. [Louise de Kéralio-Robert], *Les Crimes des reines de la France depuis le commencement de la monarchie jusqu'à Marie Antoinette, publiés par Prudhomme* (Paris, 1791), vi–vii. For a historical perspective on these stereotypes, see Natalie Zemon Davis, "Women on Top," in *Society and Culture in Early Modern France* (Stanford, 1975), 124–51; Ian Maclean, *The Renaissance Notion of Woman* (New York, 1980); Paul Hoffmann, *La Femme dans la pensée des lumières* (Paris, 1977); Landes, *Women and the Public Sphere;* Outram, *The Body in the French Revolution;* and Hunt, "The Many Bodies of Marie Antoinette," 108–30.

33. Louise Robert, *A Monsieur Louvet, député à la Convention Nationale par le Département du Loiret* (Paris, n.d. [1793]).

34. Henri Grégoire, *Rapport sur les encouragements, récompenses et pensions à*

accorder aux savants, aux gens de lettres et aux artistes (Paris, an III [1794–95]), 15–20.

35. Louise de Kéralio-Robert, *Amélia et Caroline, ou l'amour et l'amitié*, 5 vols. (Paris, 1808).

36. Kéralio-Robert's definition of the novel as *histoire* was not unprecedented. Indeed, it can be located in a tradition of feminist literary invention dating back to at least the seventeenth century. As Faith Beasley has shown, feminist writers after the Fronde, and most notably Mme de Lafayette, also exploited the double meanings of *histoire* as public history and as *histoire particulière*, in order to write their own versions of history. See Beasley, *Revising Memory*. It would be interesting to explore further the association of this narrative strategy with moments of political reaction, i.e., the post-Fronde world of Mme de Lafayette and the postrevolutionary world of Mme Kéralio-Robert. For further reflections on the relationship of women's writing to history in the revolutionary period, see Marie-Claire Hoock-Demarle, *La Rage d'écrire: Femmes-écrivains en Allemagne de 1790 à 1815* (Aix-en-Provence, 1990), especially 99–104 and 243–50.

37. The sources for her historical account are Edward Hyde, first Earl of Clarendon, *The History of the rebellion and Civil Wars in England, begun in 1641, with the precedent passages and actions that contributed thereto, and the happy end and conclusion thereof by the King's blessed restoration* (Oxford, 1704); Thomas Gumble, *The life of general Monck, duke of Albemarle, etc., with remarks upon his actions* (London, 1671) [French editions of this work appeared in London, 1672, and Cologne, 1712]; and David Hume, *The History of England, from the Invasion of Julius Caesar to the Revolution in 1688* (London, 1762).

38. For examples of this tendency, see Landes, *Women and the Public Sphere;* Outram, *The Body in the French Revolution;* Joan DeJean, "The Salons, 'Preciosity,' and the Sphere of Women's Influence," in *A New History of French Literature*, 297–303; and Sarah Maza, "Women's Voices in Literature and Art," in *A New History of French Literature*, 623–27.

39. For some very interesting recent theoretical reflections on the problem of female exceptionalism and history writing, see Christine Planté, "Femmes exceptionelles: des exceptions pour quelle règle," in the special issue of *Les Cahiers du Grif: Le Genre de l'histoire* 37/38 (Spring 1988), 91–111.

Bibliography of
Natalie Zemon Davis's Work

Books

Society and Culture in Early Modern France: Eight Essays. Stanford: Stanford University Press, 1975. British edition, London: Duckworth, 1975; Cambridge: Polity, 1987. French edition (trans. Marie-Noël Bourguet), Paris: Aubier, 1979. Italian edition (trans. Sandro Lombardini), Turin: Giulio Einaudi, 1980. Japanese edition (trans. Komao Naruse, Shiro Miyashita, and Yumiko Takahashi), Tokyo: Heibonsha, 1987. German edition (trans. Nele Löw-Beer), Frankfurt Am Main: Fischer Taschenbuch Verlag, 1987. Spanish edition (trans. Jordi Beltran Ferrer), Barcelona: Crítica, 1993. Portuguese edition (trans. Mariza Corréa), São Paolo: Paz e Terra, 1990. Spanish translation of chapter 3, "City Women and Religious Change," and chapter 5, "Women on Top," in *Historia y Género: Las mujeres en la Europa Moderna y Contemporánea,* edited and translated by James Amelang and Mary Nash, 59–92, 127–65. Valencia: Ediciones Alfons El Magnanim, 1990. Chapter 3 excerpted in *The Other Side of Western Civilization. Readings in Everyday Life. Vol. 1: The Ancient World and the Reformation.* 3d ed., edited by Stanley Chodrow, 333–51. New York: Harcourt, Brace, Jovanovich, 1984. Chapter 5 slightly revised in *The Reversible World: Symbolic Inversion in Art and Society,* edited by Barbara Babcock, 147–90. Ithaca: Cornell University Press, 1978. Serbo-Croatian translation of chapter 5 by Lydia Sklevicky in *Gordogan* 22 (1986): 85–120. Chapter 6, "The Rites of Violence," reprinted in *Social History of Western Civilization. Vol. 1: Readings from the Ancient World to the Seventeenth Century,* edited by Richard Golden, 287–301. New York: St. Martin's Press, 1988. Polish translation of chapter 6 in *Odrodzeni I Reformacia W. Polsce* 30 (1985): 33–53. Chapter 7, "Printing and the People," reprinted in *Literacy and Social Development in the West,* edited by Harvey J. Graff, 69–95. Cambridge: Cambridge University Press, 1981. Chapter 7 excerpted and translated into Italian in *Letteratura e Cultura Popolare,* edited by Elide Casali, 116–125. Bologna: Zanichelli, 1982. Chapter 7 excerpted in *Rethinking Popular Culture: Contemporary Perspectives in Cultural Studies,* edited by Chandra Mukerji and Michael Schudson, 65–96. Berkeley: University of California Press, 1991. German translation of chapter 8, "Proverbial Wisdom and Popular Errors," in *Volkskultur. Zur Wiederentdeckung des vergessen Alltags*, edited by Richard van Dülmen and Norbert Schindler, 78–116, 394–406. Frankfurt Am Main: Fischer Taschenbuch Verlag, 1984.

The Return of Martin Guerre. Cambridge: Harvard University Press, 1983; Harmondsworth: Penguin, 1985. French editions (trans. Angélique Lévi) in Natalie Zemon Davis, Jean-Claude Carrière, and Daniel Vigne, *Le Retour de Martin Guerre*, Paris: Editions Robert Laffont, 1982; Editions J'ai lu, 1982; France Loisirs, 1982. German editions (trans. Ute and Wolf Heinrich Leube), Munich: R. Piper and Co. Verlag, 1984; Frankfurt Am Main: Fischer Taschenbuch Verlag, 1989, with afterword by Carlo Ginzburg. Italian edition (trans. Sandro Lombardini), Turin: Giulio Einaudi, 1984, with afterword by Carlo Ginzburg. Spanish edition (trans. Helene Rotés), Barcelona: Antoni Bosch editor, 1984. Dutch edition (trans. G. Groot), Amsterdam: Elsevier, 1985. Japanese edition (trans. Komao Naruse), Tokyo: Heibonsha, 1985. Swedish edition (trans. Ingemar G. Nilsson), Stockholm: Ordfronts förlag, 1985. Portuguese edition (trans. Denise Bottmann), São Paolo: Paz e Terra, 1987. Russian edition (trans. A. L. Velichanskii), Moscow: Progress Publishers, 1990.

Frauen und Gesellschaft am Beginn der Neuzeit. Studien über Familie, Religion und die Wandlungsfähigkeit des sozialen Körpers, trans. Wolfgang Kaiser. Berlin: Klaus Wagenbach, 1986. Includes one essay, "Religion in the Neighborhood: The Stones of Ste Croix Parish," published here for the first time.

Fiction in the Archives: Pardon Tales and their Tellers in Sixteenth-Century France. Stanford: Stanford University Press, 1987. British edition, Cambridge: Polity Press, 1988. French edition (trans. Christian Cler), Paris: Editions du Seuil, 1988. German editions (trans. Wolfgang Kaiser), Berlin: Klaus Wagenbach, 1988; Frankfurt Am Main: Fischer Taschenbuch Verlag, 1991. Japanese edition (trans. Komao Naruse and Shiro Miyashita), Tokyo: Heibonsha, 1990. Italian edition (trans. Patrizia Guarnieri), Turin: Giulio Einaudi, 1992.

Coauthored and Edited Works

Founder and coeditor, *Renaissance and Reformation* (A Bulletin for Scholars in the Toronto Area) 1–5 (1964–69); continued as *Renaissance and Reformation. Renaissance et Réforme*, publication of the Canadian Society of Renaissance Studies.

"Memory and Countermemory" (with Randolph Starn). Special Issue of *Representations* 26 (Spring 1989).

Gender in the Academy. Women and Learning from Plato to Princeton. An Exhibition Celebrating the 20th Anniversary of Undergraduate Coeducation at Princeton University (with Stephen Ferguson, Anthony Grafton, Linda Lierheimer, Carol Quillen, and Patricia Schechter). Princeton: Princeton University Library, 1990. Introduction reprinted in *Princeton University Library Chronicle* 52, no. 1 (Autumn 1990): 126–129.

Storia delle Donne in Occidente, ed. Georges Duby and Michelle Perrot. Vol. 3:
Dal Rinascimento all'Eta Moderna (with Arlette Farge). Rome: Laterza, 1991.
French edition (trans. Anne Michel et al.), Paris: Plon, 1991. Dutch edition
(trans. Margreet Blok et al.), Amsterdam: Agon, 1992. American edition, *A
History of Women in the West,* vol 3: *Renaissance and Enlightenment Paradoxes*
(with Arlette Farge, trans. Arthur Goldhammer), Cambridge: Harvard
University Press, 1993. Spanish edition (trans. Marco Aurelio Galmarini
and Cristina Garcia Ohlrich), Madrid: Taurus, 1992. Forthcoming in German and Portuguese.

Contributions to Books

"The Protestant Printing Workers of Lyons in 1514." In G. Berthoud et al.,
Aspects de la propagande religieuse, 247–57. Geneva: E. Droz, 1957.
"The 1592 Edition of Estienne's 'Apologie pour Hérodote.'" In G. Berthoud
et al., *Aspects de la propagande religieuse,* 373–76. Geneva: E. Droz, 1957.
"Publisher Guillaume Rouillé, Businessman and Humanist." In *Editing Six-
teenth-Century Texts,* edited by R. J. Schoeck, 72–112. Toronto: University
of Toronto Press, 1966. Reissued New York, London: Garland Publishing
Inc., 1978.
"City Women and Religious Change in Sixteenth-Century France." In *A
Sampler of Women's Studies,* edited by Dorothy McGuigan, 17–45. Ann
Arbor: University of Michigan Center for Continuing Education of
Women, 1973. Reprinted in chapter 3 of *Society and Culture in Early Mod-
ern France.*
"Some Tasks and Themes in the Study of Popular Religion." In *The Pursuit
of Holiness in Late Medieval and Renaissance Religion: Papers from the University
of Michigan Conference,* edited by Charles Trinkaus and Heiko Oberman,
484–514. Leiden: E. J. Brill, 1974.
"The Historian and Popular Culture." In *The Wolf and the Lamb: Popular
Culture in France from the Old Regime to the Twentieth Century,* edited by
Jacques Beauroy, Marc Bertrand, and Edward T. Gargan, 9–16. Saratoga,
CA: Anma Libri, 1977.
"Gender and Genre: Women as Historical Writers, 1400–1820." In *Beyond
their Sex: Learned Women of the European Past,* edited by Patricia H. Labalme,
153–82. New York: New York University Press, 1980.
"Women in the Arts Mécaniques in Sixteenth-Century Lyon." In Françoise
Bayard et al., *Lyon et l'Europe. Hommes et sociétés. Mélanges d'histoire offerts à
Richard Gascon,* vol. 1, 139–67. Lyons: Presses Universitaires de Lyon, 1980.
Expanded and revised as "Women in the Crafts in Sixteenth-Century
Lyon," *Feminist Studies* 8, no. 1 (Spring 1982): 46–80; revised version re-
printed in *Women and Work in Preindustrial Europe,* edited by Barbara A.
Hanawalt, 167–97. Bloomington: Indiana University Press, 1986. German
translation of revised version in *Arbeit, Frömmigkeit und Eigenstinn. Studien
zur historischen Kulturforschung,* edited by Richard van Dülmen, 43–74, 304–
10. Frankfurt Am Main: Fischer Taschenbuch Verlag, 1990.

"Charivari, honneur et communauté à Lyon et à Genève au XVIIe siècle." In *Le Charivari. Actes de la table ronde organisée par le CNRS et L'EHESS, Paris (25 avril 1977),* edited by Jacques Le Goff and Jean-Claude Schmitt, 207–20. Paris: Mouton, 1981. English translation, "Charivari, Honor, and Community in Seventeenth-Century Lyon and Geneva." In *Rite, Drama, Festival, Spectacle: Rehearsals Toward a Theory of Cultural Performance,* edited by John A. MacAloon, 42–57. Philadelphia: Ishe Press, 1984. Spanish translation in Spanish edition of *Society and Culture* (1993), chap. 3. Japanese translation in *Shisho.*

"From 'Popular Religion' to Religious Cultures." In *Reformation Europe: A Guide to Research,* edited by Steven Ozment, 321–41. St. Louis: Center for Reformation Research, 1982. French translation in *Religion populaire, religion de clercs?,* edited by B. Lacroix and J. Simard, 393–416. Quebec: IQRC, 1984.

"Le monde de l'imprimerie humaniste: Lyon." In *Histoire de l'édition française, vol. 1. Le livre conquérant du Moyen Age au milieu du 17e siècle,* edited by Henri-Jean Martin and Roger Chartier, 255–278. Paris: Promodis, 1983.

"Introduction." In *The Knight, the Lady and the Priest. The Making of Modern Marriage in Medieval France,* by Georges Duby, trans. Barbara Bray, vii–xv. New York: Pantheon, 1983.

"'The Sense of History': A Case Study." In *Historians and Filmmakers. Toward Collaboration* (A roundtable held at the New York Institute for the Humanities, New York University, October 30), 1982, edited by Barbara Abrash and Janet Sternburg, 28–39. New York: Institute for Research in History, 1983.

"Scandale à l'Hôtel Dieu (Lyon, 1537–1543)," trans. Alain Croix. In *La France d'Ancien Régime. Etudes réunies en l'honneur de Pierre Goubert,* vol. 1, edited by Alain Croix, Jean Jacquart, François Lebrun, 175–88. Toulouse: Privat, 1984. German translation in Davis, *Frauen und Gesellschaft* (1986), 93–107, 157–59. Spanish translation in Davis, *Society and Culture* (1993), chap. 5.

"Boundaries and the Sense of Self in Early Modern France." In *Reconstructing Individualism: Autonomy, Individuality, and the Self in Western Thought,* edited by Thomas C. Heller, Morton Sosna, David E. Wellbery, 53–63, 333–35. Stanford: Stanford University Press, 1986. German translation in Davis, *Frauen und Gesellschaft* (1986), 7–18, 133–35.

"Women's History as Women's Education." In *Women's History as Women's Education: Essays . . . from a Symposium in Honor of Jill and John Conway, Smith College, April 17, 1985,* by Natalie Zemon Davis and Joan Wallach Scott, 7–22. Northampton, MA: Smith College Archives and the Sophia Smith Collection, 1985.

"Scoperta e rinnovamento nella storia delle donne," trans. P. Renzi. In *Profil di donne. Mio Immagine Realtà fra Medioveo ed Età Contemporanea* (Università degli Studi di Lecce, Dipartimento di Sciencze Storiche e Sociali, Saggi e Ricerche, 19), edited by B. Vetere and Paolo Renzi, 303–22. Galatina: Congedo Editor, 1986.

"Life-Saving Stories." In *A New History of French Literature,* edited by Denis Hollier, 139–45. Cambridge: Harvard University Press, 1989. French translation in the French edition, Paris: Bordas Editeur, 1993.

"Fame and Secrecy: Leon Modena's Life as an Early Modern Autobiography." In *The Autobiography of a Seventeenth-Century Venetian Rabbi: Leon Modena's "Life of Judah,"* translated and edited by Mark Cohen, 50–70. Princeton, NJ: Princeton University Press, 1988. Reprinted in *Essays in Jewish Historiography, History and Theory,* Beiheft 17, edited by Ada Rapoport-Albert, 103–18. Middletown, CT: Wesleyan University Press, 1988. Italian translation by Caterina Grendi Baglietto, in *Quaderni Storici* 64 (April 1987): 39–60. German translation by Wolfgang Kaiser, in *Freibeuter* 54 (1992): 9–32.

"Donne e politica." In *Dal Rinascimento all'Eta Moderna,* edited by Davis and Farge, 201–19. Rome: Laterza, 1991. French translation by Pascale de Mézamat, Paris: Plon, 1991, 175–90. Dutch translation by Margreet Blok, Amsterdam: Agon, 1992, 157–70. Spanish translation by Marco Aurelio Galmarini. Madrid: Taurus, 1992, 211–27. English version, "Women in Politics," in Davis and Farge, eds., *Renaissance and Enlightenment Paradoxes* (Cambridge: Harvard University Press, 1993). Forthcoming in German and Portuguese.

"Preface" to *Liste Otto. The Official List of French Books Banned under the German Occupation,* 1940, iii–ix. Cambridge: Harvard College Library, 1992.

"Iroquois Women, European Women." In *Women, "Race," and Writing in the Early Modern Period,* edited by Margo Hendricks and Patricia Parker, 243–58 and 349–61. London: Routledge, 1993.

Articles

"On the Protestantism of Benôit Rigaud." *Bibliothèque d'humanisme et renaissance* 17 (1955): 246–51.

"Holbein's *Pictures of Death* and the Reformation at Lyons." *Studies in the Renaissance* 3 (1956): 97–130.

"Christophe Plantin's Childhood at Saint Just." *De Gulden Passer* (1957): 107–20.

"Mathematicians in the Sixteenth-Century French Academies: Some Further Evidence." *Renaissance News* 11 (1958): 3–10.

"Sixteenth-Century French Arithmetics on the Business Life." *Journal of the History of Ideas* 21 (1960): 18–48.

"The Good Name of Martin Ponthus." *Bibliothèque d'humanisme et renaissance* 22 (1960): 287–93.

"Peletier and Beza Part Company." *Studies in the Renaissance* 11 (1964): 188–222.

"Strikes and Salvation at Lyons." *Archiv für Reformationsgeschichte* 56 (1965): 48–64. Reprinted in chapter 1 of *Society and Culture in Early Modern France.*

"A Trade Union in Sixteenth-Century France." *Economic History Review* 19 (1966): 48–69. Reprinted in *"Van oproeren en Stakingen" Sociale en politieke movilisering in Europa, 1500–1850,* edited by H. A. Diederiks, 25–52. The Hague: M. Nijhoff, 1981.

"The Protestantism of Jacques Besson." *Technology and Culture* 7 (1966): 513.

"A Finding List of Renaissance Legal Literature to 1700" [with R. J. Schoeck, J. K. McConica]. *Renaissance and Reformation* 4 (1967–68): 2–28, 33–85, 98–126.

"Gregory Nazianzen in the Service of Humanist Social Reform." *Renaissance Quarterly* 20 (1967): 455–64.

"Poor Relief, Humanism and Heresy: The Case of Lyon." *Studies in Medieval and Renaissance History* 5 (1968): 217–75. French translation in *Etude sur l'histoire de la pauvreté (Moyen âge-XVIe siècle).* 2 vols., edited by Michel Mollat, 761–822. Paris: Publications de la Sorbonne, 1974. Reprinted in chapter 2 of *Society and Culture in Early Modern France.*

"Sixteenth-Century Continental Editions of Authors in the Forbes Collection." *Renaissance and Reformation* 5, no. 1 (November 1968): 8–13.

"A Checklist of French Political and Religious Pamphlets, 1560–1635, in the University of Toronto Library" [with J. A. McLelland]. *Renaissance and Reformation* 5, no. 3 (May 1969): 18–41.

"René Choppin on More's *Utopia.*" *Moreana* 19–20 (1968): 91–96.

"The Reasons of Misrule: Youth-Groups and Charivaris in Sixteenth-Century France." *Past and Present* 50 (February 1971): 41–75. Reprinted in chapter 4 of *Society and Culture in Early Modern France.*

"Erasmus at Moscow." *Renaissance and Reformation* 7 (1971): 84–86.

"New Monarchs and Prudent Priests." *Canadian Journal of History* 6 (1971): 69–74.

"A Note on the Publishers of a Lyon Bible of 1566." *Bibliothèque d'humanisme et renaissance* 34 (1972): 501–3.

"The Rites of Violence: Religious Riot in Sixteenth-Century France." *Past and Present* 59 (May 1973): 51–91. Reprinted in *The Massacre of St. Bartholomew: Reappraisals and Documents,* edited by Alfred Soman. The Hague: M. Nijhoff, 1974. Also reprinted in chapter 6 of *Society and Culture in Early Modern France.*

"A Rejoinder" [to Janine Estebe, "Debate. The Rites of Violence: Religious Riot in Sixteenth-Century France"]. *Past and Present* 67 (May 1975): 131–35.

"'Women's History' in Transition: The European Case." *Feminist Studies* 3 (Spring-Summer 1976): 83–93. Reprinted in *Women's Lives: Perspectives on Progress and Change,* edited by Virginia Lee Lussier and Joyce Jennings Walstedt, 5–25. Newark: University of Delaware, 1977. Italian translation in *Donna Woman Femme* 3 (April-June 1977): 7–33. Dutch translation by Els Kloek and Jenneke Quast, in *Tweede Jaarboek voor Vrouwengeschiedenis,* 236–63. Nijmegen: Socialistese Uitgeveri Nijmegen, 1981. German translation in Davis, *Frauen und Gesellschaft,* 117–32, 161–71.

"Ghosts, Kin and Progeny: Some Features of Family Life in Early Modern France." *Daedalus* 106, no. 2 (Spring 1977): 87–114. Reprinted in *The Fam-*

ily, edited by Alice Ross et al., 87–114. New York: Norton, 1978. German translation in Davis, *Frauen und Gesellschaft,* 19–51, 135–44.

"Men, Women and Violence: Some Reflections on Equality." *Smith Alumnae Quarterly* (April 1977): 12–15. Reprinted in *The Role of Women in Conflict and Peace,* edited by Dorothy G. McGuigan, 19–29. Ann Arbor: University of Michigan Center for Continuing Education of Women, 1977.

"Le Milieu social de Corneille de La Haye (Lyon, 1533–1575)." *Revue de l'art* 47 (1980): 21–28.

"The Sacred and the Body Social in Sixteenth-Century Lyon." *Past and Present* 90 (February 1981): 40–70. Reprinted in *Humanities in Review,* vol. 1, edited by Ronald Dworkin, Karl Miller, and Richard Sennett, 40–79. Cambridge: Cambridge University Press, 1982. Excerpted in *The Other Side of Western Civilization: Readings in Everyday Life. Vol. 2: The Sixteenth Century to the Present,* 3d. ed., edited by Peter Stearns, 29–35. New York: Harcourt, Brace, Jovanovich, 1984. German translation in Davis, *Frauen und Gesellschaft,* 64–92, 145–57.

"Anthropology and History in the 1980s: The Possibilities of the Past." *Journal of Interdisciplinary History* 12, no. 2 (Autumn 1981): 267–75. Reprinted in *The New History. The 1980s and Beyond,* edited by Theodore K. Rabb and Robert I. Rotberg, 267–75. Princeton, NJ: Princeton University Press, 1982. Hungarian translation in *Vilagtortenet* 2 (1984): 17–27. German translation in *Vom Umschreiben der Geschichte. Neue historische perspektiven,* edited by Ulrich Raulff, 45–53. Berlin: Klaus Wagenbach, 1986.

"Misprint and Minerva: Printers' Journeymen in Sixteenth-Century Lyon." *Printing History* 3, no. 1 (1981): 72–83.

"Beyond the Market: Books as Gifts in Sixteenth-Century France." *Transactions of the Royal Historical Society,* series 5, 33 (1983): 69–88.

"About Dedications" (*Radical History Review* Special Supplement: The David Abraham Case), *Radical History Review* 32 (1985): 94–96.

"A Renaissance Text to the Historian's Eye: The Gifts of Montaigne." *Journal of Medieval and Renaissance Studies* 15, no. 1 (Spring 1985): 47–56. German translation in Davis, *Frauen und Gesellschaft,* 108–16, 159–61. Revised as "Art and Society in the Gifts of Montaigne." *Representations* 12 (Fall 1985): 24–32.

"What is Women's History." *History Today* 35 (June 1985): 40–42.

"'Any Resemblance to Persons Living or Dead': Film and the Challenge of Authenticity" (The Fifth Patricia Wise Lecture, American Film Institute). *Yale Review* 76 (Summer 1987): 457–82. Reprinted in *Historical Journal of Film, Radio and Television* 8 (1988): 269–83. German translation by Robin Cackett, in *Bilder schrieben Geschichte: Der Historiker im Kino,* edited by Rainer Rother, 37–64. Berlin: Klaus Wagenbach, 1991.

"A Symposium: Feminist Book Reviewing" [with Julia Penelope, Margery Wolf, Cynthia Neverdon-Morton, Linda Gardiner]. *Feminist Studies* 14, no. 3 (1988): 601–22.

"History's Two Bodies" (Presidential Address, American Historical Association). *American Historical Review* 93, no. 1 (February 1988): 1–30. German translation by Ebba D. Drolshagen, in Fernand Braudel et al., *Der Historiker als Menschenfresser. Uber den Beruf des Geschichtesschreibers*, 46–84. Berlin: Klaus Wagenbach, 1990. Chinese translation in *The Challenge of Modern Historiography: The Presidential Addresses of AHA Presidents, 1961–1988*, edited by Wang Jianhua, 505–29. Shanghai: Shanghai Academy of Social Sciences, 1990.

"'On the Lame'" (*AHR* Forum: The Return of Martin Guerre). *American Historical Review* 93, no. 3 (June 1988): 507–603.

"Du conte et de l'histoire." *Le débat* 54 (March-April 1989): 138–43.

"Women's history: Multiple stories." In *In de Ban van het Verhall. (Jaarboek voor Vrouwengeschiedenis)* 11 (1990): 98–106.

"The Shapes of Social History." *Storia della Storiografia* 17 (1990): 28–34. Spanish translation by M. Ferrandis Garrayo in *Historia Social* 10 (Spring-Summer 1991): 177–82. German translation forthcoming in *Mikro-Historie. Neue Pfade in die Sozialgeschichte*, edited by Hans Medick. Frankfurt Am Main: Fischer Taschenbuch Verlag, 1994.

"Rabelais Among the Censors (1940s, 1540s)." *Representations* 32 (Fall 1990): 1–32.

"Stories and the Hunger to Know." *Literaria Pragensia: Studies in Literature and Culture* 1 (1991): 12–13. Expanded and republished in *Yale Journal of Criticism* 5, no. 4 (Spring 1992): 159–63.

"Censorship, Silence and Resistance: The *Annales* during the German Occupation of France." *Literaria Pragensia: Studies in Literature and Culture* 1 (1991): 13–23. Republished in Russian in *Sur un point crucial: Débat autor des 'Annales,' ou: comment écrire l'histoire aujourd'hui et demain*. Sour la direction de You. Bessmerty. Moscow: Nauka, 1993: 166–79. Forthcoming in *Revista di Storia della Storiografia Moderna*.

"Yom Kippur in Moscow, 5750." *Radical History Review* 49 (1991): 155–60.

"The Rights and Responsibilities of Historians in Regard to Historical Films and Video" [with Daniel J. Walkowitz for the AHA Ad Hoc Committee on History and Film]. *Perspectives* 30, no. 6 (September 1992): 15, 17.

"Women and the World of the *Annales*." *History Workshop* 33 (Spring 1992): 121–37.

"Toward Mixtures and Margins" (*AHR* Forum: The Folklore of Industrial Society: Popular Culture and Its Audiences). *American Historical Review* 97 (1992): 1409–16.

"Commemorating 1492: A Roundtable" [with Sacvan Bercovitch, Aron Rodrigue, Victor Perera and Sean Wilentz]. *Tikkun* 7, no. 5 (September-October 1992): 53–62.

"Gifts, Markets and Communities in Sixteenth-Century France." Published in Russian, translated by Irina Bessmertny, in *Odysseus-92* (1993).

Reviews

Review of *Geneva and the Coming of the Wars of Religion in France, 1555–1563*, by Robert M. Kingdon. *History of Ideas Newsletter* 2, no. 4 (October 1956): 90–92.

Review of *Le Miracle de Laon en Lannoys*, edited by A. H. Chaubard. *History of Ideas Newsletter* 3, no. 2 (April 1957): 18–19.

Review of *Le Livre du recteur de l'Académie de Genève (1559–1878)*, edited by S. Stelling Michaud. *Renaissance News* 14 (1961): 43–45.

Review of *The Massacre of Saint Bartholomew*, by Henri Noguères, trans. Claire Eliane Engel. *American Historical Review* 68 (1962–63): 517–18.

Review of *Lyons 1473–1503: The Beginnings of Cosmopolitanism*, by James B. Wadsworth. *Renaissance News* 16, no. 2 (1963): 118–21.

Review of *Science and the Renaissance*, 2 vols., by W. P. D. Wightman. *Bibliothèque d'humanisme et renaissance* 25 (1963): 433–36.

Review of *Renaissance Studies*, by Wallace K. Ferguson. *Canadian Historical Review* 45, no. 4 (1964): 344–45.

Review of *The Renaissance Reconsidered: A Symposium*, by Leona Gabel et al. *American Historical Review* 70 (1964–65): 851–52.

Review of René de Lucinge's *Lettres sur les débuts de la Ligue (1585)*, edited by Alain Dufour and Eustorg de Beaulieu, and *Les Divers Rapports*, edited by M. A. Pegg. *Renaissance News* 18 (1965): 150–52.

Review of *Change in Medieval Society: Europe North of the Alps, 1050–1500*, edited by Sylvia A. Thrupp. *Canadian Journal of Economics and Political Science* 31, no. 4 (1965): 608–9.

Review of *Studies in Genevan Government (1536–1605)*, by E. William Monter. *Archiv für Reformationsgeschichte* 57, no. 1–2 (1966): 276–78.

Review of *The Political Ideas of Pierre Viret*, by Robert Dean Linder. *Renaissance News* 19, no. 4 (1966): 371–73.

Review of *The Library Catalogue of Anthony Higgin, Dean of Ripon (1608–1624)*, edited by Jean E. Mortimer. *Bibliothèque d'humanisme et renaissance* 30 (1968): 413–14.

Review of *Strasbourg and the Reform: A Study in the Process of Change*, by Miriam Usher Chrisman. *Journal of Modern History* 40, no. 4 (December 1968): 588–91.

Review of *Geneva and the Consolidation of the French Protestant Movement, 1564–1572*, by Robert Kingdon. *Renaissance Quarterly* 22, no. 1 (1969): 54–56.

"Deforming the Reformation." Review of *Religion and Regime*, by Guy E. Swanson. *New York Review of Books* 12, no. 7 (April 10, 1969): 35–38.

"Missed Connections: Religion and Regime." Review of *Religion and Regime*, by Guy E. Swanson. *Journal of Interdisciplinary History* 1 (1971): 384–94.

Review of *Grand commerce et vie urbaine au XVIe siècle: Lyon et ses marchands (environs de 1520-environs de 1580)*, 2 vols., by Richard Gascon. *American Historical Review* 79, no. 1 (February 1974): 158–61.

"Les conteurs de Montaillou." Review of *Montaillou, village occitan de 1294 à 1324*, by Emmanuel Le Roy Ladurie. *Annales. Economies. Sociétés. Civilisations* 34 (1979): 61–73.

Review of *The Renaissance Notion of Women: A Study in the Fortunes of Scholasticism and Medical Science in European Intellectual Life*, by Ian Maclean. *Renaissance Quarterly* 34, no. 2 (1981): 211–13.

"Revolution and Revelation." Review of *The Three Orders: Feudal Society Imagined*, by Georges Duby, trans. Arthur Goldhammer; and idem. *The Age of Cathedrals: Art and Society, 980–1420*, trans. Eleanor Levieux and Barbara Thompson. *New York Review of Books* 31, no. 1 (February 2, 1984): 32–34.

"The Harvest of Sorcery." Review of *The Night Battles: Witchcraft and Agrarian Cults in the Sixteenth and Seventeenth Centuries*, by Carlo Ginzburg, trans. Anne Tedeschi and John Tedeschi; and *La sorcière de Jasmin*, by Emmanuel Le Roy Ladurie. *Times Literary Supplement* 221, no. 4 (February 24, 1984): 179–80.

Review of *The Development of the Family and Marriage in Europe*, by Jack Goody. *American Ethnologist* 12, no. 1 (1985): 149–51.

Review of *Rouen During the Wars of Religion*, by Philip Benedict, and of *The Making of a State: Württemberg, 1593–1793*, by James Allen Vann. *Renaissance Quarterly* 38, no. 2 (1985): 327–32.

"Happy Endings." Review of *The Birth of Purgatory*, by Jacques Le Goff, trans. Arthur Goldhammer. *New York Review of Books* 32, no. 12 (July 18, 1985): 31–33.

"A New Montaigne." Review of *Montaigne in Motion*, by Jean Starobinski, trans. Arthur Goldhammer. *New York Review of Books* 34, no. 18 (November 19, 1987): 50–54.

"A Modern Hero." Review of *Marc Bloch: A Life in History*, by Carole Fink. *New York Review of Books* 37, no. 7 (April 26, 1990): 27–30. Japanese translation in *Misuzu* 354 (September 1990): 2–13.

Film and Television

Historical consultant for *Le Retour de Martin Guerre*, Daniel Vigne, director; Société française de production cinématographique, producer. Premiered in Paris, May 1982; in New York, June 1983.

Consultant for "RENAISSANCE" television series, created by Theodore K. Rabb and produced by the Medici Foundation. Broadcast by PBS in January-March 1993.

Interviews

Judy Coffin and Robert Harding. "Politics, Progeny and French History: An Interview with Natalie Zemon Davis." *Radical History Review* 24 (Fall 1980): 115–39. Reprinted as "Natalie Zemon Davis," in *Visions of History: Interviews with E. P. Thompson . . . by Marho*, edited by Henry Abelove et al., 99–122. New York: Pantheon, 1983. Reprinted in Italian in *Memoria. Rivista di storia delle donne* 9, no. 3 (1983): 79–93. Reprinted in German in *Freibeuter* 24 (1985): 65–75.

Ed Benson. "Martin Guerre, the Historian and the Filmmakers: An Interview with Natalie Zemon Davis." *Film and History* 13 (September 1983): 49–65.

Marine Valensise, ed. "Una Storia da Film (e poi da Libro): Intervista a

Natalie Zemon Davis." *Problemi dell' Informazione* 10, no. 2 (April-June 1985): 245–64.

William McCleery. "Natalie Zemon Davis." *Conversations on the Character of Princeton*, 33–38. Princeton, NJ: Princeton University Office of Communications, 1986.

Saskia Jansens and Anja Petrakopoulos. "Een 'old pro' over haar vak. Interview met Natalie Zemon Davis." *Skript* 12 (1990): 79–87.

Asuncion Doménch and Ana Bustelo. "Natalie Zemon Davis." *Historia 16*, 15, no. 176 (1990): 123–26.

Roger Adelson. "Interview with Natalie Zemon Davis." *Historian* 53, no. 3 (Spring 1991): 405–22.

Danielle Haase Dubosc and Eliane Viennot. "Entretien avec Natalie Davis." In *Femmes et pouvoirs sous l'ancien régime*, edited by Danielle Haase Dubosc and Eliane Viennot, 306–9. Paris: Editions Rivages, 1991.

Monika Bernold and Andrea Ellmeier. "Geschichte, Hoffnung und Selbstironie. Natalie Zemon Davis im Gespräch." *L'Homme. Zeitschrift für Feminische Geschichtswissenschaft* 3, no. 2 (1992): 98–105.

Antoinette Reerink. "Natalie Zemon Davis over: Vrouwen, Indianen en Politieke Correctheid." *Spiegel Historiael* 28, no. 1 (January 1993): 30–34.

Pieces Circulated in Mimeograph

[Natalie Zemon Davis and Elizabeth Douvan.] "Operation Mind. A Brief Documentary Account of the House Committee on Un-American Activities." Ann Arbor: University of Michigan Council of the Arts, Sciences and Professions, 1952. Circulated anonymously.

"A study of 42 women who have children and who are in Graduate Programmes at the University of Toronto. Preliminary Report" [with Josephine Grimshaw, Elizabeth Mandell, Alison Smith Prentice and Germaine Warkentin]. Toronto: University of Toronto, 1966.

"Society and the Sexes in Early Modern Europe, 15th–18th Centuries. A Bibliography" [with the assistance of Elizabeth Cohen, Sherrill Cohen, Ian Dengler, Barbara B. Diefendorf, Gillian Grebler, Alison Klairmont Lingo and Kirk Robinson.] University of Toronto, 1971, and University of California, Berkeley, 1972–73.

Contributors

James S. Amelang is Professor of Urban History at the Autonomous University of Madrid, Spain. He is the author of *Honored Citizens of Barcelona: Patrician Culture and Class Relations, 1490–1714* (1986) and the editor and translator of *Journal of the Plague Year: The Diary of the Barcelona Tanner Miquel Parets, 1651* (1991).

Andrew Barnes is Associate Professor of History at Carnegie-Mellon University. He is the author of *The Social Dimension of Piety: Associative Life and Devotional Change in the Penitent Confraternities of Marseilles, 1499–1792* (forthcoming). Currently he is working on the christianization of Africa.

Jodi Bilinkoff is Associate Professor of History at the University of North Carolina at Greensboro. She is the author of *The Avila of Saint Teresa: Religious Reform in a Sixteenth-Century City* (1989).

Elizabeth S. Cohen teaches in the Department of History at York University, North York, Ontario. She is the author, with Thomas Cohen, of *Words and Deeds in Renaissance Rome: Trials Before the Papal Magistrats* (1993). She is currently working on a book on prostitution in early modern Rome.

Jonathan Dewald is Professor of History at State University of New York at Buffalo. He is the author of *The Formation of a Provincial Nobility: The Magistrats of the Parlement of Rouen, 1499–1610* (1980), *Pont-St-Pierre: Lordship, Community and Capitalism in Early Modern France* (1987), and *Aristocratic Experience and the Origins of Modern Culture, France 1570–1715* (1993).

Barbara B. Diefendorf is Professor of History at Boston University. She is the author of *Paris City Councillors in the Sixteenth Century: The Politics of Patrimony* (1983) and *Beneath the Cross: Catholics and Huguenots in Sixteenth-Century Paris* (1991). She is currently working on female spirituality and the Catholic Reformation in Paris.

Carla Hesse is Associate Professor of History at the University of California, Berkeley. She is a member of the editorial board of *Representations* and the author of *Publishing and Cultural Politics in Revolutionary Paris (1789–1810)* (1991).

273

Alison Klairmont Lingo is a research assistant at the University of California, Berkeley. She received her Ph.D. from UC Berkeley in 1980 and is currently completing a book on women's health care literature in early modern France.

Keith P. Luria is Associate Professor of History at North Carolina State University, Raleigh. He is author of *Territories of Grace: Cultural Change in the Seventeenth-Century Diocese of Grenoble* (1991). He is now working on Protestant and Catholic relations in the seventeenth century.

Laurie Nussdorfer is Associate Professor of History and Letters at Wesleyan University. She is the author of *Civic Politics in the Rome of Urban VIII* (1992). She is currently working on literacy and the lower classes in Renaissance and Baroque Rome.

Virginia Reinburg is Associate Professor of History at Boston College. She is the author of *Popular Prayers in Late Medieval and Reformation France* (forthcoming). Her current work is a study of liturgical, legal, and political rituals in late medieval and early modern France.

Peter Sahlins is Associate Professor of History at the University of California, Berkeley. He is the author of *Boundaries: The Making of France and Spain in the Pyrenees* (1989) and *Forest Rites: Peasant Revolt and Popular Culture in Nineteenth-Century France* (forthcoming).

Index

Alvarez, Baltasar, 84, 86, 87–88, 89, 91

Ambrosio (literate surrogate to Margarita), 189–90, 196

Annales school, 1

Anne of Austria, 247

Apostles' Creed (prayer), 33

Apothecaries, 204–5

Aretino, Pietro, 195

Ariège, (department), 159–72

Auger, Emond, 32; *Formulaire de prières catholiques,* 31

Augustine, Saint, 73, 75

Autun, bishop of, 142

Ave Maria (prayer), 33

Avila, Julián de, 85, 91–93

Avila (city), 83–96

Bakhtin, Mikhail, 162, 195

Barber-surgeons, 204–5, 210

Barcelona, 119–33

Barnes, Andrew, 11

Basseville, Hugou de, 245

Basso, Keith, 182

Benedicti, Jean, 33

Benoist, René, 31

Bentham, Jeremy, 171

Berthelot du Chesnay, Charles, 149–50, 153

Beza, Theodore, 42–43, 44, 45, 51, 57n.3

Billinkoff, Jodi, 10

Binz, Louis, 144

Biography: of female penitents by male confessors, 83–84. *See also* Kéralio, Louise de

Blackstone, William, 241

Bodin, Jean, 227

Books of hours, 19–34; contents of, 20–21; ownership of, 21

Borromeo, Charles, 76

Bossy, John, 144–45, 146, 149, 151, 152

Bourgeois, Louise, 210–11

Boutry, Philippe, 153

Briggs, Robin, 149

Budé, Louis, 45

Bury, Jacques, 210, 214

Busquet (Huguenot clan), 231

Calvin, John, 29, 32, 33; on prayer, 22; and Psalms, 43, 44; use of Psalms by, 45, 46

Calvinists, French. *See* Huguenots

Campion, Henri de, 231–32

Capuchins, 69–77

Catechism, 33

Catholic reformers: on prayer, 29–34

Catholics: attitudes toward sex, 209; conflicts with Huguenots, 68–69; cooperation with Huguenots, 66–68. *See also* Saint Bartholemew's Day

Celibacy: of clergy, 141–43

Cephalic version, 213

Chandieu, Antoine de la Roche, 47

Charivari, 159, 161, 170